Literary Eats

Literary Eats

Emily Dickinson's Gingerbread,
Ernest Hemingway's Picadillo,
Eudora Welty's Onion Pie and
400+ Other Recipes from American
Authors Past and Present

GARY SCHARNHORST

McFarland & Company, Inc., Publishers
Jefferson, North Carolina

Frontispiece: Mary Roberts Rinehart at stove (Library of Congress).

LIBRARY OF CONGRESS CATALOGUING-IN-PUBLICATION DATA

Scharnhorst, Gary.
Literary eats : Emily Dickinson's gingerbread, Ernest Hemingway's picadillo, Eudora Welty's onion pie, and 400+ other recipes from American authors past and present / Gary Scharnhorst.
p.   cm.
Includes bibliographical references and index.

ISBN 978-0-7864-7548-3 (softcover : acid free paper) ∞
ISBN 978-1-4766-1252-2 (ebook)

1. Cooking.   2. Cooking, American.   3. Authors, American—Biography—Miscellanea.   4. Food habits—United States—History—Miscellanea.   I. Title.
TX714.S353 2014   641.5973—dc23   2014004099

BRITISH LIBRARY CATALOGUING DATA ARE AVAILABLE

On the cover: Baking ingredients sit on table (Max Oppenheim, Digital Vision/Thinkstock)

Manufactured in the United States of America

McFarland & Company, Inc., Publishers
Box 611, Jefferson, North Carolina 28640
www.mcfarlandpub.com

For Dieter, Regina, Karin, Udo, Nadine, Walter,
Ursula, Karl, Günter, Dietmar and Kurt

Acknowledgments

Unpublished Brownie recipe by Elizabeth Bishop. Copyright 2013 by the Alice H. Methfessel Trust. Printed by permission of Farrar, Straus and Giroux, LLC, on behalf of the Elizabeth Bishop Estate. Printed from manuscript in the Elizabeth Bishop Papers at Vassar College, folder 112.13, courtesy of Archives and Special Collections Library, Vassar College.

"Café Ellison Diabolique" by Harlan Ellison(r). Copyright 1973, 1991 by Harlan Ellison. Renewed, 2001, by the Kilimanjaro Corporation. Reprinted by arrangement with, and permission of, the Author and the Author's agent, Richard Curtis Associates, Inc., New York. All rights reserved. Harlan Ellison is a registered trademark of the Kilimanjaro Corporation.

"Case of the Caretaker's Cat Cocktail" reprinted by permission of the Erle Stanley Gardner Trust.

Recipes for Green Chile Sauce, Huevos Rancheros, and Mexican Summer Soup from *The Aficionado's Southwestern Cooking* by Ronald Johnson are copyright 1968 by the Literary Estate of Ronald Johnson and reprinted with permission.

"Crab Nebula" and "Primitive Chocolate Mousse copyright 1973, 2001 by Ursula K. Le Guin; first appeared in *Cooking Out of This World*; reprinted by permission of the author and the author's agents, the Virginia Kidd Agency, Inc. "Liriv Metadi or Valley Succotash" copyright 1985 by Ursula K. Le Guin; first appeared in *Always Coming Home*; reprinted by permission of the author and the author's agents, the Virginia Kidd Agency, Inc.

Recipes for "Veal Cutlets with Tomato Sauce" and "Vegetable Soup" by Fanny Longfellow reprinted with permission from *Early American Cooking: Recipes from America's Historic Sites* by Evelyn Beilenson, published in 1985 by Peter Pauper Press, Inc., White Plains, New York, U.S.A. Used by permission. www.peterpauper.com.

Eggs à la Nabocoque by Vladimir Nabokov. Copyright 1972 by Vladimir Nabokov, courtesy of the Vladimir Nabokov Archive at the Berg Collection, New York Public Library. Used by permission of the Wylie Agency, LLC.

Recipes for Bread Pudding, Chicken Loaf, Corn and Cheese Fondue, Jello Salad, Swedish Meatballs by Lorine Niedecker reprinted with permission of the Hoard Historical Museum, Ft. Atkinson, Wisconsin (item number 002.3.8).

All Marjorie Kinnan Rawlings recipes from *Cross Creek Cookery*, copyright 1942 by Marjorie Kinnan Rawlings, copyright renewed © 1970 by Norton Baskin. Used by permission of Brandt and Hochman Literary Agents, Inc. All rights reserved.

Recipe for "Easy Peach Cobbler" from *Dori Sanders' Country Cooking* by Dori Sanders. Copyright 1995 by Dori Sanders. Reprinted by permission of Algonquin Books of Chapel Hill. All rights reserved.

"Gormeh Salzee" reprinted by permission of the Estate of William Stafford.

Recipe for Grits by Tennessee Williams. Copyright 1981, 2012 by the University of the South. Reprinted by permission of Georges Borchardt, Inc., on behalf of the Tennessee Williams Estate. All rights reserved.

Conrad Aiken's poem used by permission of Brandt and Hochman Literary Agents, Inc. All rights reserved.

"How to Make Rhubarb Wine" from *Sure Signs: New and Selected Poems*, by Ted Kooser, copyright 1980. Reprinted by permission of the University of Pittsburgh Press.

Table of Contents

Preface

In "The Custom-House," the introduction to *The Scarlet Letter* (1850), Nathaniel Hawthorne reminisced about a gourmand in Salem, Massachusetts, with whom he was acquainted:

> It always pleased and satisfied me to hear him expatiate on fish, poultry, and butcher's meat, and the most eligible methods of preparing them for the table. His reminiscences of good cheer, however ancient the date of the actual banquet, seemed to bring the savor of pig or turkey under one's very nostrils. There were flavors on his palate that had lingered there not less than sixty or seventy years, and were still apparently as fresh as that of the mutton chop which he had just devoured for his breakfast. I have heard him smack his lips over dinners, every guest at which, except himself, had long been food for worms. It was marvelous to observe how the ghosts of bygone meals were continually rising up before him — not in anger or retribution, but as if grateful for his former appreciation, and seeking to reduplicate an endless series of enjoyment, at once shadowy and sensual: a tenderloin of beef, a hind quarter of veal, a sparerib of pork, a particular chicken, or a remarkably praiseworthy turkey.[1]

Hawthorne's attention to culinary detail is not unusual. Though he was at best an indifferent cook, he was a lusty eater — like many other American writers whose works are filled with references to food, its preparation and consumption. At the other extreme from Hawthorne, Marianne Moore once served her fellow poet Donald Hall a minimalist lunch:

> On a tray she placed three tiny paper cups and a plate. One of the cups contained about two teaspoons of V-8 juice. Another had about eight raisins in it, and the other five and a half Spanish peanuts. On the plate was a mound of Fritos, and when she passed them to me she said, I like Fritos. They're so good for you, you know.[2]

Titles such as *Breakfast at Tiffany's*, *Naked Lunch*, and *Dinner at Eight* are rife in American literature, and even Washington Irving's title *Salmagundi* alludes to a salad dish. The poet Vachel Lindsay bartered volumes of his poetry for food, in particular "Rhymes to Be Traded for Bread" (1912).

Yet until now no one has compiled a comprehensive collection of recipes for the dishes American writers are known to have consumed. One reason is that, historically, Americans are presumed to have no distinctive cuisine. According to the British traveler Frances Trollope in her *Domestic Manners of the Americans* (1832), Americans "rarely dine in society, except in taverns and boarding houses" and "eat with the greatest rapidity and in total silence."[3] Fast food, it seems, was not a twentieth-century invention. Two years before the publication of his novel *The Virginian* (1902), Owen Wister lamented the haste with which passengers were expected to eat their meals at stops along the railway in his story "Twenty Minutes for Refreshments." James Fenimore Cooper remarked in *The American Democrat* (1838), written after living several years in Paris, that "Americans are the grossest feeders of any civilized nation known. As a nation, their food is heavy, coarse, and indigestible."[4]

1

Washington Irving's dining room at Sunnyside near Tarrytown, New York (Library of Congress).

The United States was a nation of gluttons and dyspeptics, or so was the stereotype. Why would anyone want to record their recipes? No "really indigenous cookbook, born on its own soil and conscious of its own resources," appeared in America "until after the Declaration of Independence," according to Waverly Root and Richard de Rochemont,[5] and unlike institutes for the culinary arts today, the first cooking schools in the U.S., established in New York in 1876 and Boston in 1879, did not train professional chefs but prepared working-class women for careers in the kitchens of the leisure class.

Every past compilation of American literary recipes has been specialized, moreover — limited by period (e.g., *Early American Cooking: Recipes from America's Historic Sites*), region (e.g., Marjorie Kinnan Rawlings' *Cross Creek Cookery*), ethnicity (e.g., Lafcadio Hearn's *La Cuisine Creole* or Pearl S. Buck's *Oriental Cookbook*), genre (e.g., *John Keats's Porridge: Favorite Recipes of American Poets*), gender (e.g., *Favorite Recipes of Famous Women*), individual author (e.g., *Emily Dickinson: Profile of the Poet as Cook*), ingredients (e.g., Ryan Berry's *Famous Vegetarians and Their Favorite Recipes*), or even restaurant (e.g., Frank Case's *Feeding the Lions: An Algonquin Cookbook*). I wish to break the mold: *Literary Eats* is purposefully decentered, organized not thematically or chronologically but alphabetically.

Still other literary cookbooks and cooking blogs make no pretense to the authenticity of their recipes: they have been "adapted" or "derived" from the originals or "inspired" by dishes merely mentioned by an author (e.g., Andrew Beahrs' *Twain's Feast*, Troy Gilbert and Greg Picolo's *Dinner with Tennessee Williams*, or Suzanne Rodriguez-Hunter's *Found Meals of the Lost Generation*). Occasionally the dishes are given precious names such as Ezra Pound cake, Elmer Rice pilaf, or Sam Shepard's pie. These recipes no more describe the preparation of the actual dishes the authors ate than Civil War re-enactors fight actual battles. The writers of such volumes implicitly assume that any dish — say, corn timbales — prepared according to the instructions in a contemporary cookbook must have resembled the dish the author knew.

Instead, in this book I have reproduced more than 400 authentic recipes for drinks and dishes enjoyed by more than 100 American authors since the late eighteenth century. Recipes for specific dishes—from simple to complex, from many different cuisines, from soups to desserts, from home cooking to grand cookery—are listed in the table of contents and alphabetized in the index. I have foresworn recipes for such delicacies as Louisa May Alcott's apple slump or Herman Melville's poor man's pudding because *bona fide* recipes for them simply do not exist. My editorial interventions are limited to spelling out abbreviated portion sizes for purposes of consistency ("pound" for "lb.," "tablespoon" for "T" or "tbsp.," "teaspoon" for "t" or "tsp.," etc.) and standardizing the spelling of "catsup" and "barbeque." I have designed the book to appeal to amateur chefs and so-called "foodies" who may want to test some of the recipes in their kitchens; to American literature instructors and scholars, some of whom may use it as a teaching tool; and general readers who will read it for pleasure. In several cases, when I have located a menu for a dinner, a list of attendees at the dinner that includes American writers, and recipes for the dishes served on the occasion — either at Delmonico's or the Waldorf-Astoria — I've included these recipes. In order to suggest the complexity of these dishes and the intricacy of their preparation, I cite their specific components by the recipe numbers used by the chefs Alessandro Filippini in *The Table* (1889) and Charles Ranhofer in *The Epicurean* (1894). This volume is, above all, a cookbook to be read — an anthology of recipes, a unique literary genre.

The most famous recipe ever published appears at the beginning of Act IV of *Macbeth* when the witches boil a stew with such ingredients as "Eye of newt and toe of frog, / Wool of bat and tongue of dog, / Adder's fork and blind-worm's sting, / Lizard's leg and owlet's wing." This recipe epitomizes two additional types of recipes in this book — parodies and those in verse. To be sure, there is sometimes a fine line between a genuine recipe and a parodic one (e.g., see Nabokov's recipe for a hard-boiled egg or Gail Hamilton's for brown bread cakes or David Amram's for an omelet).

In addition to tracing a rich American literary tradition, this volume silhouettes the transition from hearth to wood-stove to gas-stove cooking and the introduction of such innovations as commercial canning and refrigeration. New cooking technologies required new cooking procedures and protocols. The book also documents the evolution of the recipe formula from a mere list of ingredients with inexact measurements (e.g., "a lump of butter the size of an egg" or "a handful of salt") to exact measurements and instructions in the imperative mood ("stir," "mix," "slice," "boil," etc.). Many of the recipes feature native ingredients, such indigenous fruits and vegetables as apples, yams, corn (long regarded as animal food in Europe), and tomatoes (often considered a carcinogen prior to the twentieth century). Some of them adjure the economical cook to waste nothing — not even the hooves or internal organs of slaughtered animals. As Lydia Maria Child wrote in *The American Frugal Housewife* (1830), "Nothing should be thrown away so long as it is possible to make use of it, however trifling that use may be."[6] Elsewhere Marion Harland similarly bragged that "not an edible atom of the genial porker went to waste in the household of the notable housewife."[7] Hooves might be utilized in jellies and sauces, ears and muzzles in head cheese, intestines as sausage casings.

To be sure, many of the dishes I mention can no longer be duplicated, or duplicated only with difficulty, because the components are impossible to obtain or are available only at great trouble and expense (e.g., raw milk and many species of terrapin, fowl, and seafood). Some of the recipes consist of little more than a list of ingredients because, prior to the introduction of gas stoves with rheostats in the 1920s, the directions for baking specified not a specific heat but a "fast," "quick," "moderate," "slack," "gentle," or "slow" oven. In fact, I omitted several recipes that purport to authenticity because they specify an exact oven temperature, proving they had been written after 1920, much as if a recipe from the 1880s required a food processor or blender instead of a mortar and pestle or a manual grinder.

In effect, then, this is a celebrity cookbook to which many celebrities, some living but most long dead, have contributed. I've learned a great deal about cuisine in the course of compiling it. When I began this project, I knew what a roux was but not how to spell it. While researching it, I discovered that nearly two dozen American author-chefs— Child, Sarah Josepha Hale, Onoto Watanna, Rex Stout, Lillian Hellman, and Maya Angelou among them — have published cookbooks, with dozens of American poets, playwrights, and novelists contributing to them since the rise of celebrity culture in the mid-nineteenth century. Dozens of male writers have authored or contributed to cookbooks, moreover, complicating the assumption that domestic labor has always been almost exclusively a woman's responsibility. Over the months I've tapped such resources as the menu collection at the New York Public Library and online archives of historical cookbooks at the University of Michigan and the Library of Congress. That is, I have gleaned all the recipes in this volume from cookbooks by authors, cookbooks or periodicals to which an author or an author's immediate family member contributed, and cookbooks by chefs who prepared public dinners attended by authors and for which there are extant menus. I have hardly scratched the surface, however. For example, I have not yet consulted any manuscript cookbooks such as those of Grace Ellery Channing in the Schlesinger Library at Radcliffe College, Dorothy Thompson in the Syracuse University Library, Rose Wilder Lane in the Hoover Presidential Library near Iowa City, Ellen Glasgow in the University of Virginia Library, and Gloria Anzaldúa at the Harry Ransom Center at the University of Texas.

By arrangement with the publisher, all royalties from the sale of this book have been directed to Desert Harvest and the Roadrunner Food Bank, a pair of food charities in Albuquerque, New Mexico. I wish to acknowledge the help of Tara Calishain, Heather Cole, and Amber Paranick in the preparation of this volume. My sincere thanks to Gary Snyder, Harlan Ellison, Ted Kooser, Leslie Marmon Silko, Bobbie Ann Mason, Ursula Le Guin, Elmore Leonard, David Amram, Rudolfo Anaya, Gerald Vizenor, Denise Chávez, Luci Tapahonso, and the many agents, heirs, trustees, executors, and publishers who granted me permission to reprint copyrighted works without fee.

The Recipes

CONRAD AIKEN

Conrad Aiken (1889–1973) received the Pulitzer Prize for Poetry in 1930 and served as the poetry consultant at the Library of Congress from 1950 to 1952.

Scrapple

The only recipe by Aiken —
One not derived from Shakespeare-Bacon —
Is: any really sensible chap'll
Fry an apple with his scrapple.

— Barr, *Artists' and Writers' Cookbook*, 14.

BRONSON AND LOUISA MAY ALCOTT

Bronson Alcott (1799–1888) was a vegetarian both by conviction and of necessity. His cousin William Andrus Alcott was a dietary reformer and disciple of Sylvester Graham, who advocated the consumption of raw fruits and vegetables and bread made with whole bran and unbleached flour and the avoidance of meat, seafood, and spices. Bronson's daughter Louisa May Alcott (1832–1888), the author of *Little Women* (1868–69), reminisced in "Transcendental Wild Oats" (1873), a fictionalized memoir of Fruitlands, a vegetarian community her father helped found, that the "elders" there ordained a diet of "unleavened bread, porridge, and water for breakfast; bread, vegetables, and water for dinner; bread, fruit, and water for supper."[1] The same restrictions were incorporated into the manuscript recipes compiled by Abigail May Alcott, Bronson's wife and Louisa May's mother.

In *Little Men* (1871), the narrator notes, "It was maddening [for Jo's boys] to smell the dinner, to know that there was to be succotash and huckleberry pudding."[2]

Berry Pudding Without Eggs

1 pint of berries, pint of flour, pint of sour milk, spoon of saleratus [baking soda], one of salt. Boil two hours. Turn often in pot to prevent settling.— Abigail May Alcott, *Receipts and Simple Remedies*, ed. Nancy Kohl (Concord, Mass.: Louisa May Alcott Memorial Association, 1980), 5.

Biscuit Without Milk

Rub a piece of butter the size of an egg into a quart of flour. Add teaspoonful of salt, scatter in two teaspoonfuls of cream of tartar. Have ready a large pint of cold water in which

5

teaspoonful of saleratus has been dissolved, pour it into the flour stirring quickly with your hand, then add flour enough to mould it smooth. Roll out an inch thick and bake quickly.— Alcott, *Receipts and Simple Remedies*, 7.

Cake Without Eggs

1 cup of butter
2½ cups sifted sugar
1 pint sour cream or buttermilk

1 quart flour
1 spoonful of saleratus
Bake ¾ hour.

— Alcott, *Receipts and Simple Remedies*, 2.

Ginger Snaps

Half pound butter, half [cup] sugar, two and one half [cups] flour, 1 pint molasses, teaspoon soda, caraway seed or ginger.

Roll very thin and bake a few minutes.— Alcott, *Receipts and Simple Remedies*, 4.

Graham Cake

1 teacup sour milk, nutmeg, 1 brown sugar, ½ spoon salt, 2½ flour (graham), spoonful saleratus.— Alcott, *Receipts and Simple Remedies* 2.

Tomato Catsup

In the nineteenth century, catsup was made from a variety of ingredients other than tomatoes, including lemons, anchovies, walnuts, cucumbers, mushrooms, oysters, currants, cherries, plums, liver, and lobster. Tomatoes were often shunned because they were considered carcinogenic,[3] though the Alcotts ignored the risk.

Slice the tomatoes, and sprinkle them with salt, boil, let them stand a while, then boil and strain through a sieve, slice two good-sized onions very thin, to every gallon add not large spoonful of ginger, two of pounded clove, two of allspice, one of pepper. Boil twenty minutes after the spices are in. Keep in a covered jar.— Alcott, *Receipts and Simple Remedies*, 6.

HORATIO ALGER, JR.

Horatio Alger, Jr. (1832–1899), a writer of juvenile fiction best known for his novel *Ragged Dick; or, Street Life in New York* (1868), resided in Natick, Massachusetts, with his sister Olive Augusta Cheney (1833–1916), a prominent suffragist, and her husband Amos for long periods of time as a guest or invalid. In July 1899, he died in their home, where he had been fed such healthy, high-fiber dishes as Egg Plant Pilau and Graham Muffins.

Egg Plant Pilau

Take one medium-sized egg plant. After paring cut in half-inch slices. Cut the slices in three quarter inch dice. Put in a two-quart enamel pan, sprinkle well with salt, cover with boiling water and let it stand for ten minutes, then drain. Chop fine two good sized onions and a tablespoonful of parsley and add to the egg plant. Then put in one-half cup well washed rice, and one quart hot water and bring slowly to the boiling point. Boil slowly until all the liquid has been absorbed. Add salt to taste. Put in one teaspoonful of butter, two teaspoonfuls of sugar and one-half cup of strained tomato. Place at the side of the fire where it cannot possibly burn for fifteen minutes. Turn out in a hot dish.— Boston *Woman's Journal*, October 17, 1908, 168.

Graham Muffins

One egg, one-quarter cup molasses, two and one-quarter cups sour milk, one-half an even teaspoonful of soda, two even cups of graham, and one even cup of flour. Add the egg, well beaten, to the molasses and sour milk, reserving a tablespoonful of the milk with which to dissolve the soda. Add the soda when dissolved, and afterward the graham and the flour. If you have no sour milk, add a teaspoonful of vinegar to the milk to sour it. Bake in muffin rings or a gem pan. They are delicious.— Hattie A. Burr, *The Woman Suffrage Cook Book* (Boston: Burr, 1890), 15.

DAVID AMRAM

Best known as a musician, David Amram (b. 1930) composed classical scores for the movies *Splendor in the Grass* (1961) and *The Manchurian Candidate* (1962). He is also the author of three autobiographies: *Vibrations: The Adventures and Musical Times of David Amram* (1968), *Offbeat: Collaborating with Kerouac* (2002), and *Upbeat: Nine Lives of a Musical Cat* (2008). In the first of these volumes, Amram reminisced about preparing an omelette for the jazz saxophonist Charlie Parker in 1952.

Omelette

I cooked up [a crazy omelette] with fried onions, marmalade, maple syrup, bacon, tomatoes, covered with hot mayonnaise with some garlic fried in it and a little cheese sauce. Bird was fascinated by my cooking and we both wolfed down portions of it, chased with some borscht and orange soda.— Amram, *Vibrations* (1968; rpt. Boulder: Paradigm, 2010), 103.

RUDOLFO ANAYA

The dean of Chicano writers, Rudolfo Anaya (b. 1937) is best known as the author of the coming-of-age novel *Bless Me, Ultima* (1972) and a series of tales featuring the detective Sonny Baca, and was a longtime creative writing professor at the University of New Mexico. His recipe for sardine sandwiches underscores the importance of sardines in Hispano culture, such as the Spanish ceremony *El Entierro de la Sardina*.

Sardinas de Lata (Sardines from the Can)

I don't know where to begin my praise of a mouth-watering sardine sandwich after a long morning of writing, especially if the novel is going nowhere. It begins with the opening of the can. There is an art to opening the can without spilling the precious oil in which the tasty friends are packed. I suggest each person experiment with the process, and do share it with a loved one. That first essence of sardines can be intoxicating.

A pre-sandwich aperitif is a shot of tequila.

Gingerly remove each sardine from its oily home and place them lengthwise on a warm tortilla. Add hot mustard, your preference, and thick slices of onions. I prefer Vidalia onions to complement the green chile which has been prepared with plenty of garlic.

A person can write all day on an easy to fix sardine sandwich. If you can't find green chile at your deli, add extra Dijon mustard.

As to the brand, I buy American; Portuguese sardines are for connoisseurs. I do love slightly smoked sardines, but today sardines come in a variety of sauces, so I leave that exploration of fine dining up to each sardine lover. Go on, don't be afraid to explore; I trust you'll find the right sardine flavor you can share with your friends.

The complimentary drink is a stout beer. Californians prefer a Chardonnay, full bodied, gay and busy, and with a nutty flavor. Don't sweat the bouquet because the sardines will kill it. Quite honestly, if a royalty check has just arrived and there's a hardy Merlot or Cabernet in the house, these reds pull their weight with sardines.

Palate cleanser: I take another shot of tequila. If you're on your way to meet your agent or publisher (which few of us are nowadays) breath mints will do. A caution, breath mints do tend to clash with the satisfying aftertaste of sardines.

(If you thought I was going to give a recipe for tacos or enchilades, plates laden with spicy New Mexico chile verde or chile Colorado as only my wife can prepare, sorry. When left alone to my devices and deep in a novel I go for the quick and easy to prepare protein. Su amigo de Nuevo Mexico, where we have never heard the phrase, "We sail with the tide." Ciao.) — *The New Great American Writers' Cookbook*, ed. Dean Faulkner Wells (Jackson: University Press of Mississippi, 2003), 117.

Having breakfast together at a Manhattan diner in 1959 are (left to right) painter and poet Larry Rivers, Jack Kerouac, David Amram, Allen Ginsberg, and Gregory Corso with his back to the camera (photograph by John Cohen, courtesy L. Parker Stephenson Gallery).

SHERWOOD ANDERSON

Baked Ham

The author of *Winesburg, Ohio* (1919), Sherwood Anderson (1876–1941) remarks in chapter 17 of his novel *Poor White* (1920) on the "three small houses where hams were smoked" in a backwater Missouri village on the banks of the Mississippi.[1] In the heyday of cooking contests during the Great Depression, he offered a prize-winning recipe for ham steak.

A good cured ham is best. You cut thick slices across the ham, almost an inch thick. Put them in a heavy iron frying pan and float them in fresh milk. Let them simmer for four hours. Add more fresh milk if needed. Cook until ham is well cooked through and through. Serve like a thick steak.— *Chicago Tribune*, April 5, 1936, E2.

ANONYMOUS

Boston Brown Bread

The Bostonians, you know, are most cultured, 'tis said.
And it's greatly on account of their Boston brown bread.
The secret of making, I'm privileged to tell,
So, add one cup of corn meal, dear sisters, scald well;
Then add to the same one cup of graham,
And a cup and a half of white flour;
Of molasses a cup, and an egg beaten up,
And one cup of milk that is sour;
One teaspoon and a half of soda to raise it
And one of salt, or none would praise it;
Stir it up well, and four hours steam it;
And rest assured all will deem it
A greater treat than the finest cake
That one could eat or cook could bake.

—*Marshall Ladies' Choicest and Best* (Marshall, Minn.:
Ladies of St. Cecelia Guild, 1898), 51; rpt. in Jan Longone,
"The Mince Pie That Launched the Declaration of Independence
and Other Recipes in Rhyme," *Gastronomica* 2 (Fall 2002), 88.

Breakfast Dish

Cut smoothly from a wheaten loaf
    Ten slices, good and true,
And brown them nicely o'er the coals,
    As you for toast would do.

Prepare a pint of thickened milk,
    Some codfish shredded small;
And have on hand six hard-boiled eggs,
    Just right to slice withal.

Moisten two pieces of the bread,
    And lay them in a dish,
Upon them slice some hard-boiled egg,
    Then scatter o'er with fish.

And for a seasoning you will need
    Of pepper just one shake,
Then spread above the milky juice,
    And this one layer make.

And thus, five time, bread, fish and egg,
    Or bread and egg and fish,
Then place one egg upon the top,
    To crown this breakfast dish.

            — Burr, *The Woman Suffrage Cook Book*, 20.

Cheese Relish

Six Boston crackers split and dried,
And buttered well upon one side,
One pound of cheese, be sure it's nice —
Cut first in slices, then in dice.
One pint of milk, if fresh, use cold,
But scald if it's a little old.
A baking dish to hold a quart.
One of the round and shallow sort.
Now first put in some bits of cheese,
Then crumble cracker over these.
Then cheese, then cracker, and when you stop,
Be sure the cracker comes on top.
With salt and pepper season lightly,
Also with cayenne very slightly.
The milk add last, bake half an hour,
And serve it hot, if in your power.

            —*A Book of Practical Recipes* (Pittsburgh, Pa.: Ladies of the
            South Side Presbyterian Church, 1907), 46; rpt. in Longone, 89.

Chowder, an Old Recipe

To make a good chowder and have it quite nice,
Dispense with sweet marjoram parsley and spice;
Mace, pepper and salt are now wanted alone.
To make the stew eat well and stick to the bone,
Some pork is slice thin and put into the pot;
Some say you must turn it, some say you must not;
And when it is brown, take it out of the fat,
And add it again when you add this and that.
A layer of potatoes, sliced quarter inch thick,
Should be placed in the bottom to make it eat slick;

A layer of onions now over this place,
Then season with pepper and salt and some mace.
Split open your crackers and give them a soak.
In eating you'll find this the cream of the joke.
On top of all this, now comply with my wish,
And put, in large chunks, all your pieces of fish;
Then put on the pieces of pork you have fried —
I mean those from which all the fat has been tried.
In seasoning I pray you, don't spare the cayenne;
'Tis this makes it fit to be eaten by men.
After adding these things in their reg'lar rotation,
You'll have a dish fit for the best of the nation.

> — Jessup Whitehead, *The Steward's Handbook* (1899); rpt. in Susan Williams, *Savory Suppers and Fashionable Feasts* (New York: Pantheon, 1985), 227.

Colonial Punch

Of oranges four and lemons two
You take the juice to make your brew;
Eight tablespoons of sugar fine,
A quart of good red Bordeaux wine,
A large spoonful of choice Jamaica
Will give a flavor delicious later.
Then a generous wine glass of old Cognac
Will make your lips begin to smack,
But wait until you add the sparkling champagne
A pint at least or your labor's in vain.

> —*Famous Old Receipts*, 186.

Corn Bread

Two cups Indian; one cup wheat;
One cup sour milk, one cup sweet;
One good egg that you will beat;
One-half cup molasses, too;
One-half cup sugar add thereto,
With one spoon butter, new
Salt and soda each a teaspoon
Mix up quick and bake it soon;
Then you'll have corn bread complete,
Best of all corn bread you meet.

> —*Marshall Ladies' Choicest and Best* (Marshall, Minn.: Ladies of St. Cecelia Guild, 1898), 49; rpt. in Longone, 88.

Corn Pone

Take a cup of cornmeal, and the meal should be yellow;
Add a cup of wheat flour for to make the corn mellow;

Of sugar a cup, white or brown at your pleasure,
(The color is nothing, the fruit is the measure);

And now comes a troublesome thing to indite,
For the rhyme and the reason they trouble me quite;
For after the sugar, the flour and the meal
Comes a cup of sour cream, but unless you should steal
From your neighbors, I fear you will never be able
This item to put upon your cook's table;
For "sure and indeed," in all town I remember,
Sour cream is as scarce as June buds in December.

So here an alternative nicely contrived
Is suggested your mind to relieve,
And showing how you without stealing at all
The ground that is lost may retrieve.
Instead of sour cream take one cup of milk,
"Sweet milk!" what a sweet phrase to utter!
And to make it creamlike put into the cup
Just three tablespoonfuls of butter.

Cream of tartar, one teaspoonful, rules dietic —
How nearly I wrote it down tartar emetic! —
But no; cream of tartar it is without doubt,
And so the alternative makes itself out.
Of soda the half of a teaspoonful add,
Or else your poor corn cake will go to the bad;
Two eggs must be broken without being beat,
Then of salt a teaspoonful your work will complete.
Twenty minutes of baking are needed to bring
To the point of perfection this "awful good thing."

To eat at the best this remarkable cake
You should fish all day long on the royal-named lake,
With the bright waters glancing in glorious light
And beauties outnumbered bewild'ring your sight,
On mountain and lake, in water and bay;
And then, when the shadows fall down from on high,
Seek "Sabbath Day Point," as the light fades away,
And end with this feast the angler's long day,
Then, there you will find, without any question,
That an appetite honest awaits on digestion.

— Brander Matthews, "Recipes in Rhyme,"
Harper's Bazar [*sic*] 38 (February 1904), 191.

Eve's Pudding

If you want a good pudding, mind what you are taught,
Take of eggs six in number when bought for a groat,
The fruit with which Eve her husband did cozen,

Well pared and well chopped, at least half a dozen,
Six ounces of bread, let Moll eat the crust,
And crumble the rest as fine as the dust,
Six ounces of currants from the stems you must sort,
Lest you break out your teeth and spoil all the sport,
Six ounces of sugar won't make it too sweet,
Some salt and some nutmeg will make it complete,
Three hours let it boil, without any flutter,
But Adam won't like it without wine and butter.

—*Famous Old Receipts*, 351.

Oatmeal Pudding

Of oats decorticated take two pounds,
And of new milk enough the same to drown;
Of raisins of the sun, stoned, ounces eight;
Of currants, cleanly picked, an equal weight;
Of suet, finely sliced, an ounce at least;
And six eggs, newly taken from the nest:
Season this mixture well with salt and spice;
'Twill make a pudding far exceeding rice;
And you may safely feed on it like farmers,
For the recipe is learned Dr. Harmer's.

— Maria Moss, *A Poetical Cookbook*
(Philadelphia: Caxton, 1864), 103.

Old Virginia Mince Pie

Our much respected Uncle Sam
Loves pies—of pumpkin, fruit or jam;
Potato, apple, lemon, cherry;
Peach, plum, and every kind of berry.
These are but courtiers to the prince
Of pies—the "Old Virginia Mince."
There is but one right way to make it;
Ere in its flaky crust you bake it:
Use neither tongue nor other meat
(As some cooks do), but boil the feet
Of calf or pig: then softly press
Through colander the pearly mess.
Of this fill cup, with dainty touch,
To mix with fruit and spice and such.
A cup of raisins, stoned, prepare;
A cup of currants then wash with care
(For things that grow in foreign lands
May have been packed by germy hands.)
A cup of apple chopped — no rind:
A cup of sugar — heaping, mind!

A cup of finely shredded suet,
A dash of pepper from the cruet;
A pinch of salt, of nutmeg, mace,
Of cloves— to give a zest and grace;
One lemon, orange, juice and rind
(Only the yellow grated fine).
Some citron shavings, crisp and thin;
Then pour a glass of brandy in.
Glass large or small, no matter which,
Enough to make all moist and rich.
(Should Uncle Sam object, thus meet it:
"He isn't asked to drink, just eat it.")
Line a deep dish with pastry, light
As feathers, soft and creamy white.
Cover as simply as you will
For worth and beauty need no frill.
Five minutes slowly bake, then heat
Your oven three hundred Fahrenheit.
Watching, you rest upon your chair,
And festive odors fill the air!
You almost see the mistletoe!
You almost hear the fiddle-bow!
The rhythmic tap of little feet,
The rippling laughter, low and sweet,
As perfumed incense rises high
From Old Virginia's own mince pie.
The old-time Randolphs made these pies
For Christmas dinners. They were wise.
They made some other things, they tell,
Tobacco, laws, and made them well.
Our Independence Declaration,
The prop and bulwark of our nation,
Standing today as then it stood,
Was writ by one of Randolph blood.[1]
That Democratic son of yore
Ate a mince pie the day before.

        — *Our Girls' Cook Book* (Evansville: Journal
        Job Printing, 1910), 75; rpt. in Longone, 88.

Oyster Cocktail

If the right amount you take,
This will just seven cocktails make.
In each glass three raw oysters toss,
And stand aside till you make your sauce.
Take of catsup one-half cup,
Same of vinegar and stir up,

One tablespoon of Worcestershire,
It must be hot and burn like fire.
Ten drops of Tabasco add,
Of course this last is just a fad,
And if it is not on your shelf,
To red pepper help yourself.
Now over each glass of oysters pour
Just three teaspoons and no more.
Serve as first course to your dinner,
It will please both saint and sinner.

—*Congressional Club Cookbook* (Washington,
D.C.: Congressional Club, 1927), 151.

Plum Pudding

If you wish to make a pudding in which everyone delights,
Of six pretty new laid eggs you must take the yolks and whites;
Beat them well up in a basin till they thoroughly combine,
And be sure you chop the suet up particularly fine;
Take a pound of well-stoned raisins, and a pound of currants dried,
A pound of pounded sugar, and some lemon peel beside;
Rub them well all up together, with a pound of wheaten flour,
And then set them to settle for a quarter of an hour,
Then tie the mixture in a cloth, and put it in a pot —
Some people like the water cold, and some prefer it hot:
But though I don't know which of these two plans I ought to praise,
I know it ought to boil an hour for every pound it weighs.
Oh! if I were Queen of England, or still better, Pope of Rome,
I'd have a vast plum pudding every day I dined at home.
All the world should have a piece, and if any did remain,
Next morning for my breakfast I would fry it up again.

—*Southern Planter* 12 (May 1852), 154.

Plum Pudding

Aunt Betsy makes good pudding,
    And you can likewise do it
If you follow her directions:
    "Take half a pound of suet,
Three quarter pounds of bread crumbs fine,
Two tablespoons of brandywine,
One and a quarter pounds of fruit,
A pinch of grated ginger root,
Quarter-pound moist sugar — brown —
A single nutmeg grated down,
Two tablespoons of milk or cream
(The latter is best, I deem),
Four eggs — and just enough molasses

To fill one of your small wineglasses—
Then steam five hours." I'm sure you'll say
"No better cook than Betsy Leigh."
— Matthews, "Recipes in Rhyme," 189.

Stewed Duck and Peas

I give thee all my kitchen lore,
Though poor the offering be;
I'll tell thee how 'tis cooked, before
You come to dine with me.
The duck is truss'd from head to heels,
Then stew'd with butter well,
And streaky bacon, which reveals
A most delicious smell.
When duck and bacon, in a mass,
You in a stewpan lay,
A spoon around the vessel pass,
And gently stir away;
A tablespoon of flour bring,
A quart of water plain,
Then in it twenty onions fling,
And gently stir again.
A bunch of parsley, and a leaf
Of ever verdant bay,
Two cloves, — I make my language brief, —
Then add your peas you may;
And let it simmer till it sings
In a delicious strain;
Then take your duck, nor let the strings
For trussing it remain.
The parsley fail not to remove,
Also the leaf of bay;
Dish up your duck, — the sauce improve
In the accustom'd way,
With pepper, salt, and other things
I need not here explain;
And if this dish contentment brings,
You'll dine with me again.
— Moss, 48; rpt. Longone, 87.

SUSAN B. ANTHONY

Even Susan B. Anthony (1820–1906), the most prominent suffragist of the nineteenth century, co-author of the six-volume *History of Woman Suffrage* (1881), and the heroine of Gertrude Stein's opera *The Mother of Us All* (1949), was not exempt from the expectation that she conform to conventional gender roles. Anthony was "an excellent cook and housekeeper," according to Jenny June Croly, "and it was a proverb at home that, when Susan did the housekeeping the meals were always punctual and well served. She believes in a plain, simple diet."[1] Anthony contributed a recipe for Apple Tapioca Pudding to Jennie June's cookbook.

Apple Tapioca Pudding

Peel and core eight apples, fill them with sugar in which a little nutmeg has been grated. Take a cupful of tapioca, which has all night been soaking in water, add to it a little milk or water if needed, and pour it round the apples, which have been laid in a buttered dish. Bake slowly one hour and serve with cream and powdered sugar. It is good hot or cold, the tapioca forming a jelly round the apples.— Jane C. Croly, *Jennie June's American Cookery Book* (New York: American News, 1870), 330–31.

CATHARINE BEECHER

Catharine Beecher (1800–1878), one of thirteen children of Lyman and Roxana Beecher, was the sister of Henry Ward Beecher, Harriet Beecher Stowe, and Isabella Beecher Hooker. Like her siblings, she was a devoted domestic reformer, and with Harriet she collaborated on the advice manual *American Woman's Home* (1869). There the sisters conceded, "Of a piece of beef at twenty-five cents a pound, fifty cents' worth is often lost in bone, fat, and burnt skin."[1] So the next year Catharine Beecher published a recipe for a low-quality cut of beef.

Cheapest Beef

Take eight pounds of the cheapest beef, no matter how tough. Put it on a trivet or a time plate, in a close-covered pot, with four quarts of water, two great-spoonfuls of salt, and one great-spoonful of sugar. Simmer gently and steadily five hours, or till the water is reduced to about three pints. Then bake it in an oven, or put coals on the pot cover, and continue the simmering till the water is reduced to about half a pint, which is to be thickened for the gravy with a little potato or cornstarch.

The above is varied by adding these flavors in a muslin bag, placed in the water at first: Two leeks, or one onion sliced; one teaspoonful of dried and powdered thyme; half a teaspoonful of summer savory, dried and powdered; half a teaspoonful of dried and powdered sweet-marjoram, or sage, or rosemary.— *Harper's Bazar* [sic], September 3, 1870, 567.

Coffee

In chapter 18 of Harriet Beecher Stowe's *Uncle Tom's Cabin* (1851–52), the slave cook Dinah "makes superb coffee."[2] Ironically, in *A Treatise on Domestic Economy* (1845), Catharine Beecher had blamed tea and coffee for causing "much of the nervous debility and suffering endured by American women."[3] Still, she printed a coffee recipe in her *Miss Beecher's Domestic Receipt Book* five years later.

Mocha and Old Java are the best, and time improves all kinds. Dry it a long time before roasting. Roast it quick, stirring constantly, or it will taste raw and bitter. When roasted, put in a bit of butter the size of a chestnut. Keep it shut up close, or its loses its strength and flavor. Never grind it till you want to use it, as it loses flavor by standing.

To prepare it, put two great spoonfuls to each pint of water, mix it with the white, yolk, and shell of an egg, pour on hot, but not boiling water, and boil it not over ten minutes. Take it off, pour in half a teacup of cold water, and in five minutes pour it off without shaking. When eggs are scarce, clear with fish skin, as below. Boiled milk improves both tea and coffee, but must be boiled separately. Much coffee is spoiled by being burned black instead of brown, and by being burned unequally, some too much and some too little. Constant care and stirring are indispensable.

Fish Skin for Coffee

Take the skin of a mild codfish which has not been soaked, rinse and then dry it in a warm oven, after bread is drawn. Cut it in inch squares. One of these serves for two quarts of coffee, and is put in the first thing.— *Miss Beecher's Domestic Receipt Book* (New York: Harper and Bros., 1850), 187–88.

French Pot au Feu

> In *The American Woman's Home*, Catharine Beecher and her sister Harriet remarked on one of the advantages of open-hearth cooking: The "kettle may be maintained in a constant position on the range, and into it the cook may be instructed to throw all the fibrous trimmings of meat, all the gristle, tendons, and bones, having previously broken up these last with a mallet. Such a kettle, the regular occupant of a French cooking-stove, which they call the *pot au feu*, will furnish the basis for clear, rich soups, or other palatable dishes."[4]

Put three pounds of fresh meat into three quarts of cold water, with two teaspoonfuls of salt. When it begins to simmer, add a gill of cold water, and skim thoroughly. Then add a medium-sized carrot, sliced, two small turnips, one middle-sized leek, one stalk of celery, one of parsley, a bay leaf, one onion with two cloves stuck in it, and two cloves of garlic. Simmer five hours. Strain the broth into a soup dish, and serve the meat and vegetable on a platter. If more water is needed, add that which is boiling.— *Harper's Bazar* [sic], September 3, 1870, 567.

Fricassee Chickens

Wash the chickens and divide them into pieces, put them in a pot or stew pan with several slices of salt ham or pork and sprinkle each layer with salt and pepper; cover them with water, and let them simmer till tender, keeping them covered. Then take them up, and mix with the gravy a piece of butter the size of a hen's egg, and a paste made of two teaspoonfuls of flour wet up with the gravy. Put back the chickens and let them stew five minutes. Then spread crackers or toasted bread on the platter, put the chickens on it, and pour the gravy over.

In case it is wished to have them browned, take them out when nearly cooked and fry them in butter till brown, or pour off all the liquid and fry them in the pot.— *Miss Beecher's Domestic Receipt Book*, 50–51.

Mush or Hasty Pudding

Wet up the Indian meal in cold water, till there are no lumps, stir it gradually into boiling water which has been salted, till so thick that the stick will stand in it. Boil slowly, and so as not to burn, stirring often. Two or three hours' boiling is needed. Pour it into a broad, deep dish, let it grow cold, cut it into slices half an inch thick, flour them, and fry them on a griddle with a little lard, or bake them in a stove oven.—*Miss Beecher's Domestic Receipt Book*, 108.

Shoulder of Lamb

Check the shoulder with cuts an inch deep, rub on first butter, then salt, pepper, and sweet herbs, over these put the yolk of an egg and bread crumbs, and then bake or roast it a light brown. Make a gravy of the drippings, seasoning with pepper, salt, and tomato catsup, and also the grated rind and juice of a lemon; thicken with a very little flour.—*Miss Beecher's Domestic Receipt Book*, 49.

Spanish Olla-Podrida

Fry four ounces of salt pork in the pot, and when partly done add two pounds of fresh meat and a quarter of a pound of ham, with water enough just to cover the meat. Skim carefully the first half hour, and then add a gill of pease (if dried, soak them an hour first), half a head of cabbage, one carrot, one turnip, two leeks, three stalks of celery, three stalks of parsley, two stalks of thyme, two cloves, two onions sliced, two cloves of garlic, ten peppercorns, and a pinch of powdered mace or nutmeg. Simmer steadily for five hours. When the water is too low, add that which is boiling. Put the meat on a platter, and the vegetables around it. Strain the liquor on to toasted bread in a soup dish.—*Harper's Bazar* [*sic*], September 3, 1870, 567.

Succotash

Succotash, from the Narragansett word *msíckquatash*, is an Indian dish, a medley of corn and beans. As Ben Franklin wrote the London *Gazetteer:* "Indian corn, take it all in all, is one of the most agreeable and wholesome grains in the world; that its green leaves roasted are a delicacy beyond expression; that samp, hominy, succotash, and nokehock [hot cornmeal] made of it, are so many pleasing varieties; and that johny or hoecake, hot from the fire, is better than a Yorkshire muffin."[5]

If you wish to make succotash, boil the beans from half to three-quarters of an hour, in water a little salt, meantime cutting off the corn and throwing the cobs to boil with the beans. Take care not to cut too close to the cob, as it imparts a bad taste. When the beans have boiled the time above mentioned, take out the cobs, add the corn, and let the whole boil from fifteen to twenty minutes for young corn, and longer for older corn. Make the proportions two-thirds corn and one-third beans. When you have a mess amounting to two quarts of corn and one quart of beans, take two tablespoonfuls of flour, wet it into a thin paste, and stir it into the succotash, and let it boil up for five minutes. Then lay some butter in a dish, take it up into it, and add more salt if need be.—*Miss Beecher's Domestic Receipt Book*, 77.

Tomato Catsup

Pour boiling water on the tomatoes, let them stand until you can rub off the skin, then cover them with salt, and let them stand twenty-four hours. Then strain them, and to two quarts put three ounces of cloves, two ounces of pepper, two nutmegs. Boil half an hour, then add a pint of wine.—*Miss Beecher's Domestic Receipt Book*, 72.

HENRY WARD BEECHER

Henry Ward Beecher (1813–1887) was the minister of the Plymouth Church in Brooklyn for forty years before his death and perhaps the most eminent American divine of the 1870s and '80s. As a young pastor in Indianapolis in the mid–1840s, he edited the *Western Farmer and Gardener*, an agricultural paper in which he published his own recipes and, much as his sisters offered advice on domestic economy, he later published an agricultural manual, *Plain and Pleasant Talk About Fruits, Flowers, and Farming* (1859). He also penned a novel, *Norwood* (1868).

Barbeque

Any animal split in two down the back and laid on a gridiron is "barbequed," according to the dictionary sense of that work; but, as the term is usually understood, it is roasting the animal whole for social gatherings or some great public occasions. It is an excellent and easy way for hunters camping out to cook their small game or fish. In ancient and more barbarous times the animals were literally roasted whole, but a more decent and palatable mode is after the following fashion:

First dress and clean the animal; wash thoroughly, and drain, and wipe dry; and if desired, fill the interior with any stuffing that may be fancied—vegetables, with forcemeat balls, small birds, etc.; for it will take hours to cook the whole.

Meanwhile dig a hole in the ground in size to suit the body to be cooked. Drive four stakes or posts just far enough outside the hole to be in no danger of burning. On these posts build a rack of poles to support the carcass; these should be selected of dried wood of a kind that will not impart any flavor to the meat. This being done, build a large fire of hard wood in the hole. When the wood has burned down to clear coals, without any smoke, lay the animal to be roasted on the rack over the coals. Have ready a bent stick, with a large well-cleansed sponge fastened to one end, and the other end of the stick made fast to one corner of the rack. Arrange this stick so that it will hang directly over the sheep, calf, or ox to be roasted. Have ready a mixture of ground mustard, vinegar, salt, and pepper; add to it sufficient water to fill the sponge as often as it drips dry, so that it can drip constantly over the meat until done. Have another fire burning near at hand, so as to replenish the coals under the carcass as often as needed.

Before putting the body over the coals, fasten it to three strong poles extending far enough beyond the carcass, one as a stay or support down the back to prevent the meat, when nearly done, breaking apart, and the others as handles by which three or four men can turn over the roast, so that all parts may be roasted evenly, and occasionally sprinkled with flour, and basted, if desired, with butter or clarified drippings.

The rack should not be raised so high from the coals as to make it inaccessible to this last operation, nor placed so close to the pit as to scorch.

This mode of cooking is all very well in the excitement of some great public occasion, but is lacking in the delicacy of flavor imparted that best suits an epicure's palate. But for *hunters* it is an excellent way to cook small game or fish. Clean them nicely, but leave them as nearly whole as may be, and season them well. After the wood in the pit, which need not be large, is burned to a coal, wrap the game in several thicknesses of clean coarse paper. Have the last wrapper wet. Rake the coals one side; scrape the ashes back, leaving only a small portion on the hot earth; lay the game or fish, thus carefully wrapped up, on this bed, cover first with the hot ashes, then with the coals. A fish will be deliciously cooked in this manner, and all the juices preserved. Undo the wrappers, and when the last paper is loosened, the skin will all peel off, leaving the fish almost like a jelly.

With birds, ducks, turkeys, etc., which take the longer to cook, it may be necessary to keep the pit hot by burning more small wood on top of the closely covered game. But when done, the result will be the same. The game will be most delicately cooked, almost jellied with its own juice, in which it has been *sodden*; and with the skin, which will peel off easily, any taste of paper that may be possible will disappear.— *Harper's Bazar* [*sic*], April 23, 1881, 269.

Biscuits

Peel and boil two large potatoes in just water enough to cover. When done, mash smoothly, and adding a half a pint of the water in which they were boiled while hot, rub it through a "colander" or coarse sieve; add half a pint sweet milk, half a teaspoonful salt, one tablespoonful sugar, and flour to make a stiff batter. When cool, add half a penny's worth of baker's or half a cup homemade yeast, which is better. Let it rise thoroughly; then rub a teacup of butter into sufficient flour to mould. (If warm weather, it will be well to dissolve a half-teaspoonful of soda, and stir into the batter.) Beat the white of one egg stiff, and stir in with the butter and flour, being careful to use as little flour as possible, and have it stiff enough for moulding; then knead half an hour. If light too early for tea, put it into the cellar or refrigerator, till within an hour of tea-time — when it should be kneaded fifteen minutes, cut into small biscuits, and set to rise till as light as possible without souring; bake in a quick oven. When done, cover over closely with a clean breadcloth, and let them remain in the pan a few minutes to soften; then send to the table. They should be light as a puff, and very tender.—*Jennie June's American Cookery Book*, 328.

Reed-Birds

Cut sweet potatoes lengthwise; scoop out in the center of each a place that will fit half the bird. Now put in the birds, after seasoning them with butter, pepper, and salt, tying the two pieces of potato around each of them. Bake them. Serve them in the potatoes. Or, they can be roasted or fried in boiling lard like other birds.— Mary F. Henderson, *Practical Cooking and Dinner Giving* (New York: Harper and Bros., 1877), 188.

Succotash, or Corn and Beans

We give directions for a mess sufficient for a family of six or seven. To about half a pound of salt pork add three quarts of cold water and set it to boil. Now cut off three quarts of green corn from the cobs, set the corn aside and put *the cobs* to boil with the pork, as they will add much to the richness of the mixture. When the pork has boiled, say half an hour, remove the cobs and put in one quart of freshly-gathered, green, shelled beans; boil again for fifteen minutes; then add the three quarts of corn and let it boil another fifteen minutes. Now turn the whole out into a dish, add five or six large spoonfuls of butter, season it with pepper to your taste, and with salt also, if the salt of the pork has not proved sufficient. If the liquor has boiled away, it will be necessary to add a little more to it before taking it away from the fire, as this is an essential part of the affair.— *Western Farmer and Gardener*, August 1, 1846, 231.

Tomatoes

Beecher published a recipe for tomatoes in the *Western Farmer*, and it was "universally copied" and "beguiled thousands to the love of tomatoes. It has been introduced to cookbooks under the name of 'Indiana Recipe for Cooking Tomatoes.'"[1]

Take six pounds of sugar to the peck, or sixteen pounds, of the fruit. Scald and remove the skin in the usual way. Cook them over a fire, their own juice being sufficient without the addition of water, until the sugar penetrates and they are clarified. They are then taken out, spread on dishes, flattened, and dried in the sun. A small quantity of the syrup should be occasionally sprinkled over them whilst drying, after which pack them down in boxes, treating each layer with powdered sugar. The syrup is afterwards concentrated and bottled up for use. They keep well from year to year, and retain surprisingly their flavor, which is nearly that of the first quality of fresh figs! The pear shaped or single tomatoes answer the purpose best. Ordinary brown sugar may be used, a large portion of which is retained in the syrup.—*Western Farmer and Gardener*, August 5, 1844, 15.

Turtle Bean Soup

Soak one and a half pints of turtle beans, in cold water, overnight. In the morning drain off the water, wash the beans in fresh water, and put into the soup digester, with four quarts of good beef stock, from which all the fat has been removed. Set it where it will boil steadily but slowly, till dinner, or five hours, at the least—six is better. Two hours before dinner put in half a can of tomatoes, or eight fresh ones, and a large coffee-cup of tomato catsup. One onion, a carrot, and a few of the outside stalks of celery, cut into the soup with the tomatoes, improves it for most people. Strain through a fine colander, or coarse sieve, rubbing through enough of the beans to thicken the soup, and send to table hot.

In a note accompanying this recipe, Mrs. Beecher says: "After straining, I sometimes return the soup to the 'digester,' bring to a boil, and break in four or five eggs, and as soon as the *whites* have 'set'—a *very little*—dish the soup and bring to the table with the slightly cooked eggs floating on the top. There should be eggs enough to take one out for every person at the table."—*Jennie June's American Cookery Book*, 327.

ELIZABETH BISHOP

Brownies

In December 1957, the poet Elizabeth Bishop (1911–1979) wrote the poet Robert Lowell, "Since Brazilians are mad about anything chocolate (and get a special thrill from it because it's so bad for their 'livers') I have been requested to bring along 4 dozen brownies (something I've introduced to Brazil) and a large chocolate cake. You see how innocent our lives are here—just making money and eating sweets."[1] Bishop's brownie recipe survives among her papers at Vassar College.

4 squares bitter chocolate (or about a cup of cocoa)
4 eggs
½ cup butter
2½ cups white sugar

1 cup flour

2 teaspoons vanilla

2 cups chopped nuts

Melt the chocolate and butter together — or, if you use cocoa, melt along with half the sugar and a little water. Cool slightly and beat in eggs and rest of sugar.

Sift in flour, add vanilla and nuts and beat. The batter is fairly stiff — doesn't run much. Spread about <————> this thick in square pan.

Bake in a *slow* oven — about 45 minutes to an hour, depending on pan, thickness, etc. They should be dry on top, just pulling away from edges, but still rather damp in the middle. Cut in squares in pan and remove with spatula.

This makes *chewy* brownies — for a harder kind, use brown sugar and an extra egg — or half brown sugar — Can be made thicker and used hot with whipped cream on top for a dessert. — Archives and Special Collections Library, Vassar College

LILLIE DEVEREUX BLAKE

Like many other eminent women at the time, the novelist Lillie Devereux Blake (1833–1913), author of *Fettered for Life* (1874), was expected to demonstrate her femininity by cooking or at least publishing her own recipes.

Last Century Blackberry Pudding

Quart of molasses, teaspoonful each of allspice, cloves and cinnamon, same of salt, three pints of blackberries, two eggs, two teaspoonfuls of baking powder, flour enough to make the spoon stand in the batter; stir the blackberries in the last thing, boil in a bag four to five hours. Can be made just as well without eggs. Blackberries or huckleberries may be used, and, in winter, the same recipe makes an excellent cheap plum pudding. — Burr, *The Woman Suffrage Cook Book*, 57.

Tropic Delicacy

Slice four bananas, sprinkle profusely with powdered sugar, and squeeze the juice of two lemons over them. Put on ice till served. — Burr, *The Woman Suffrage Cook Book*, 112.

EDWIN BOOTH — BREAKFAST AT DELMONICO'S

In June 1880, before he left New York for London, where he performed during the next theatrical season, the actor Edwin Booth (1833–1893), older brother of Abraham Lincoln's assassin, was the guest of honor at a breakfast at Delmonico's. The attendees included the actors Joseph Jefferson and Lawrence Barrett, the playwright James Steele Mackaye, the impresarios Lester Wallach and P. T. Barnum, the theatrical critic William Winter, the poet E. C. Stedman, and the editors Parke Godwin and Lawrence Hutton.[1]

Terrine de fois gras (Terrine entière de foies-gras)

Unmold a terrine of foies-gras; scrape it neatly with a knife on top and sides to remove all the exterior grease, and keep it on ice. Procure a mold of the same shape but an inch wider in diameter and an inch deeper; incrust it in pounded ice; decorate the bottom and sides with fanciful cuts of truffles, tongue, egg white, and pistachios, dipping each piece into half-set jelly before fastening them on; cover this decoration with a layer of jelly, and pour in more to lay half an inch thick in the bottom. Place the foies-gras exactly in the center and finish filling the mold with cooled-off jelly; keep on ice. Put a rice foundation bottom one inch and a half in height on a plated metal tray with a half-inch high straight edge (the rice foundation should be one inch and a half less in diameter than the tray), turn the aspic out of its mold on to the rice foundation, fastening a small basket on top secured by a skewer, and filling it with small glazed truffles. Decorate around the rice foundation with triangular jelly croûtons, as shown in the drawing.—Charles Ranhofer, *The Epicurean* (New York: Ranhofer, 1894), 724.

Fig. 447.

Terrine de fois gras, from **The Epicurean.**

Kay Boyle

Kay Boyle (1902–1992), the last surviving major American expatriate writer of the '20s and the author of more than 40 books, lived in Rawayton, Connecticut, in the early 1960s.

Ratatouille Rowayton

There is aways a question as to whether a woman should or should not reveal the secrets which distinguish her. I do not know the answer entirely, but I do know that I am as loath to receive guests without my earrings on as I am to have my guests sit down to dinner without having my Ratatouille Rowayton in the oven with a generous sprinkling of freshly-grated parmesan cheese encrusting the top. I have never divulged the recipe for this dish, and I do not intend to do so now. But put the depicted ingredients together, and you will have prepared one of the most satisfactory casseroles that ever accompanied a meat dish (preferably broiled chicken or baked ham), or — with fresh, briefly-boiled shrimp added — ever constituted an entire dinner in itself.

In either case, a garden of raw peas, lettuce and spinach leaves, tossed with olive oil, garlic salt, and lemon juice, must be present, as fresh and inevitable as apple blossoms in May.

1. [rice] White and long-grained and beloved in China.

2. [artichokes] Drab green, hearts of, and they may be frozen, their natural habitat, France or Italy.

3. [peppers] Emerald green and varnished (come in red, if you prefer).

4. [tomatoes] Bright red, and should be skinned for participation in the Ratatouille.

5. [zucchini] Green, mottled like snakes. They might be taken for cucumbers by the undiscerning.

6. [mushroom] Golden, and filled with forest darkness and evening dew. Take a squirrel's advice on the edible varieties.

5 must first be washed slightly in cold water, hand-dried, and sliced.

3 must be gutted of seeds and chopped fine.

2 may be split in two, broken hearts being more tender than others.

Now boil 1, 2, 3, 4, and 5 in a minimum of salted water for precisely fifteen minutes.

Remove from fire and add 6, which has been previously broiled in butter. Place entire mixture in a glass casserole so that the colors show, sprinkle with Parmesan, and place in middle of oven. Bake at 350° for fifteen minutes, broil for time required to brown the Parmesan. Serve with Beaujolais, 1959.— Beryl Barr and Barbara Turner Sachs, *Artists' and Writers' Cookbook* (Sausalito: Contact Editions, 1961), 222–23.

OLIVER BELL BUNCE

> Oliver Bell Bunce (1828–1890) was a playwright best known for the comedy *Love in '76* (1857) and for editing *Appleton's Journal* between 1872 and 1881. His widow worked as a home economist after his death and syndicated some of her recipes.

Dandelion Wine

This homemade beverage is a New England drink. To make it in perfection gather four quarts of fresh dandelion blossoms, then cover with four quarts of cold water and add four oranges, peeled and cut into small bits, also four lemons, unpeeled, cut into smaller pieces, with seeds removed. Cover closely and let stand for two days, then put into a preserving kettle and allow to heat slowly until the boiling point is reached, but do not boil. Strain and add four pounds of coffee sugar. When it has cooled to blood heat add a slice of toast saturated with yeast and let all stand where the temperature will remain unchanged for four days, then again strain and bottle. The longer it stands the better it will be found.— *Atlanta Constitution*, July 1, 1900, A3.

Orange Loaf Cake

Mix the juice and grated rind of four oranges, let stand for ten minutes, then rub well with a spoon and strain. Add one pound of powdered sugar and work to a thick syrup. Cut one pound of butter into dice; wash in cold water. Squeeze and remove all water and milk, then add to the orange syrup and beat to a light cream.

Beat ten eggs until they are like soft custard and sift fourteen ounces of flour; stir them alternately with the cream a little at a time. Beat as long and as steadily as your strength will allow; pour into a buttered mold, and bake in a brisk oven until it shrinks from the pan. Turn it out from the mold, dust with flour, wipe it off; then cover with the following icing while warm:

Roll one small orange on a plate so as to cause the oil to exude. Then take a little powdered sugar to which there are no lumps, and rub gently and evenly in the hand, and then rub over and over the orange till it becomes saturated with oil, repeating the process till three pounds of sugar have been used, or the oil becomes exhausted.

Squeeze out the juice of the oranges and strain. Then break the whites of two eggs into a shallow china dish, and whisk them until they foam, but do not whiten; then sift in the sugar, a little at a time, add the juice with half a teaspoonful of lemon juice, little by little till it has been used.—*Atlanta Constitution* September 9, 1900, B5.

Robert E. Lee Cake

> In the old plantation days when dinner parties were many and family economies few, and the life of the Southern planter was one of pleasure rather than toil, Saturday was always "cake-day." … These cakes, rich, well-raised and light, were made from the recipes given here…. With many of the recipes, the cake-makers and bakers of today have substituted baking powder for the soda and cream of tartar, necessary in the days when the formulas were greatly in use.[1]

Nine eggs, the weight of seven eggs in sugar, the weight of four eggs in flour, down weight. Add the sugar to the well-beaten yolks of the nine eggs. Then add the whites, beaten very light. Stir in the flour gently and season with fresh lemon. Bake in jelly-cake tins. When cold spread each layer with the following filling: Strain the grated rind and juice of two oranges and one lemon through a fine sieve into a pound of pulverized sugar. Add to this a grated coconut and the white of one egg beaten very light.

This recipe will make two cakes of three layers each, and is exceptionally fine.—*Los Angeles Times*, April 13, 1893, 10.

JOHN BURROUGHS

> John Burroughs (1837–1921) was a nature writer in the tradition of Thoreau and John Muir. His collected writings total over twenty volumes with such titles as *Locusts and Wild Honey* (1879), *Bird and Bough* (1906), and *Under the Apple Trees* (1916). He lived during his last summers in a rustic cabin he built in the western Catskills.

A Frickasie (Colonial Recipe)

Take ye fowls, cut them in pieces and clean them. Season with pepper and salt, a little mace, nuttmeg cloves, some parslay, a little bit of onion. Let them lay 2 hours, then flowr them very well, fry in sweet butter and make ye butter hott before you put them in. Fry a fine brown. Wash ye pan and put them in again with a pint of gravy. Lett them swimyer in ye gravy. Take the yolks of 3 eggs with a little grated nuttmeg and a little juce of lemon and 2 spoonfulls of wine. Shake it over the fire till it is as thick as cream, pour over ye frickasie and so serve it to ye table hott.—*Famous Old Receipts*, ed. Jacqueline Harrison Smith (Philadelphia: Winston, 1908), 123.

Hearth and fireplace of John Burroughs' Woodchuck Lodge, built in 1908 in the western Catskills of New York (Library of Congress).

John Cage

Though John Cage (1912–1992) is best-known as an avant-garde musician and composer, he was also a painter and poet. Late in his life, afflicted with various ailments, he adopted a macrobiotic diet.

Homemade Bread

5 cups vegetable purée or gruel (see note)
5 cups stone-ground wholewheat flour
4 tablespoons fresh minced dill
1 teaspoon salt

1. Combine purée and flour in a large mixing bowl. Mix thoroughly. If the mixture is too liquid to knead add more flour. If too dry add more liquid.

2. Knead the mixture for 10 minutes. Turn into an 8½-by–4½-by–2½ breadpan.

3. Bake in a pre-heated 375 degree oven for 1 hour 15 minutes.

4. Turn out onto a rack and cool.

Note: Mr. Cage uses leftover cooked vegetables such as broccoli, kale, spinach, carrots, celery, celery root and squash, which he purées in a food processor with vegetable stock or water. The bread has the consistency of a dense German pumpernickel and goes well with smoked salmon.—*New York Times*, March 18, 1981, C6.

HELEN CAMPBELL

Helen Campbell (1839–1918) was the author of *The Problem of the Poor* (1882), *Prisoners of Poverty* (1889), and *Women Wage-Earners* (1893), the novel *Ballantyne* (1901), and co-editor with Charlotte Perkins Stetson (Gilman) of *The Impress* (1894). She held the position of professor of domestic science at Kansas State Agricultural College during the academic year 1896–97.

Candied or Crystallized Fruit or Nuts

Boil one cup of granulated sugar and one cup of boiling water together for half an hour. Then dip the point of a skewer into the syrup and then into cold water. If the thread formed breaks off brittle, the syrup is ready. The syrup must never be stirred, and must boil slowly, not furiously. When done, set the saucepan in boiling water, or pour the syrup into a bowl placed in hot water to keep the syrup from candying. Take the prepared fruit or nuts on the point of a large needle or fine skewer, dip them into the syrup, and then lay them on a dish, which has been lightly buttered or oiled; or string them on a thread, and after dipping in the syrup suspend them by the thread. When oranges are used, divide them into eighths and wipe all moisture. Cherries should be stoned. English walnuts are especially nice prepared in this way.—*Mrs. Lincoln's Boston Cookbook* (Boston: Roberts Bros., 1883), 436.

Deviled Ham

For this purpose use either the knuckle or any odds and ends remaining. Cut off all dark or hard bits, and see that at least a quarter of the amount is fat. Chop as finely as possible, reducing it almost to a paste. For a pint-bowl of this, make a dressing as follows:—

One even tablespoonful of sugar; one even teaspoonful of ground mustard; one salt-spoonful of cayenne pepper; one spoonful of butter; one teacupful of boiling vinegar. Mix the sugar, mustard, and pepper thoroughly, and add the vinegar little by little. Stir it into the chopped ham, and pack it in small molds, if it is to be served as a lunch or supper relish, turning out upon a small platter and garnishing with parsley.

For sandwiches, cut the bread very thin; butter lightly, and spread with about a teaspoonful of the deviled ham. The root of a boiled tongue can be prepared in the same way. If it is to be kept some time, pack in little jars, and pour melted butter over the top.— Campbell, *The Easiest Way in Housekeeping and Cooking* (Boston: Roberts Bros., 1893), 170.

Gingersnaps

One cup of butter and lard or dripping mixed, or dripping alone can be used; one cup of molasses; one cup of brown sugar; two teaspoonfuls of ginger, and one each of clove, all-spice, and mace; one teaspoonful of salt, and one of soda dissolved in half a cup of hot water; one egg.

Stir together the shortening, sugar, molasses, and spice. Add the soda, and then sifted flour enough to make a dough,—about three pints. Turn on to the board, and knead well. Take about quarter of it, and roll out thin as a knife-blade. Bake in a quick oven. They will bake in five minutes, and will keep for months. By using only four cups of flour, this can be baked in a loaf as spiced gingerbread; or it can be rolled half an inch thick, and baked

Helen Campbell in her laboratory kitchen circa 1896 (Library of Congress).

as a cookie. In this, as in all cakes, experience will teach you many variations.— Campbell, *The Easiest Way in Housekeeping and Cooking*, 229.

Irish Stew

This may be made of either beef or mutton, though mutton is generally used. Reject all bones, and trim off all fat and gristle, reserving these for the stock-pot. Cut the meat in small pieces, not over an inch square, and cover with cold water. Skim carefully as it boils up, and see that the water is kept at the same level by adding as it boils away. For two pounds of meat allow two sliced onions, eight good-sized potatoes, two teaspoonfuls of salt, and half a teaspoonful of pepper. Cover closely, and cook for two hours. Thicken the gravy with one tablespoonful of flour stirred smooth in a little cold water, and serve very hot. The trimmings from a fore-quarter of mutton will be enough for a stew, leaving a well-shaped roast besides. If beef is used, add one medium-sized carrot cut fine, and some sprigs of parsley. Such a stew would be called by a French cook a ragoût, and can be made of any pieces of meat or poultry.— Campbell, *The Easiest Way in Housekeeping and Cooking*, 151.

Tomato Catsup

Boil one bushel of ripe tomatoes, skins and all, and when soft strain through a colander to remove the skins only. Mix one cup of salt, two pounds of brown sugar, half an ounce of cayenne pepper, three ounces each of ground allspice, mace, and celery seed, two ounces of ground cinnamon, and stir into the tomato. Add two quarts of best cider vinegar, and when thoroughly mixed strain through a sieve. Pour all that runs through into a large kettle, and boil slowly till reduced one half. It is an improvement to add a pint of brandy ten minutes before the catsup is done, but many think it unnecessary. Put it in small bottles, seal, and keep in a cool, dark place.— *Mrs. Lincoln's Boston Cookbook*, 404.

ALICE CARY AND PHOEBE CARY

The poets Alice Cary (1820–1871) and Phœbe Cary (1824–1871) were well-regarded by their contemporaries, including Poe and Whittier, and lived together their entire lives.

Boiled Apple Dumplings

Peel and core large greening apples, of a uniform size, and fill the cavity with clear lemon marmalade. Enclose each one in a nice paste, rolled rather thin, and draw small knitted clothes over them, which give them a very pretty effect. Tie them close, and boil three quarters of an hour, or an hour, if the crust is made with suet. Serve with hard sauce, flavored with nutmeg.— *Jennie June's American Cookery*, 329.

Compote of Apples

Make a syrup of one pound of loaf sugar and a pint of water into which squeeze the juice of two lemons. When it is clear, and boiling, drop into it a dozen or more fine, sound, tart apples, peeled and cored, and let them boil gently until they are perfectly tender. When done, take them up with a skimmer, throw into the syrup a few thin strips of lemon rind, let them boil a few minutes, and then pour them, with the syrup, over the apples. Set away to cool.—*Jennie June's American Cookery*, 329

Minced Chicken

Mince all that is left of cold roast or boiled chickens. Warm it with half a cup of cold gravy and a tablespoonful of mushroom sauce. Pile it in the center of a dish and place round it alternately small and very thin slices of broiled ham and poached eggs on toast.—*Jennie June's American Cookery*, 91

Plum Pudding

To eight ounces of fine bread crumbs add six of beef suet, fresh and chopped small; six of raisins, weighed after they are mixed, two of candied citron, a whole nutmeg grated, four eggs, a pinch of salt, and a small wineglass of brandy. Soak the bread crumbs in a small pint of milk half an hour; add the other ingredients, mix well, boil three hours in a mould, and serve with rich wine sauce.—*Jennie June's American Cookery*, 328.

Snow Balls

Peel and take out the cores of six large baking apples, equal size. Fill the holes with quince marmalade, and roll the apples in pounded loaf sugar. Then cover them with a smooth, good paste, of equal thickness, and bake them a light brown in a moderate oven. Have an icing prepared, flavored with lemon, with which cover them thickly, and set them near enough to the first to harden, but not to become brown.—*Jennie June's American Cookery*, 330.

WILLA CATHER

In a 1925 interview, Willa Cather (1873–1947) remarked, "Preparation of food is one of the most important things in life."[1] Susan Rosowski adds that "storytelling and food" were "inseparable in Cather's fiction."[2] Cather's family owned three standard, well-thumbed cookbooks during her adolescence in Nebraska: Elizabeth Ellicott Lea's *Domestic Cookery* (1854), F. L. Gillette's *The White House Cook Book* (1887), and James Edson White and Mrs. M. L. Wanless's *The Home Queen Cook Book* (1893).

Christmas Plum Pudding

Shortly after Christmas 1921, Willa Cather thanked her friend Carrie Miner Sherwood for sending her a holiday pudding. The recipe for it survives among Sherwood's papers.

1 cup finely chopped beef suet
2 cups bread crumbs
1 cup sugar
1 cup raisins
1 cup washed currants
1 cup blanched almonds, chopped
½ cup citron, sliced thin
1 teaspoon salt

Willa Cather (right) at lunch in Ville d'Avray in 1923, with Isabelle McClung and Jan Hambourg (Willa Cather Archive, Archives & Special Collections, University of Nebraska-Lincoln Libraries).

1 teaspoon [ground] cloves
2 teaspoons cinnamon
½ teaspoon grated nutmeg
4 well-beaten eggs
1 cup milk
1 teaspoon soda, dissolved in 1 tablespoon warm water
flour as needed, about 1½ cups

Put fruit in a bowl and sprinkle with flour to coat. In a large bowl, mix the eggs, sugar, spices, and salt with milk. Stir in the fruit, chopped nuts, bread crumbs, and suet. Add the dissolved soda and enough flour to make the fruit stick together (about 1½ cups). Boil or steam for 4 hours.—*At Willa Cather's Tables*, ed. Ann Romines (Red Cloud, Neb.: Cather Foundation, 2010), 141.

Cream Pie

A recipe for cream pie also appears in *The Home Queen Cook Book*, where it is scored and labeled "fine."[3]

Boil 1½ pts. Milk and add to it 3 tablespoons corn starch dissolved in a little milk, 1 cup sugar and butter the size of a small egg. Pour this mixture over the beaten yolks of 3 eggs, and add lemon extract or flavoring of some kind to taste. Pour this into the pie plates lined with paste, and bake about 20 minutes. Beat the whites of the 3 eggs with a little sugar, spread over the pie, and brown lightly in the oven.—White and Wanless, *The Home Queen Cookbook* (Chicago: Donahue, 1893), 392.

RAYMOND CHANDLER

Gimlet

One of the founders, with Dashiell Hammett, of the so-called hard-boiled school of detective fiction, Raymond Chandler (1888–1959) offers a recipe for a gimlet in the voice of one of his characters in *The Long Goodbye* (1953).

A real gimlet is half gin and half Rose's Lime Juice and nothing else. It beats martinis hollow.—Chandler, *Later Novels and Other Writings* (New York: Library of America, 1995), 432.

DENISE CHÁVEZ

Denise Chávez (b. 1948), author of *The Last of the Menu Girls* (1986), is a novelist, short story writer, playwright, actor, and teacher based in southern New Mexico.

Delfina Spanish — Really Mexican — Rice

1 small onion, diced
2 tablespoons cooking oil. I use canola oil, but my Mother used whatever leftover grease was in her tinita on top of the stove.
1 cup white rice. It's not necessary to have fancy, expensive, health food rice; as I recall we never did.
1 cup juicy tomatoes, canned or fresh, chopped
2 cups hot water or broth
Comino/cumin to taste
Salt to taste
Sauté onions in a faithful sartén. Two tablespoons of oil should do it, but since onions vary, you will have to check, and you may need more. When the onions are soft, add rice. Add the cup of tomatoes. Stir gently and add 2 cups boiling or very hot water or broth. After the initial stirring of rice, tomatoes and water or broth, add the comino and salt, about a teaspoon each. After this, cover the rice and leave it alone. Don't look, don't touch and don't mess with the rice! Don't even think of looking at it until it is done. And how will you know when it is done? You'll just know. Something in your body will start twitching and itching and you'll know, you'll just know it's ready. If for some reason you don't start twitching, it should take about 20 minutes. That is, if you use simple white rice and not brown rice. If you use brown rice, we know what kind of person you are, and it will take longer, about 45 minutes.

Take the rice from the heat and let it rest. If you are my Mother, your rice will be perfect. If you are like me, the rice will be pretty good, my husband's phrase for so-so or merely acceptable. His arbitrary "so-so" is what I fear my rice tastes like.—Chávez, *A Taco Testimony: Meditations on Family, Food and Culture* (Tucson: Rio Nuevo, 2006), 76–77.

LYDIA MARIA CHILD

Writers of domestic fiction often penned cookbooks, as Monika Elbert and Marie Drews remind us.[1] A case in point is Lydia Maria Child (1802–1880), an ardent abolitionist and author of the sentimental romance *Hobomok* (1824). Child's only book of cookery, *The Frugal Housewife*, was reprinted at least 35 times in the U.S. between 1829 and 1850 and appeared in England and Germany. Herbert Edwards describes it as "one of the most popular ... books published in New England in the 1830s."[2]

Beef

Beef soup should be stewed four hours over a slow fire. Just water enough to keep the meat covered. If you have any bones left of roast meat, &c., it is a good plan to boil them with the meat, and take them out half an hour before the soup is done. A pint of flour and water, with salt, pepper, twelve or sixteen onions, should be put in twenty minutes before the soup is done. Be careful and not throw in salt and pepper too plentifully; it is easy to add to it; and not easy to diminish. A lemon cut up and put in half an hour before it is done, adds to the flavor. If you have tomato catsup in the house, a cup full will make soup rich. Some people put in crackers; some thin slices of crust, made nearly as short as common shortcake; and some stir up two or three eggs with milk and flour, and drop it in with a spoon.

A quarter of an hour to each pound of beef is considered a good rule for roasting; but this is too much when the bone is large and the meat thin. Six pounds of the rump should roast six quarters of an hour; but bony pieces less. It should be done before a quick fire.

The quicker beefsteak can be broiled the better. Seasoned after it is taken from the gridiron.—Child, *The Frugal Housewife* (Boston: Carter and Hendee, 1830), 50–51.

Currant Wine

Those who have more currants than they have money will do well to use no wine but of their own manufacture. Break and squeeze the currants, put three pounds and a half of sugar to two quarts of juice, and two quarts of water. Put in a keg or barrel. Do not close the bung tight, for three or four days, that the air may escape while it is fermenting. After it is done fermenting close it up tight. Where raspberries are plenty, it is a great improvement to use half raspberry juice and half currant juice. Brandy is unnecessary, when the above mentioned proportions are observed. It should not be used under a year or two. Age improves it.—Child, *The Frugal Housewife*, 87.

Mince Meat

There is a great difference in preparing mince meat. Some make it a coarse, unsavory dish; and other make it nice and palatable. No economical housekeeper will despise it; for broken bits of meat and vegetables cannot so well be disposed of in any other way. If you wish to have it nice, mash your vegetables fine, and chop your meat very fine. Warm it with what remains of sweet gravy, or roast meat drippings, you may happen to have. Two or three apples, pared, cored, sliced and fried, to mix with it is an improvement. Some like a little sifted sage sprinkled in.

It is generally considered nicer to chop your meat fine, warm it with gravy, season it, and lay it upon a large slice of toasted bread to be brought upon the table without being mixed with potatoes; but if you have cold vegetables, use them.—Child, *The Frugal Housewife*, 53.

Plum Pudding

The heroine of Child's *Hobomok* declares that she "must learn to eat hominy and milk and forget the substantial plum puddings of England,"[3] though Child also printed a recipe for plum pudding in *The Frugal Housewife.*

If you wish to make a really nice, soft custard-like plum pudding, pound six crackers, or dried crusts of light bread, fine, and soak them overnight in milk enough to cover them, put them in about three pints of milk, beat up six eggs, put in a little lemon brandy, a whole nutmeg, and about three quarters of a pound of raisins which have been rubbed in flour. Bake it two hours, or perhaps a little short of that. It is easy to judge from the appearance whether it is done.

The surest way of making a light rich plum pudding is to spread slices of sweet, light bread plentifully with butter; on each side of the slices spread abundantly raisins, or currants, nicely prepared; when they are all heaped up in a dish cover them with milk, eggs, sugar and spice, well beat up, and prepared just as you do for custards. Let it bake about an hour.

One sauce answers for common use for all sorts of puddings. Flour and water stirred into boiling water sweetened to your taste with either molasses or sugar, according to your ideas of economy; a great spoonful of rosewater, if you have it, butter half as big as a hen's egg. If you want to make it very nice put in a glass of wine, and grate nutmeg on the top.

When you wish better sauce than common, take a quarter of a pound of butter and the same of sugar, mould them well together with your hand, add a little wine, if you choose. Make it into a lump, set it away to cool, and grate nutmeg over it.—Child, *The Frugal Housewife*, 67.

Pumpkin and Squash Pie

For common family pumpkin pies, three eggs do very well to a quart of milk. Stew your pumpkin, and strain it through a sieve, or colander. Take out the seeds, and pare the pumpkin, or squash, before you stew it; but do not scrape the inside; the part nearest the seed is the sweetest part of the squash. Stir in the stewed pumpkin, till it is as thick as you can stir it round rapidly and easily. If you want to make your pie richer, make it thinner, and add another egg. One egg to a quart of milk makes very decent pies. Sweeten it to your taste, with molasses or sugar; some pumpkins require more sweetening than others. Two teaspoonfuls of salt; two great spoonfuls of sifted cinnamon; one great spoonful of ginger. Ginger will answer very well alone for spice, if you use enough of it. The outside of a lemon grated in is nice. The more eggs, the better the pie; some put an egg to a gill of milk. They should bake from forty to fifty minutes, and even ten minutes longer, if very deep.— Child, *The Frugal Housewife*, 70.

ROBERT P. TRISTRAM COFFIN

The New England poet Robert P. Tristram Coffin (1892–1955) was awarded the Pulitzer Prize for Poetry in 1936.

Lobster Stew

Bring two cups of Maine sea water to a boil in a steamer and lay in twelve medium lobsters shellside down to steam in their own juice; cover tightly, keep heat high ten to fifteen minutes.

Remove and pick meat from shell while hot, discarding intestinal vein and lungs. Let picked meat cool overnight. Melt half a pound of butter in a large pot and in it heat lobster meat until it seethes. Turn heat low and slowly add one quart of milk, stirring clockwise to keep mixture from coagulating. Add a second quart of milk a little at a time. Bring the liquid to a froth and immediately pour in a third quart of milk, stirring constantly. Let the stew come to a boil and stir in one pint of cream; when this starts to bubble add another pint of cream. Let it simmer a few minutes without permitting it to boil, then remove from heat. Cool twelve to twenty-four hours while flavor develops. Reheat, season to taste, and serve to ten or twelve.— Evan Jones, *American Food: The Gastronomic Story* (New York: Dutton, 1975), 24.

JOHN ESTEN COOKE

The Virginia poet, novelist, and biographer John Esten Cooke (1830–1886) was outspoken in his defense of the cavalier tradition. He was not immune to the benefits of brand-name product endorsement.

Perfection Salad

1 envelope Knox Sparkling Gelatine
½ cup cold water
½ cup mild vinegar
2 tablespoonfuls lemon juice
2 cups boiling water
½ cup sugar
1 teaspoonful salt
1 cup cabbage, finely shredded
2 cups celery, cut in small pieces
2 pimentoes, cut in small pieces

Soak gelatin in cold water five minutes. Add vinegar, lemon juice, boiling water, sugar, and salt. Strain, and when mixture begins to stiffen, add remaining ingredients. Turn into mold, first dipped in cold water, and chill. Remove to bed of lettuce or endive. Garnish with mayonnaise dressing, or cut in cubes, and serve in cases made of red or green peppers, or turn into molds lined with canned pimentos. A delicious accompaniment to cold sliced chicken or veal.— Janet McKenzie Hill, *Dainty Desserts for Dainty People* (Johnstown, N.Y.: Charles B. Knox, 1909) 26.

ROSE TERRY COOKE

Frizzled Dried Beef

In "Liab's First Christmas" (1886) by the New England regional writer Rose Terry Cooke (1827–1892), a character prepares "a savory supper of cream toast and dried beef with gravy."[1] Cooke contributed a pair of recipes, one for Frizzled Dried Beef, to one of the standard American cookbooks of the late nineteenth century.

Cut your beef very thin, then pull it into small pieces, taking out all the strings of sinew, fat, and bits of outside; put it in a frying pan, and cover with cold water; let it simmer on the back of the stove till perfectly tender; then pour off the water, and cover the beef with cream, add pepper, celery salt, and salt if needed; mix one tablespoonful of melted butter with one heaped tablespoon of flour, and stir into the hot cream; cover, and keep very hot till served.— Maria Parola et al., *Universal Common Sense Cookery Book* (Boston: Charles E. Brown, 1892), 33–34.

Scalloped Fish

Any cold fresh fish, or cold boiled salt codfish, must be pulled into fine flakes, carefully taking out skin and bones and dark parts; mix in a bowl with equal quantity of bread or cracker crumbs; season with salt, pepper, celery salt, a little nutmeg, a very little juice squeezed from a cut onion, and a very little red pepper if preferred; moisten the mixture well with a gravy made of melted butter, flour, and hot water; put into a baking dish, cover with dry crumbs and thickly strewn bits of butter; bake till brown. This is a pretty dish for supper, baked in small tin or earthen shells, or in the great sea clam shells found on the ocean shore, or in the blue crockery dishes that are sold for such purposes. Serve very hot.— Parola et al., *Universal Common Sense Cookery Book*, 20.

SUSAN COOLIDGE

Susan Coolidge, aka Sarah Chauncy Wooley (1835–1905), was a prolific writer for children, best known today for her novel *What Katy Did* (1872). In 1895 she contributed a sheaf of recipes for New England dishes to *The Century Cookbook*, many of them never before published. "They are copies from old grandmother and great-grandmother receipt-books," she averred, "tested by generations of use, and become, at this time, traditional in the families to which they belong. They are now given to the public as examples of the simple but dainty cooking of a by-gone day, which, while differing in many points from the methods of our own time, in its way is no less delicious."[1]

Browned Oysters

Take thirty large oysters (about three pints); wash them in their own liquor. Add to one pint of milk three tablespoonfuls of the oyster liquor, well strained, a very little mace, and a bit of butter about the size of an English walnut, and make the mixture scalding hot. Rub two tablespoonfuls of flour perfectly smooth with a little of the milk; pour in and stir until the whole is thick. Then drop in the oysters; cook five minutes or so, till they are well plumped out, and add a little salt, white pepper, and a tablespoonful of Worcestershire sauce. Serve on a platter on slices of buttered toast.— Mary Ronald, *The Century Cook Book* (New York: Century, 1895), 231.

Easy Chicken Salad

Take a two-pound can of Richardson & Robbins's compressed chicken; remove the skin, and cut the chicken into small dice.

Add twice as much celery cut into small pieces, salt to taste, and marinate the whole with a mixture of three tablespoonfuls of vinegar to nine of oil. Have it very cold, and just before serving pour over it a Mayonnaise made by the following receipt. This quantity is enough for twenty-five persons.

Cream dressing: Rub together in a china bowl a large tablespoonful of butter, four table-spoonfuls of vinegar, a half teaspoonful of salt, and a half teaspoonful of dry mustard.

Place the bowl in a saucepan full of boiling water over a spirit lamp, or on the range. Stir the mixture carefully till very hot, to prevent the butter from oiling. When hot add two well-beaten eggs; stir till thick, then pour in a half pint of cream, stir, remove from the fire, and allow it to get perfectly cold.

Cold sweetbreads are excellent served with this cream Mayonnaise.— Ronald, *The Century Cook Book*, 235.

Molasses Pie

This is a genuine New England dainty, dear to the hearts of children. Mix half a pint of the best molasses with a tablespoonful of flour, and add the juice of a large lemon, and the rind and pulp chopped fine. Bake with an under and an upper crust.— Ronald, *The Century Cook Book*, 243.

Rhode Island Johnny-Cake

For this, Rhode Island meal, ground between stones, is required. Take one pint of meal and one teaspoonful of salt, and scald thoroughly with boiling water till it is a stiff, smooth batter. Thin with cold milk till about the consistency of sponge-cake batter, and drop in tablespoonfuls on a hot buttered griddle. When the under side is brown, turn the cakes and brown the other side. Eat with butter.— Ronald, *The Century Cook Book*, 237.

Spiced Shad

Scale the fish, cut off the heads and tails, and divide them into four pieces.

Chop four or five small onions, and sprinkle a layer on the bottom of a stone jar; on this place a layer of fish, packing closely. Spice with black and cayenne pepper, cloves, allspice, whole peppers, and a little more onion. Then add another layer of fish, and so on till the jar is full. Arrange the roe on top, spice highly, and fill the jar with the strongest vinegar procurable. Place thick folds of paper on the jar under the cover, and bake for twelve hours. The vinegar will dissolve the bones, and the fish can be sliced for a tea-table relish.— Ronald, *The Century Cook Book*, 233.

Squash Pies

Pare and cut into pieces a Hubbard squash, and steam it till thoroughly soft; then rub it through a coarse sieve.

To a quart of the squash, which should be as thick and dry as chestnuts when prepared for stuffing, add three quarters of a pint, heaping full, of granulated sugar, the peel and juice of a large lemon, half a nutmeg grated, a tablespoonful of powdered ginger, about as much powdered cinnamon, a small teaspoonful of salt, six drops of rosewater, half a pint of cream, and four beaten eggs. Stir thoroughly, and add about three pints of scalded milk. The mixture should be tasted, and a little more sugar, or lemon, or spice added if required.

Line a deep tin pie-dish with paste, lay a narrow strip around the edge, and fill the dish with the mixture. Bake till the filling is set. This quantity will make four pies.— Ronald, *The Century Cook Book*, 238.

WILLIAM A. CROFFUT

William A. Croffut (1835–1915) edited the New York *Graphic*, a forerunner of the "yellow" newspapers, in the 1870s and the *Washington Post* in the mid–1880s. He was also the author of *Bourbon Ballads* (1880), *A Midsummer Lark* (1883), and *The Prophecy and Other Poems* (1894).

Clam Soup

First catch your clams—along the ebbing edges
Of saline coves you'll find the precious wedges,
With backs up, lurking in the sandy bottom;
Pull in your iron rake, and lo! you've got 'em!
Take thirty large ones, put a basin under,
And cleave, with knife, their stony jaws asunder;
Add water (three quarts) to the native liquor,
Bring to a boil (and, by the way, the quicker
It boils the better, if you'd do it cutely.)
Now add the clams, chopped up and minced minutely.
Allow a longer boil of just three minutes,
And while it bubbles, quickly stir within its
Tumultuous depths where still the mollusks mutter,
Four tablespoons of flour and four of butter,
A pint of milk, some pepper to your notion,
And clams need salting, although born of ocean.
Remove from fire; (if much boiled they will suffer—
You'll find that India rubber isn't tougher.)
After 'tis off, add three fresh eggs, well beaten,
Stir once more, and it's ready to be eaten.
Fruit of the wave! O, dainty and delicious!
Food for the gods! Ambrosia for Apicius!
Worthy to thrill the soul of seaborn Venus,
Or titillate the palate of Silenus!

—Wilcox, *Buckeye Cookery*, 267.

Peas Stewed in Cream

Put two or three pints of young green peas into a sauce pan of boiling water; when nearly done and tender, drain in a colander quite dry; melt two ounces of butter in a clean stew pan, thicken evenly with a little flour, shake it over the fire, but do not let it brown, mix smoothly with a gill of cream, add half a teaspoon of white sugar, bring to a boil, pour in the peas, keep moving for two minutes until well heated, and serve hot. The sweet pods of young peas are made by the Germans into a palatable dish by simply stewing with a little butter and savory herbs.—Estelle Woods Wilcox, *Buckeye Cookery* (Minneapolis: Buckeye, 1877), 294.

Stuffed Cabbage

Take a large, fresh cabbage and cut out the heart; fill the vacancy with stuffing made of cooked chicken or veal, chopped very fine and highly seasoned and rolled into balls with yolk of egg. Then tie the cabbage firmly together (some tie a cloth around it), and boil in a covered kettle two hours. This is a delicious dish and is useful in using up cold meats.— Wilcox, *Buckeye Cookery*, 285.

Sweet Pickle

Take eight pounds of green tomatoes and chop fine, add four pounds brown sugar and boil down three hours, add a quart of vinegar, a teaspoon of mace, cinnamon and cloves, and boil about fifteen minutes; let cool and put into jars or other vessel. Try this recipe once and you will try it again.— Wilcox, *Buckeye Cookery*, 235.

BERNARD DEVOTO

> Bernard DeVoto was a western historian, editor, and Mark Twain's second literary executor.

Lobster

> Avis DeVoto, Bernard's wife, corresponded with Julia Child for nearly 40 years, and in one letter she described the proper way to prepare lobster.

The only real way to cook lobsters is in three or four inches of sea water, in a covered kettle, for about twelve minutes (pound and a quarter lobsters being the ideal size). You then drape these dazzling creatures over the rocks until they cool off a bit, tear them apart with the bare hands, dip each piece in melted butter, and guzzle. There should be from two to six lobsters per person. While the lobsters cook and cool off, two dry Martinis à la DeVoto should be served. Nothing whatever else should be served — we are eating all the lobster we went, we are not fooling around with salad or strawberry shortcake or even coffee. All you need are the martinis, plenty of lobsters, millions of paper napkins, and a view.—*As Always, Julia: The Letters of Julia Child and Avis DeVoto*, ed. Joan Reardon (Boston: Houghton Mifflin, 2010), 14.

Martinis à la DeVoto

There is a point at which the marriage of gin and vermouth is consummated. It varies a little with the constituents, but for a gin of 94.4 proof and a harmonious vermouth it may be generalized at about 3.7 to one. And that is not only the proper proportion but the critical one; if you use less gin it is a marriage in name only and the name is not martini. You get a drinkable and even pleasurable result, but not art's sunburst of imagined delight becoming real. Happily, the upper limit is not so fixed; you may make it four to one or a little more than that, which is a comfort if you cannot do fractions in your head and an assurance when you must use an unfamiliar gin. But not much more. This is the violet hour, the hour of hush and wonder, when the affections glow and valor is reborn, when the shadows deepen along the edge of the forest and we believe that, if we watch carefully, at any moment we may see the unicorn. But it would not be a martini if we should see him.

So made, the martini is only one brush stroke short of the perfect thing, and I will rebuke no one who likes to leave it there. But the final brush stroke is a few drops of oil squeezed from lemon rind on the surface of each cocktail. Some drop the squeezed bit into the glass; I do not favor the practice and caution you to make it rind, not peel, if you do. And, of course, you will use cocktail glasses, not cups of silver or any other metal, and they will have stems so that heat will not pass from your hand to the martini. Purists chill them before the first round. If any of that round (or any other) is left in the pitcher, throw it away.—*The Hour* (Boston: Houghton Mifflin, 1951), 67–69.

CHARLES DICKENS — DINNER AT DELMONICO'S

On April 18, 1868, at the close of his second U.S. speaking tour, Charles Dickens was feted with a dinner at Delmonico's at the corner of 14th Street and Fifth Avenue in New York. As the historian Daniel Boorstin explains, Lorenzo Delmonico's restaurants "set a standard for New York gourmets which … made that city, next to Paris, the restaurant capital of the world."[1] Charles Ranhofer, the chef at Delmonico's almost without interruption between 1862 and 1896, "was at the cusp of the restaurant industry in America."[2] The guests at the Dickens dinner included the leading authors, editors, and publishers in the country, among them Horace Greeley, Charles Scribner, Thomas Nast, James T. Fields, J. B. Lippincott, E. C. Stedman, S. S. McClure, Whitelaw Reid, E. L. Godkin, Henry Holt, and J. R. Osgood.[3] The restaurant remained fashionable until it was finally forced to close for lack of business during Prohibition. The critic Edmund Wilson noted in his journal in August 1923 that a "for rent" sign hung on "the distinguished toned-yellow building, with its columned and ornamented windows and its dulled green row of lamps."[4]

Delmonico's at the corner of 14th Street and Fifth Avenue in New York circa 1903 (Library of Congress).

Aspic of Foies-Gras (Aspic de foie-gras)

Incrust a plain cylindrical mold in ice. Unmold on a small baking sheet a terrine of foies-gras; remove all the grease and keep it for one hour on ice. Cut this foies-gras into three-eighths of an inch thick slices, using a knife dipped in hot water, and then cut these slices into inch and a quarter rounds with a pastry cutter also dipped in hot water. Lift up these rounds one by one with a fork and immerse them in a brown chaudfroid sauce (**No. 594**), having it thin and almost cold; range them at once on a baking sheet and let this sauce get quite stiff on the ice. Cut out some rounds of cooked truffles very nearly the same diameter as the foies-gras, only have half as many; glaze them with a brush and range them at once

DÎNER DE 175 COUVERTS.
En l'Honneur de Charles Dickens.

MENU.

Huîtres sur coquilles.

POTAGES.

Consommé Sévigné. Crème d'asperges à la Dumas.

HORS-D'ŒUVRE CHAUD.

Timbales à la Dickens.

POISSONS.

Saumon à la Victoria. Bass à l'Italienne.
Pommes de terre Nelson.

RELEVÉS.

Filet de bœuf à la Lucullus. Laitues braisées demi-glace.
Agneau farci à la Walter Scott. Tomates à la Reine.

ENTRÉES.

Filets de brants à la Seymour.
Petits pois à l'Anglaise.
Croustades de ris de veau à la Douglas.
Quartiers d'artichauts Lyonnaise.
Epinards au velouté.
Côtelettes de grouses à la Fenimore Cooper.

ENTRÉES FROIDES.

Galantines à la Royale.
Aspics de foies-gras historiés.

INTERMÈDE.

Sorbet à l'Américaine.

RÔTS.

Bécassines. Poulets de grains truffés.

ENTREMETS SUCRÉS.

Pêches à la Parisienne (chaud).

Macédoine de fruits. Moscovite à l'abricot.
Lait d'amandes rubané au chocolat.
Charlotte Doria.
Viennois glacé à l'orange. Corbeille de biscuits Chantilly.
Gâteau Savarin au marasquin.

———

Glaces forme fruits Napolitaine.
Parfait au Café.

PIÈCES MONTÉES.

Temple de la Littérature. Trophée à l'Auteur.
Pavillon international. Colonne Triomphale.
Les armes Britanniques. The Stars and Stripes.
Le Monument de Washington. La Loi du destin.

———

Fruits. Compotes de pêches et de poires. Petits fours.
Fleurs.
Dessert.

Menu for Dickens' dinner at Delmonico's on April 18, 1868, from *The Epicurean.*

on a baking sheet. Pour a quarter-inch thick layer of jelly into the mold, and when it has become quite hard dress on it a ring of the foies-gras rounds, the smooth side uppermost and slightly overlapping each other, but alternating every two with a round of truffle; cover this crown exactly the same as the first one in order to fill up the mold, pouring jelly between each. Keep the mold on ice for one hour or more. In order to turn it out it is only necessary to dip the mold into warm water, wipe dry, and invert in on a cold dish.

594. Chaudfroid Brown and Game (Chaudfroid brun et chaufroid de gibier)

Put into a sauce pan, one pint of very clear well-colored espagnole sauce (**No. 414**), reduce it with some veal blond (**No. 423**), and dilute with half its quantity of aspic jelly (**No. 103**). Boil up the sauce and remove it at once to the side of the fire, in order to despumate it for ten minutes, skimming it well in the meantime; then take it off entirely and pass through a tamp. Before using try a little to find out whether it coats properly; if not strong enough add some gelatin.

414. Brown, Espagnole or Spanish Sauce (Sauce brune espagnole)

Espagnole or Spanish sauce is a leading sauce from which many smaller ones are made. To obtain a good espagnole, it is necessary to have good stock (**No. 421**); in case there be no stock specially prepared for this purpose, use good clear broth. For four quarts of stock, melt in a saucepan one pound of butter, stir into it the same weight of very dry, good flour, so as to obtain a clear paste; then let it cook for four or five minutes on the fire, without ceasing to stir, and afterward set it back on to a very slow fire, or in a slack oven, to let it get a good dark brown color, being careful to move it about often. When the roux is cooked, take it from the oven and dilute with the prepared stock, not having it too hot, and stir the liquid again over the fire to bring it to a boil. Should the sauce not be sufficiently smooth — should any lumps appear in it, then strain it through a fine sieve, and put it back into the saucepan; and at the first boil, set it on one side so that it only boils partially, and let it despumate in this way for two or three hours. Skim off well the fat, and strain the broth into a vessel to let get cold, meanwhile stirring frequently.

103. To Prepare, Clarify and Filter Aspic Jelly (Pour préparer la gelée d'aspic, la clarifier et la filtrer)

Aspic or meat jelly is prepared with chicken or game broth, obtaining it as clear as possible, and mixing it with a certain quantity of gelatin made either with calf's feet or pig skin, or even with isinglass. Aspics are also prepared with special stocks made under the following conditions: brown in a saucepan half a pound of breast of veal, one knuckle, and two fowls, suppressing the breasts; when the meats are lightly colored moisten them amply with some light broth, free of all fat, and add to it four or five boned and blanched calf's feet, also some roots and onions, a garnished bouquet, but no salt, boil the liquid while skimming remove it to the side of the range, and finish cooking the meats, lifting them out as soon as they are done. Strain the liquid through a sieve, skim off all the fat, try a little of it on ice to judge of its consistency, and should it not be sufficiently firm, then heat it up once more, and stir into it a few gelatine leaves softened in cold water and dissolved in a small separate saucepan. The aspic should never be reduced with the idea of rendering it firmer, because the boiling only wastes it without thickening it; chop one pound of lean beef, one pound for two quarts of liquid, add to it four egg whites or two whole eggs and one pint of white wine, dilute it gradually with the aspic jelly, put it into a saucepan

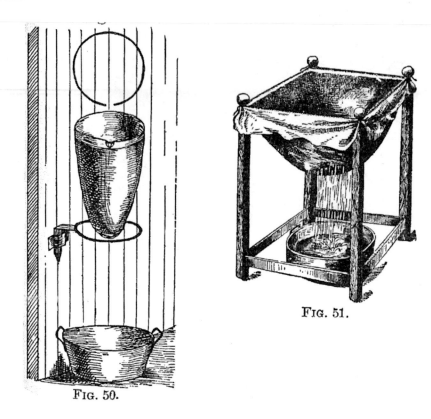

FIG. 51.

FIG. 50.

A filtering method for Aspic Jelly from *The Epicurean.*

on the fire, stir the liquid with a whisk until the instant boiling point is reached, then remove it to one side, and let it simmer very slowly, till it becomes perfectly clear, then strain it through a flannel bag; or moisten a clean napkin and arrange it on a kitchen filtering stool as shown; should the jelly not be sufficiently limpid, pour it through again until perfectly clear.

423. Veal Blond Stock (Fond de blond de veau)

Butter the bottom of a saucepan capable of containing sixteen quarts; set in four sliced onions, and on top of these four pounds of split knuckle of veal and four pounds of shoulder of veal, two fowls, after removing the breasts, and moisten all with one quart of beef stock (**No. 194a**). Place the saucepan on a brisk fire, keeping the lid on, and reduce the moisture by moderating the heat of the fire, and letting the liquid fall slowly to a glaze; now moisten again with six quarts more of beef stock, season with salt and whole peppers, and add four leeks, two carrots, cut in pieces, a bunch of parsley, some celery, one bay leaf and as much thyme. Cook all slowly for six hours, then skim off the fat and strain through a fine sieve. Chop up the breasts taken from the two fowls with the same quantity of lean beef, and mix this in a little cold water, and with this meat clarify the veal blond the same as consommé; then strain it through a napkin.

Veal blond should be clear, succulent and of a nice color, the grease should be thoroughly removed from it; added to clear soups it greatly improves them; it is also used in reducing sauces.

421. Brown, Espagnole or Spanish Sauce Stock (Fond pour sauce brune espagnole)

Butter the bottom of a thick bottomed saucepan and garnish it with slices of onions, placing on top half a pound of ham, some slices or parings of fat pork, twelve pounds of knuckle of veal, shoulder, and trimmings, six pounds of beef or parings, and moisten with one quart of beef stock (**No. 194a**); leave the saucepan on the fire until the broth is half reduced, then cover the saucepan and moderate the fire, continue to boil till all the moisture is reduced and falls to a glaze, which is easily perceived as the grease then becomes clear; moisten it once more with eighteen quarts of beef stock; boil, skim off the fat, and add a bunch of parsley, garnished with two bay leaves and as much thyme, basil, celery, and two cloves of garlic, also one pound of carrots cut lengthwise in four, salt, ground pepper, and a little sugar. Cook all together for six hours, skim off the fat and strain through a sieve to keep for further use. This stock is used for moistening brown roux.

194a. Beef Stock or Broth (Grand bouillon de bœuf)

Put ten quarts of water into a stockpot, add eight pounds of beef meat (trimmings and bone), let there be at least two-thirds meat, being careful to have both meat and trimmings well freed of fat; and a quarter of a pound of scalded chicken legs, after removing the outer skin. Heat this up slowly so that it comes gradually to a boil, then skim carefully and add twenty grains of whole black peppers and one and one quarter ounces of salt. Put into a net six ounces of carrots, three ounces of turnips, six ounces of leeks, half an ounce of parsnips, one half an ounce of soup celery, and two ounces of onions in which two cloves should be stuck. Close the net and set it in the pot; after the vegetables have cooked for two hours, remove the net containing the vegetables and continue boiling the soup for two hours longer, making four hours in all. Take off all the fat from the surface and strain the soup either through a silk tammy or a napkin; pour it into another pot to make consommé; and in case it should be needed the following day only, pour it into vessels and set it to cool. The following is an economical way of doing so: set the vessels in a water reservoir supplied continually with cold water from melting ice in the refrigerators and brought through a pipe in the bottom of the tank, have a larger overflow pipe placed near the top so as to allow the water as it heats to flow off.— Ranhofer, *The Epicurean*, passim.

Bécassines (English Snipe, Broiled)

Pick, singe, draw, and dry well six fine English snipe; remove the skin from the heads, split them in two without detaching the parts, and put them on a dish. Season with a pinch of salt, half a pinch of pepper, and a tablespoonful of oil. Roll them in well, then put them to broil (with the bills stuck into the breasts), and let them cook for four minutes on each side. Prepare a hot dish with six toasts, arrange the snipe over, spread a gill of maître d'hôtel butter (**No. 145**) on top, decorate the dish with a little watercress, and serve.

145. Butter, Maître d'Hôtel

Put one ounce of good butter in a bowl with a teaspoonful of very finely chopped parsley, adding the juice of half a sound lemon. Mingle well with a little nutmeg, and keep it in a cool place to use when needed.— Ranhofer, *The Epicurean*, passim.

Consommé à la Sévigné

With chicken forcemeat (**No. 226**) fill six very small timbale-molds; let them poach for two minutes in hot water, then set them aside to cool, turn them out, and put them into the tureen with two tablespoonfuls of cooked asparagus-tops, and two tablespoonfuls of cooked green peas; pour over it one quart of boiling consommé (**No. 100**), and serve.

226

Cut in large pieces two raw chicken breasts, pound them in a mortar, adding the same quantity of bread soaked in milk, a teaspoonful of fresh butter and four egg yolks, seasoning with half a tablespoonful of salt, a scant teaspoonful of pepper, and a teaspoonful of nutmeg. Mix all together; strain, and put it in a bowl with three tablespoonfuls of velouté sauce (**No. 152**).

100

Chop up a shin of beef of twelve pounds, *using a machine if practicable*; put it in a large soup kettle with two sound, well-scraped, good-sized carrots, two peeled, sound onions, three well-washed and pared leeks, a few branches of celery, and one bunch of parsley roots, all well-scraped, washed, and shred, six cloves, eighteen whole peppers, a bay leaf, and the whites of six raw eggs, including their shells. Mix all well together, and then moisten with two gallons of cold white broth (**No. 99**), one quart of cold water (all this should be done before the soup kettle has been placed on the hot range). Stir thoroughly for two or three minutes without ceasing; and then place it on the hot range, add some débris of chicken if any at hand. Boil slowly for about four hours, skim the grease off thoroughly, and then strain through a wet cloth into a china bowl or stone jar, and put away in a cool place for general use. Should the white broth that you employ be hot, replace the cold water by a piece of ice well cracked, and the equivalent of a quart of water, adding it to the consommé very gradually at the beginning, but continually increasing, and stirring till all added. (Always taste if sufficiently seasoned before serving.)

152. Sauce Velouté

Melt one ounce of good butter in a saucepan, adding two tablespoonfuls of flour, and stir well, not letting it get brown. Moisten with a pint and a half of good veal and chicken stock, the stronger the better. Throw in a garnished bouquet (**No. 254**), half a cupful of mushroom liquor, if at hand, six whole peppers, half a pinch of salt, and a very little nutmeg. Boil for twenty minutes, stirring continuously with a wooden spatula; then remove to the side of the fire, skim thoroughly, and let it continue simmering slowly for one hour. Then rub through a fine sieve. This sauce will make the foundation for any kind of good white stock.

254. A Bouquet

Take four branches of well-washed parsley stalks— if the branches be small, take six — one branch of soup celery, well-washed; one blade of bay leaf, one sprig of thyme, and two cloves, placed in the center of the parsley, so as to prevent cloves, thyme, and bay leaf from dropped out of the bouquet while cooking; fold it well, and tightly tie with a string, and use when required in various recipes.

99. Bouillon Blanc — White Broth

> Alice B. Toklas explains that "*Bouillon* is a 'boiling,' a stock made of veal, chicken or beef bones simmered in water with the special vegetables and herbs appropriate to the dish."[5]

Place in a large stock-urn on a moderate fire a good heavy knuckle of a fine white veal with all the débris, or scraps of meat, including bones, remaining in the kitchen (but not of game); cover fully with cold water, adding a handful of salt; and as it comes to a boil, be very careful to skim all the scum off — no particle of scum should be left on — and then put in two large, round, well-scraped carrots (whole), one whole, cleaned, sound turnip, one whole, peeled, large, sound onion, one well-cleaned parsley root, three thoroughly washed leeks, and a few leaves of cleaned celery. Boil very slowly for six hours on the corner of the range; keenly skim the grease off; then strain well through a wet cloth into a china bowl or a stone jar, and put it away in a cool place for general use.— Alessandro Filippini, *The Table* (New York: Charles L. Webster, 1889), 165.

Salmon à la Victoria (Saumon à la Victoria)

Trim slices of fish, each about half an inch in thickness; cook them in a mirepoix stock (**No. 419**), moistened with red wine, and when done, which will take from eight to ten minutes, drain them off, and strain the stock; reduce this, and despumate it; just when ready to serve stir in a piece of lobster butter (**No. 580**).

419. Mirepoix Stock (Fond de mirepoix)

This is the essence of meats and vegetables. Put into a saucepan half a pound of chopped fat pork, fry it until melted, and then add half a pound of butter, one pound of lean veal cut in three-eighths of an inch squares, and one pound of unsmoked ham, also a pound of carrots and six ounces of onions cut in quarter inch squares, and a bunch of parsley garnished with a bay leaf and as much thyme, some basil, a clove of garlic, two cloves, and mace. Add to this a few mushroom parings, season with a little salt and mignonette, and when all the ingredients are well friend and of a fine golden color, moisten them with three quarts of remoistening (**No. 189**), and one pint of white wine, and a pint of Madeira wine; boil the whole slowly for two hours, then strain it forcibly through a tammy without removing the fat. Mirepoix is used for moistening meats, fishes, etc.

580. Lobster and Spiny Lobster Coral Butter (Beurre au corail de homard ou de langouste)

Pound one pound of very red spiny lobster shells with two pounds of butter until they are reduced to a paste; put this into a saucepan till the butter be cooked and clarified, then strain it through a piece of muslin into a bowl. As soon as the butter has thrown off its first heat, begin beating it with a spoon till it gets cold, and if needed to be dyed a deeper red shade, then add to it a little orchanet, melted in a small quantity of butter, or clear vegetal carmine. Serve the fish, surrounding it with sautéd lobster escalops, and small anchovy tartlets; cover the lobster with half of the sauce, and pour the remainder in a sauceboat to be served at the same time.

189. Clarified Consommé and Remoistening (Consommé clarifié et remouillage)

Proportions. When the stock (**No. 194a**) is ready put five quarts of it into a soup pot, adding two pounds of lean meat and three pounds of cleansed and washed fowls. Boil it up slowly, and just when ready to come to a boil, carefully remove the scum arising on the surface and then add half a pound of roasted veal. Simmer slowly until the fowl is cooked, which will take from two and a half to three hours, lifting it out as soon as it is done so as to save the breasts which will be found useful for garnishing, purées, salads, sandwiches, etc.; return what remains of the fowls to the broth once again and continue boiling for half an hour longer, skim the fat off very carefully and mix in the clarification.

Clarification. Trim off the fat, remove the nerves from a piece of beef sufficient to obtain two pounds after it is chopped up, and mix in with this chopped meat half a quart of cold stock (or water); pour this clarification into the broth, add two ounces of minced carrots, and two ounces of minced leeks; season with salt and color the soup with caramel (**No. 18**); keep the liquid in a boiling state for one hour. The consommé should be perfectly clear, sapid and tasty; strain it through a silk sieve or a fine napkin and use when needed, serve in cups, or in a soup tureen with any garnishing desired.

Remoistening. After the stock on consommé has been taken out of the pot, pour in sufficient water to have the meats entirely re-covered and boil again for three hours; remove all the fat and strain it through a napkin; do not salt this. This remoistening is used for diluting certain soups, and to moisten veal or chicken stock with which meat extract is made (**No. 368**).

18. To Prepare Liquid Caramel (Caramel liquide)

Liquid caramel is most necessary; it is used for coloring broths, gravies and even sauces, when their tints are found to be too light, still caramel should be used with discretion, for it is apt to give a bitter taste to the colored liquids into which it is added. Put a few spoonfuls of powdered sugar into a copper pan, stir it over a slow fire, then remove it onto a slower one to let cook until it becomes quite brown, and the smoke arising from it is whitish, this is a sign that it is thoroughly done. Take the pan from off the fire, moisten the sugar proportionately with hot water, and allow the liquid to boil while stirring, and cook till the consistence of a light syrup is obtained. Caramel should be kept in a small, well-closed bottle, having a cork perforated lengthwise, so that when the bottom is turned over, the liquid can drop out slowly without it being necessary to uncork it.

368. Plain Extract of Beef (Extrait de bœuf simple)

Chop up very fine one pound of lean beef, put it into a saucepan and dilute it gradually with three pints of cold bouillon (**No. 187**); set it on a slow fire, and stir until it comes to a boil, then place it on the back of the stove where it will not boil, leave it there for half an hour, and strain it through a fine sieve or napkin.

187. Clear Bouillon (Bouillon clair)

There is nothing that resembles consommé more than clarified bouillon, and if it does not entirely take its place as regards quality, still it is often used instead. Clarified bouillon is in reality only an imitation of consommé, it is equally true that with care it can easily be prepared in excellent conditions, the principal one being to operate with good bouillon, either of chicken, beef or game, etc. To obtain clear bouillon, only lean meats must be used for clarification; in order to obtain four quarts of bouillon, have one pound of lean beef free of all fat and nerves, chop it finely, and mix in with it two raw eggs and one pint of cold bouillon; place the strained bouillon on the fire, skimmed free of all its fat, and when it reaches boiling point, pour into it the clarification, beating it well with a whip. As soon as the bouillon boils, keep it to the same degree of heat without allowing it to boil for one hour; skim the fat off, season with salt and a little sugar, and color it with caramel (**No. 18**), then remove and strain through a wet napkin stretched and fastened to the four legs of a kitchen stool, or else a silk sieve. These bouillons are to be served with gar-

FIG. 455.

A mold used for Tenderloin of Beef à la Lucullus, from *The Epicurean*.

nishing of Italian pastes and farinas, also garnishing of vegetables, etc., for various soups.—
Ranhofer, *The Epicurean*, passim.

Tenderloin of Beef à la Lucullus
(Filet de bœuf à la Lucullus)

In order to arrange this tenderloin it will be necessary to have eight molds in two series of
four each, four to be decorated and four in which the tenderloins are molded, these being
an inch narrower in diameter than those to be decorated. Prepare and cook the tenderloin
as explained in l'Ambassade (**No. 1441**); when done, cut it into slices and reshape the meat
into its original form and fill the four smallest molds with it. Reduce the stock with aspic
jelly (**No. 103**), (if necessary add some isinglass to have it very firm), pour over the meat in
the molds and set on ice to get very cold. Decorate the four larger molds intended to receive
the tenderloin after they are decorated; cover the decoration with a layer of thick jelly,
unmold the smaller ones, put their contents inside the larger ones and fill up with very firm
jelly. After the jelly is very firm unmold the whole on a cloth, set at the bottom of the slope

on each side of the bridge a strong tin square three and a half inches in width and three inches high, having rounded corners and bent in the center to form a right angle; these squares are intended to keep up the tenderloins on the inclined slope, and are most necessary; place the small molds at the ends, and set around the piece twenty-four small croustades made of short paste, and filled with goose livers taken from a terrine of foies-gras; around these throw some chopped jelly, making a very regular border of croutons of the same. Stick two hatelets, one at each end, and in the center put a small figure holding up a cup filled with glazed truffles.

1441. Tenderloin of Beef à l'Ambassade — Whole (Filet de bœuf à l'Ambassade — entier)

Pare a fine tenderloin using the same care as if intended for larding (**No. 112**); cover it with thin slices of fat pork, tie it well so as to keep the latter in position; fill the bottom of a narrow baking pan with slices of pork, laying minced carrots and onions on top, pour over some good, melted fat, set the tenderloin over, and put it in the oven for forty to forty-five minutes, basting it several times while it is cooking, and turn the baking pan frequently so that the meat cooks evenly and colors well, letting it be done rare.

112. To Lard Meat, Poultry and Game (Pour Piquer les viandes la volaille et le gibier)

If it be butcher's meat, pare it properly by removing in strips the skin covering the meat, then all the superfluous fat.

The way to lard a tenderloin is to pare a fine tenderloin of beef, weighing six pounds after it is trimmed; remove the fat, slide the blade of a thin knife between the skin and the meat, and press it on the skin so as to avoid injuring the flesh; remove also the superfluous fat on the side, then cut the two ends round shaped. Choose a larding needle of suitable size to hold the larding pork that should be cut into pieces of three-sixteenths by two and a quarter inches long; lay the tenderloin lengthwise on a heavy towel, place this over the left arm, then proceed to lard the meat with the larding needle threading with a piece of the pork, boring the meat from right to left. The needle containing the pork must be stuck in the flesh to a depth depending upon its length, but the needle must be withdrawn with one stroke, so that the pork remains in the meat visible of an equal length on both sides. After the first row is larded, the next one should be slipped exactly between those of the first row; then instead of larding between the two lards of the last row, begin the operation from the start, which means lard two more rows the same as the first, observing that the second ones are arranged contrariwise to the first two, then continue until the whole tenderloin is filled. Proceed exactly the same for fricandeau, racks of veal, grenadins or sweetmeats.

When a piece of poultry or game is required to be larded, it must first be drawn, singed and trussed, then singe the breast once more, or else dip this part into boiling water to harden the meat; after this is cold, lard with lardons adapted to their size. This in fact is the whole theory of larding, and by examining various larded pieces, one can easily become an adept in the art. — Ranhofer, *The Epicurean*, passim.

EMILY DICKINSON

Emily Dickinson (1830–1886) was better known during her life for her cooking than for her poetry. Like most young women of her class, she was instructed in the "domestic arts" by her mother, who owned a copy of Child's *The Frugal Housewife*.

Black Cake

Dickinson sometimes shared recipes with her relatives and neighbors in Amherst, Massachusetts, as when she sent a copy of her recipe for Black Cake to Nellie Sweetser in the summer of 1883, and even in her verse she often invoked a food trope. As Vivian R. Pollack explains, Dickinson used "thirst and starvation metaphorically to represent a broad spectrum of needs: spiritual, emotional, and intellectual,"[1] as in the poem that begins "God gave a loaf to every bird." In the play *The Belle of Amherst* (1976), Dickinson is portrayed as she prepares a Black Cake.

2 pounds Flour —
2 Sugar —
2 Butter —
19 Eggs—
5 pounds Raisins—
1½ Currants

1½ Citron
½ pint Brandy
½— Molasses—
2 Nutmegs—
5 teaspoons Cloves— Mace — Cinnamon
2 teaspoons Soda —

Beat Butter and Sugar together —
Add Eggs without beating — and beat the mixture again —
Bake 2½ or three hours, in Cake pans, or 5 to 6 hours in Milk pan, if full —*Letters of Emily Dickinson*, ed. Thomas H. Johnson (Cambridge: Belknap, 1958), II 783.

Chocolate Dessert

Please break an Ounce Isinglass in a Quart of fresh Milk, placing in boiling Water till quite dissolved, adding afterward four table spoons Chocolate shavings and two of Sugar, boiling together fifteen minutes and straining before turning into molds.—*Letters of Emily Dickinson*, II 376.

Cocoanut Cake

On the back of one of Dickinson's poems appeared her handwritten recipe for Cocoanut [*sic*] Cake.

1 cup coconut
2 cups flour
1 cup sugar
½ cup butter
½ cup milk
2 eggs
½ teaspoonful soda
1 teaspoonful cream tartar
This makes one half the rule — Nancy Harris Brose, *Emily Dickinson: Profile of the Poet as Cook* (Amherst: privately printed, 1976), 20.[2]

Gingerbread

1 Quart Flour,
½ Cup Butter,
½ Cup Cream,

1 Table Spoon Ginger,
1 Tea Spoon Soda
1 Salt
Make up with Molasses—*Letters of Emily Dickinson*, II 493.

Dorothy Dix

Dorothy Dix (1861–1951) was a pioneering Southern-born woman journalist and advice columnist. Like many Southern cooks, she specified the use of Tabasco in her recipe for Barbequed Chicken—a mixture of capsicum peppers, salt, and vinegar first produced by the McIlhenny Co. on Avery Island, Louisiana, in 1868 and patented in 1870.

Barbequed Chicken

Broil the chickens in the usual way, and when they are dished pour over them this sauce: Melt 2 tablespoons of butter in a saucepan, add the same quantity of vinegar, a teaspoonful of made mustard, a strong dash of Tabasco, a teaspoonful of Worcestershire sauce, a teaspoonful of sugar, a saltspoonful of salt, and half as much pepper. Blend all together, heat to a boil, and pour over the chickens. Let stand for five minutes before serving.— Florence Stratton, *Favorite Recipes of Famous Women* (New York and London: Harper, 1925), 48.

Abigail Scott Duniway

The suffragist and journalist Abigail Scott Duniway (1834–1915) crossed the continent with her family along the Oregon Trail in 1852, a trip she commemorated both in her first of some two dozen novels, *Captain Grey's Company* (1859), and in her last, *From the West to the West* (1905).

Chicken and Gravy as Mother Did It

Cut the chicken into pieces convenient for serving. Have ready a frying pan half full of boiling lard or butter. Roll the pieces, first slightly salting them, in fine flour or corn meal. Fry quickly till thoroughly done; dish on to a large platter and pour the surplus "fryings" into a bowl for future use, leaving less than a gill in the bottom of the frying pan. Into this stir rapidly a heaping tablespoonful of flour, then add a pint of fresh milk, stirring constantly till it boils and thickens. Salt and pepper to taste. Pour the gravy over the chicken in the platter, or, if preferred, in a separate gravy dish. Any kind of young fowl is delicious cooked in this way, and no child forgets the delights of the side dish of gravy that accompanies it.— Burr, *The Woman Suffrage Cook Book*, 36.

Pure Salt Rising Bread

When the kitchen fire is lighted in the morning put a quart cup, one-third full of fresh water, on the range and heat it quickly to 95°. Remove from the fire, add a teaspoonful of salt, a pinch of brown sugar, and coarse flour or middlings sufficient to make a batter of about the right consistency for griddle cakes. Set the cup, with the spoon in it, in a closed vessel half filled with water moderately hot but not scalding. Keep the temperature as nearly even as possible, and add a spoonful of flour once or twice during the process of fermentation. The yeast ought to reach the top of the bowl in about five hours. Dip your flour into a tray or pan, make an opening in the centre and pour in your yeast. Have ready a pitcher of warm milk, salted, or milk and water (not too hot, or you will scald the yeast germs), and stir rapidly into a pulpy mass with a spoon. Cover this sponge closely and keep warm for an hour, then knead into loaves, adding flour to make the proper consistency. Place in warm well-greased pans, cover closely, and leave till it is light. Bake in a steady oven, and when done let all the hot steam escape. Wrap closely in damp towels and keep in closed earthen jars till wanted. There is no sweeter, nicer, better, or more wholesome bread than this; but it takes time, patience and thought to make it. Try it, and be convinced.—Burr, *The Woman Suffrage Cook Book*, 4.

Transparent Jelly (No. 1)

To make transparent jellies from strawberries, raspberries, currants, grapes, blackberries, or any small fruit, carefully select that which is sound and not too ripe, and without adding water, put to press overnight, previously bruising in a wooden bowl with your potato masher, and using as a strainer a jelly-bag made of cheese cloth. You will find your clothes wringer a most convenient press for extracting the juice, as it will take the open end of the bag between the rollers and hold it securely at any stage of pressure desired. Allow the juice to escape into earthen or wooden vessels, but on no account into tin or other metal, as the contact would color the jelly, and it is your object to make it clear. The next morning measure the juice, allowing a cupful of granulated sugar to each cupful of the liquid if the fruit is sour, or three cupfuls of sugar to four of juice if the fruit is sweet, and boil rapidly in a porcelain kettle for five minutes. Dip carefully into glasses, and if not thoroughly stiff when cold, set away for a few days in the sunshine.

This recipe will never fail if the directions are strictly observed.—Burr, *The Woman Suffrage Cook Book*, 109.

Transparent Jelly (No. 2)

To make transparent jelly from apples, peaches, pears, quinces, and crabapples, cut the sound, barely ripe fruit into quarters with paring (though it is well to remove the seeds), and place in a porcelain kettle. Add boiling water to cover the fruit and cook rapidly till soft, adding more boiling water if necessary. Then place in a new jelly-bag and hang up to drip into earthen vessels. The juice, which for such fruits should be colorless, is to be treated as for making jellies of small fruits, except that it should be boiled after sugar is added till it turns to a bright amber — perhaps twenty minutes.—Burr, *The Woman Suffrage Cook Book*, 109–10.

ELIZABETH FRIES ELLET

The poet and historian Elizabeth Fries Ellet (1818–1877) is best known today for her three-volume *The Women of the American Revolution* (1845). *The Practical Housekeeper*, her monumental encyclopedia on domestic economy, appeared in 1857.

Jugged Hare

Skin the hare and cut it in pieces, but do not wash it; strew it over with pepper and salt, fry it brown. Make a seasoning of two anchovies, a sprig of thyme, a little parsley, a nutmeg grated, a little mace, a few cloves pounded, and a teaspoonful of grated lemon peel. Strew this over the hare, after having carefully taken it out of the pan clear of fat, slice half pound of bacon very thin, put it into a jug or jar, a layer of hare and one of bacon upon it, until the whole is put in, then add rather less than half a pint of ale; cover the jug very closely, so as perfectly to keep in the steam; put it into a kettle of cold water, lay a tile on the top of the jug, and let it boil three hours if the hare be young, or four or five if an old one. Take the jug out of the kettle, pick out all the bacon which has not melted, and shake the hare up in a stewpan, with a little mushroom catsup, a glass of port wine, a little mushroom powder if at hand, and a little butter and flour, well mixed together to thicken the gravy. A teaspoonful of lemon-pickle, and one of browning, will heighten the flavor.— Ellet, *The Practical Housekeeper* (New York: Stringer and Townsend, 1857), 372–73.

Scotch Haggis

Take the stomach of a sheep. The washing and cleaning is of more consequence than all, as it will be of a bad color and a bad taste if not well cleansed; when clean, turn it inside out, then let it lie for a day or two in salt and water. Blanch the liver, lights, and heart of the sheep, lay them in cold water, chop all very fine; the liver you had better grate, chop a pound of the suet very fine, dry in the oven a pound of oatmeal; mix all this well together, season with pepper and salt, a little chopped parsley, and a little chopped onion; then sew up the bag; before you finish sewing it, add a few spoonfuls of good white stock; put it in a stewpan with a drainer; boil it in water, keeping it well covered all the time, prick it all over with a small larding pin to keep it from bursting; it will take several hours to boil; be careful in taking it up, and let your dish be large enough.— Ellet, *The Practical Housekeeper*, 304.

Seven-Years' Catsup

Take two quarts of the oldest strong beer, put to it one quart of red wine, three-quarters of a pound of anchovies, three ounces of shalots peeled, half an ounce of mace, the same of nutmegs, quarter of an ounce of cloves, three large races of ginger cut in slices, and boil all together over a moderate fire till one-third is wasted. When quite cold put into a large jar, covered up, and leave it there for a week or two until the sediment is wasted, and the clear liquor is perfectly transparent; then strain it through a fine hair sieve, taste it, and add to it a little of any essence of spice, oil, or vinegar, which you think may improve it, and, if the liquid be not lucidly clear, give it one smart boil: let it rest till cool, and bottle it in very small bottles to prevent its frequent exposure to the air.

It will improve by age, and may be carried on a voyage round the world.— Ellet, *The Practical Housekeeper*, 404.

HARLAN ELLISON

Harlan Ellison (b. 1934) is a prolific writer of short stories, novellas, screenplays, and teleplays, many in the science-fiction genre.

Café Ellison Diabolique

10-ounces coffee mug
Mortar and pestle
Maxim freeze-dried instant coffee
El Popular Mexican-style cake chocolate
Ferrara Italian anisette sugar
Granulated sugar
Water (boiling)
Cream

Into a 10-ounces coffee mug spoon 1½ teaspoons of Maxim freeze-dried instant coffee, 3 teaspoons of granulated sugar, and ¼ teaspoon of Ferrara Italian anisette sugar.

With a mortar and pestle break off and hand-crush sufficient El Popular Mexican chocolate from the brick cakes in the 15-ounces package to produce 3 full tablespoons of finely-crushed chocolate grind. Add it to the coffee mug's contents.

Add boiling water to mug's contents, leaving one-sixth of the mug empty for cream or half-and-half. Stir well.

This is my personal coffee recipe, refined over the last ten years to produce a balance between the harsh, often oily and unpleasant taste of regular coffee and the cloying sweetness of hot chocolate. While it bears lineal ties with Russian coffee and *Café Chocolat*, the bite of the newly-developed freeze-dried coffees (*never* use standard-ground instants of the powdered variety) and the addition of anisette sugar give it a special piquancy all its own. I find that coffee prepared in this way, first thing in the morning, soothes the jangled stomach lining yet furnishes the push to get to work at whatever's in the typewriter from the night before. In the evening, coffee prepared in this way is an aphrodisiac that has had estimable results with ladies of my acquaintance. Thus the adjective of its title.—*Cooking Out of This World*, ed. Anne MacCaffrey (New York: Ballantine, 1973), 72–73.

NORA EPHRON

Heartburn (1983), the debut novel by Nora Ephron (1941–2012), was not only a fictionalized account of her failed marriage to the journalist Carl Bernstein of Watergate fame but a continuation of the "cooking novel" tradition launched in the mid-nineteenth century by Catherine Owen and Marion Harland. Ephron was also a successful movie director: her last film, *Julie and Julia* (2009), was based on the story of a woman who prepared all 524 recipes in Julia Child's *Mastering the Art of French Cooking* in a single year.

Mashed Potatoes

You can, of course, train children to mash potatoes, but you should know that Richard Nixon spent most of his childhood making mashed potatoes for his mother and was extremely methodical about getting the lumps out. A few lumps make mashed potatoes more authentic, if you ask me, but that's not the point. The point is that perhaps children should not be trained to mash potatoes.

For mashed potatoes: Put 1 large (or 2 small) potatoes in a large pot of salted water and bring to a boil. Lower the heat and simmer for at least 20 minutes, until tender. Drain and place the potatoes back in the pot and shake over low heat to eliminate excess moisture. Peel. Put through a potato ricer and immediately add 1 tablespoon heavy cream and as much melted butter and salt and pepper as you feel like. Eat immediately. Serves one.— Ephron, *Heartburn* (New York: Knopf, 1983), 127.

William Faulkner

William Faulkner (1897–1962) received two Pulitzer prizes and the Nobel Prize for Literature in 1949.

Curing Hams Shoulders Bacon

After the pieces are trimmed and thoroughly cooled, either by 24 hours of natural temperature or by artificial temperature NOT LOW ENOUGH TO FREEZE IT, that is, about 35 degrees F.

Lay the pieces flat, flesh side up, cover thoroughly with plain salt, about ¼ inch deep. Work saltpeter into the bone-joints and into the ends where the feet were removed, and into any other crevices or abrasions. Do this well and carefully, to prevent "blowing." A slightly higher temperature will help the salt penetrate. Leave 24 hours.

After 24 hours, turn the pieces over SKIN SIDE UP, to drain. Sprinkle skin side with salt. I punch holes through the skin with an ice pick, to help draining. Leave 24 hours.

After 24 hours, turn the pieces flesh side up again, make a paste

½ plain salt

½ molasses, sugar, red and black pepper

just moist enough to spread over the pieces without flowing off. Leave 7 days.

After 7 days, make a paste

¼ plain salt

¾ molasses, sugar, red and black pepper

slightly more fluid than the first mixture, so that it will flow slowly over the pieces, penetrating the remains of last week's treatment, dripping down the sides. Leave 7 days.

After 7 days, make a paste WITHOUT SALT

molasses, sugar, red and black pepper

fluid enough to cover the pieces without flowing off too much, cover the pieces and the residue of the two former treatments, leave seven days.

Hang the pieces and smoke with hickory or oak chips, keep it in smoky atmosphere for 2 to 7 days. The meat may be treated either before smoking or afterward with a preparation to prevent blow flies. Then wrap or enclose in cloth or paper bags and leave hanging until used.—*Faulkner Journal* 2 (Fall 1986), 74.

Hot Toddy

Faulkner's niece remembered his medicinal use of bourbon.

When grownups in the Faulkner family were sick, Pappy had an instant cure—his ever-popular Hot Toddy. It was guaranteed to cure or ease anything from the aches and pains of a bad spill from a horse to a bad cold, from a broken leg to a broken heart. Pappy alone decided when a Hot Toddy was needed, and he administered it to his patient with the best bedside manner of a country doctor.

He prepared it in the kitchen in the following way: Take one heavy glass tumbler. Fill approximately half full with Heaven Hill bourbon (the Jack Daniel's was reserved for Pappy's ailments). Add one tablespoon of sugar. Squeeze ½ lemon and drop into glass. Stir until sugar dissolves. Fill glass with boiling water. Serve with potholder to protect patient's hands from the hot glass.

Pappy always made a small ceremony out of serving his Hot Toddy, bringing it upstairs on a silver tray and admonishing his patient to drink it quickly, before it cooled off. It never failed.— *The Great American Writers' Cookbook*, ed. Dean Faulkner Wells (Oxford, Ms.: Yoknapatawpha Press, 1981), 17–18.

ERNA FERGUSSON

Erna Fergusson (1888–1964) was a regional historian prominent in the so-called "Southwest Renaissance" of the thirties and sister of the novelist Harvey Fergusson. She was also instrumental in popularizing Southwest cuisine in the U.S. While the size of the "larder" in the desert was limited compared to other regions of the country, she observed, the foodstuffs available to the Southwestern cook were many and diverse: "Beef, mutton, pork, and fowl were varied by game and dried buffalo meat from the plains."

> Vegetables grew but were used in gravies or sauces rather than alone. Fruit was eaten fresh in its short season, and dried on wide trays for storing. Corn was used in every way, from soup to desserts, and the lowly brown bean appeared at every meal. Sugar was scarce, as were coffee and chocolate, as they all came up from Mexico and only the rich could afford them. Chile grew in every man's garden and was the only condiment. A limited diet, surely, but good cooks invented many a savory combination and the modern epicure rates New Mexico cookery — when properly done — with the best.[1]

In her pioneering *Mexican Cookbook* (1934), Fergusson introduced Mexican-American foods to the entire nation. Since the "American occupation" of El Norte formalized by the Treaty of Guadalupe Hildalgo in 1848, she observed, Mexican food has "been a part of the Southwestern diet. At first chile and beans and corns in many guises were all one could get. Later the deliciousness of slowly-cooked and richly condimented dishes won them fame among people who could not even pronounce their names."[2]

Buñuelos or Sopaipillas (Fried Puffs)

2 eggs
1 cup milk
¾ teaspoon salt
1 teaspoon baking powder
4 cups flour

Sift dry ingredients together. Beat eggs well, add milk, and stir in dry ingredients, adding as much flour as it will absorb.

Roll as thin as possible, cut and fry in deep fat until a delicate golden brown. Cut into small squares, they make *sopaipillas*. Cut large and round and with a hole pinched in the middle, they make *buñuelos*.

Served with the following sauce, *buñuelos* were used as a dessert.

Sauce for *Buñuelos*

6 tablespoons *piloncillo*
½ cup water
½ cup wine
½ cup seeded raisins
½ teaspoon cinnamon

Combine ingredients and boil until it begins to thicken. Pour over hot *buñuelos* and serve at once.— Fergusson, *Mexican Cookbook* (Albuquerque: University of New Mexico Press, 1945), 91.

Chile con Carne

2 pounds mutton or beef
1 pound fresh pork
4 cloves garlic, chopped
2 tablespoons lard or drippings
3 bay leaves
1 quart ripe tomatoes or 1 large can tomatoes
1 onion chopped
1 cup chile pulp or 6 tablespoons chile powder
1 tablespoon *orégano*
1 tablespoon salt
1 pint ripe olives
1 teaspoon *comino*

Cut the meat into small cubes. Brown onion and garlic in fat, add meat. Cover and steam thoroughly. Rub tomatoes through colander, add to meat, stir in chile pulp, and cook for 20 minutes. Add seasoning and cook slowly for 2 hours. Cut olives from the pits, add and cook for another ½ hour. Serve with *frijoles*.

If chile powder is used, mix with 1 tablespoon flour, stir into fat in which onion and garlic were browned, stir until smooth. Then add meat and proceed as above.— Fergusson, *Mexican Cookbook*, 39.

Chiles Rellenos

1 pound round steak
2 tablespoons lard
½ cup sugar
¼ teaspoon cloves
½ teaspoon cinnamon
½ teaspoon salt
½ cup seedless raisins
6 green chiles, chopped
½ cup vinegar or red wine
3 eggs

Boil round steak and grind. Brown in hot lard. Add sugar, spices, salt, raisins, chiles, and liquid. Mix thoroughly and mould into egg-shaped croquettes. Beat egg whites very stiff, Add yolks and beat, Roll each croquette in flour, then in the beaten egg and fry in deep fat.

2 cups of dry native mushrooms may be substituted for the steak. This is an excellent

variation for Lent. Boil mushrooms about 10 minutes, chop, or grind.— Fergusson, *Mexican Cookbook*, 31

Corn Meal Tortillas

2 cups corn meal or *masa*
1 teaspoon salt
Warm water

Mix corn meal or *masa* and salt. If dry meal is used, add enough water to make a stiff dough, even the *masa* may require a little moisture. Adding 1 cup white flour to this recipe will make the dough easier to handle.

Set dough aside for 20 minutes, wet hands in water, mold balls of dough the size of hens' eggs, pat into thin cakes, and bake on soapstone or lightly greased griddle, turning until brown on both sides.— Fergusson, *Mexican Cookbook*, 87

Enchiladas with Flour Tortillas

2 cups flour
1 teaspoon salt
1½ teaspoons baking powder
1 tablespoon fat
Cold water

Mix and sift dry ingredients, cut in the fat and add cold water to make a stiff dough, ⅔ cup. Knead on lightly floured board, make small balls, pat thin, bake on soapstone or lightly greased griddle.

Serve with the following sauce.

2 tablespoons lard
1 large onion, chopped
3 cloves garlic, chopped
4 cups chile pulp
2 tablespoons vinegar
4 tablespoons olive oil
1 teaspoon *orégano*
½ tablespoon salt
½ pound cheese
1 pint ripe olives

Brown onion and garlic in hot lard. Add chile pulp, olive oil, *orégano*, and salt. Cook for at least 30 minutes; longer is better. While sauce is cooking, grate cheese, pit and chop olives.

Heat lard in a large skillet as for deep fat frying. When boiling hot, dip *tortillas* in fat, then in the hot sauce, and lay on a platter. Cover each *tortilla* with grated cheese and olives and add another until there are four in a pile. Top pile with a fried egg, and set in oven until cheese is melted.

A dish of chopped onions and a dish of chile sauce should be placed on the table when *enchiladas* are served. *Frijoles* complete the meal.— Fergusson, *Mexican Cookbook*, 28, 88.

Frijoles (Beans)

2 cups frijoles (Mexican beans)
⅓ pound salt pork

1 pinch *oregano*

Pick over beans carefully and soak overnight. Drain and cover with fresh cold water. Add salt pork and *oregano*, boil slowly until tender, 4 to 6 hours. If possible, cook at simmering temperature all day. As water boils away, add boiling water, never cold.

Frijoles may be served just as they come from the pot. If a larger quantity is cooked, they may be used the second day with chile.

This quantity will make ten servings.—Fergusson, *Mexican Cookbook*, 59.

Green Corn with Green Chile

3 cups green corn
2–4 green chiles
½–1 clove garlic, chopped fine
3 tablespoons lard or olive oil
¾ teaspoon salt
⅛ teaspoon pepper

Cut corn from the cob. Heat the fat in a frying pan. Add corn, chiles, and garlic. Cover and cook slowly until corn is tender, 10 to 15 minutes. Add seasoning. If corn seems too dry, add several tablespoons of boiling water while cooking.—Fergusson, *Mexican Cookbook*, 69.

Posole (Hog and Hominy)

"Posole is a traditional cold weather stew in the New Mexico Pueblos and mountain villages," according to Pulitzer Prize-winning author N. Scott Momaday. "There is nothing like it in the evenings before and after Christmas."[3] Fergusson published her own recipe.

2 pounds pork, cubed
2 onions, chopped
1 bay leaf
1 tablespoon fat
½ teaspoon *oregano*
1 cup red chile pulp or 4–6 tablespoons chile powder
1 cup *nixtamal* (hominy)
1 teaspoon salt

Fry onions in fat, add pork and blend. Add *nixtamal* or hominy, chile, and seasoning. Add hot water and simmer until pork is thoroughly tender, about 4 hours. Serve steaming hot. If chile powder is used, mix with 1 tablespoon of flour and stir into fat.

If canned hominy is used, cook pork first until almost done before adding hominy. Then simmer until done.—Fergusson, *Mexican Cookbook*, 43.

Quesadillas

1¾ cups fresh goats' cheese (¼ cake)
⅛ teaspoon salt
Pastry (see below)
½ cup sugar

Grind cheese, add sugar and salt, and mix well.

Roll out one half the pastry thin and lay on baking sheet. Spread the cheese mixture on this and cover with other half the pastry. Press edges together. Brush over with melted lard or milk and sprinkle with sugar. Mark into small squares and prick each square with a fork.

Bake in moderate over until brown, about 20 minutes.
Cool and cut as marked.

Pastels (Pastry)

2 cups flour
½ teaspoon baking powder
¾ teaspoon salt
⅔ cup butter or lard
4 to 6 tablespoons cold water

Mix and sift dry ingredients. Cut in shortening until mixture is like coarse meal. Add only enough water to bind together. Roll out thin on a slightly floured board. Line pie pan and fill with a cooked fruit mixture. Cover with interlacing strips and bake in a quick oven for 10 minutes. Continue baking in a moderate oven for 20 minutes.

Pasteles are also made with all kinds of dried fruits.

Prepare fruit as directed below.

Anise may be sprinkled over just before serving.

Pastelitos

1 pound dried apricots (2½ cups fruit pulp)
1¼ cups sugar
3 teaspoons sugar
1 teaspoon cinnamon

Wash dried apricots and soak overnight, or for several hours. Cook until soft enough to press through colander or ricer or mash well. (If mashed, pulp contains the skins and less dried fruit need be cooked.) Add sugar to pulp and cook until very thick. Let cool.

Roll out one half the pastry large enough to line a baking sheet. Spread fruit mixture on this and cover with other half of pastry. Press edges together. Sprinkle with mixture of sugar and cinnamon. Mark in small squares before baking, and prick each square with fork.

Bake in hot oven about 20 minutes. Cool and cut as marked.

Pastelitos should be about as thick as the little finger. Any kind of dried fruit or combination of dried fruits may be used. Raisins may be added to the apricot pulp.

This makes about 35 *pastelitos.*— Fergusson, *Mexican Cookbook*, 85, 98, 99–100.

Tortillas, Corn Meal

2 cups corn meal or *masa*
1 teaspoon salt
Warm water

Mix corn meal or *masa* and salt. If dry meal is used, add enough water to make a stiff dough. Even the *masa* may require a little moisture. Adding 1 cup white flour to this recipe will make the dough easier to handle.

Set dough aside for 20 minutes, wet hands in water, mold balls of dough the size of hens' eggs, put into thin cakes, and bake on soapstone or lightly greased griddle, turning until brown on both sides.— Fergusson, *Mexican Cookbook*, 87.

ANNIE ADAMS FIELDS

Annie Adams Fields (1834–1915) was the wife of James T. Fields, an author and publisher whose firm issued the books of the foremost New England literati, including Emerson, Thoreau, Hawthorne, Longfellow, Stowe, Whittier, Holmes, and Lowell. She was at the center of Boston literary life for half a century, and after the death of her husband in 1881 she became the companion of Sarah Orne Jewett. She was also the author or editor in her own right of such volumes as *James T. Fields: Biographical Notes and Personal Sketches* (1881), *Whittier: Notes of His Life and of His Friendship* (1883), *The Letters of Celia Thaxter* (1895), and *Life and Letters of Harriet Beecher Stowe* (1897).

French Toast

Spread slices of hot, dry toast with roast beef or chicken gravy, pile them up and set in oven till gravy is absorbed. Serve hot. An excellent breakfast or lunch dish.— Sophie D. Coe, *The Kirmess Cookbook* (Boston: Women's Educational and Industrial Union, 1887), 15.

Walnut Cake

Whites of four eggs beaten to a froth, one and one half cups of sugar, half a cup of butter, half a cup of milk, two cups of flour, one teaspoonful of Royal baking powder, one pint of chopped walnuts.— Coe, *The Kirmess Cookbook* 55.

ZELDA FITZGERALD

Zelda Fitzgerald (1900–1948) was a Southern belle, the author of *Save Me the Waltz* (1932), and the wife of F. Scott Fitzgerald.

Breakfast

See if there is any bacon, and if there is ask the cook which pan to fry it in. Then ask if there are any eggs, and if so try and persuade the cook to poach two of them. It is better not to attempt toast, as it burns very easily. Also in the case of bacon do not turn the fire too high, or you will have to get out of the house for a week. Serve preferably on china plates, though gold or wood will do if handy.— Stratton, *Famous Recipes of Famous Women*, 98.

BENJAMIN FRANKLIN

Benjamin Franklin (1706–1790) famously praised the virtue of temperance in his *Autobiography*: "Eat not to Dullness, drink not to elevation." Despite his reputation for asceticism and austerity, however, Franklin "was a man who liked his food and his drink"— so much so that during his tenure as the first U.S. ambassador to France between 1776 and 1785 he suffered from gout, the so-called "rich man's disease." While "he never evidenced the systematic interest" in Gallic *haute cuisine* displayed by Jefferson,[1] he preserved among his papers many handwritten recipes, including 16 pages translated into French from Hannah Glasse's *The Art of Cookery* (1747).

Apple Pudding
(Pour faire un pudding de pommes)

Make a good puff paste, roll it out half an inch thick, pare your apples, and core them, enough to fill the crust, and close it up, tie it in a cloth and boil it. If a small pudding, two hours: if a large one three or four hours. When it is enough turn it into your dish, cut a piece of the crust out of the top, butter and sugar it to your palate; lay on the crust again, and send it to table hot. A pear pudding make the same way. And thus you may make a damson pudding, or any sort of plums, apricots, cherries, or mulberries, and are very fine.— Franklin, *On the Art of Eating*, ed. Frank Chinard (Philadelphia. American Philosophical Society, 1958), 57.

Beer with Essence of Spruce (Maniere de faire de la biere avec de l'essence de spruce)

For a Cask containing 80 Bottles, take one Pot of Essence and 13 Pounds of Molasses.— or the same amount of unrefined Loaf Sugar; mix them well together in 20 Pints of hot Water: Stir until they make a Foam, then pour it into the Cask you will then fill with Water: add a Pint of good Yeast; stir it well together and let it stand 2 or 3 Days to ferment, after which close the Cask, and after a few Days it will be ready to be put into Bottles, that must be tightly corked. Leave them 10 to 12 Days in a cool Cellar, after which the Beer will be good to drink.— Franklin, *On the Art of Eating*, 57.

Broiled Steaks (Tranches de bœuf grillées)

First have a very clear brisk fire; let your gridiron be very clean; put it on the fire, and take a chaffing dish with a few hot coals out of the fire. Put the dish on it which is to lay your steaks on, then take fine rump steaks about half an inch thick; put a little pepper and salt on them, lay them on the gridiron, and (if you like it) take a shallot or two, or a fine onion and cut it fine; put it into your dish. Don't turn your steaks till one side is done, then when you turn the other side there will soon be fine gravy lie on the top of the steak, which you must be careful not to lose. When the steaks are enough, take them carefully off into your dish, that none of the gravy be lost; then have ready a hot dish and cover, and carry them hot to table, with the cover on.— Franklin, *On the Art of Eating*, 47

A Cheap and Good Soup

Pounds	Cents
Take 4 of beef from the neck, which will cost	3
2 of barley, or 4 of indian meal,	4
3 or half peck of potatoes, 3	
4 of beans, or pease,	4
2 of onions, 3	
2 of bread, or if of wheat or indian meal,	
four pounds	6
15 gallons of water,	
Salt and pepper,	2
24 pounds of solid food.	30 Cts.

Soak the pease or beans in water kept warm, till they are swelled, and then put them, together with all the vegetables except the bread, into fifteen gallons of water. (It should be pure rain, or spring water, of if manhattan or hard water, add a spoonful of pearl-ash to it.) Boil them in a tightly covered vessel two hours. Let the beef now be chopped into small pieces, and fried in fat for a few minutes, and then, with the gravy added to the soup. Continue to boil the whole two hours longer, and after seasoning with salt and pepper, it will be fit for use. The bread should be cut into small pieces, and added last; and the harder and drier it is, the better.

There will be at least when done, 13 gallons, or 104 pints of good soup: an allowance of three pints a day, for five persons for a week; and the whole, exclusive of the expense of cooking, will have cost but 30 cents.— Franklin, *Plain Directions on Domestic Economy* (New York: S.Wood and Sons, 1821), 5–6.

Mince Pie (Recette d'un pâté haché)

Take three pounds of suet shred very fine, and chopped as small as possible, two pounds of raisins stoned, and chopped as fine as possible, two pounds of currants nicely picked, washed, rubbed, and dried at the fire, half a hundred of fine pippins; pared, cored, and chopped small, half a pound of fine sugar pounded fine, a quarter of an ounce of mace, a quarter of an ounce of cloves, two large nutmegs; all beat fine; put all together into a great pan, and mix it well together with half a pint of brandy, and half a pint of sack; put it down close in a stone–Pot, and it will keep good four months. When you make your Pies, take a little dish, something bigger than a soup-plate, lay a very thin crust all over it, lay a thin layer of meat, and then a thin layer of citron cut thin, over that a little meat, squeeze half the juice of a fine Seville orange or lemon, and pour in three spoonfuls of red wine; lay on your crust, and bake it nicely.— Franklin, *On the Art of Eating*, 55.

Orange Shrub

To a Gallon of Rum two Quarts of Orange Juice and two pounds of Sugar — dissolve the Sugar in the Juice before you mix it with the Rum — put all together in a Cask & shake it well — let it stand 3- or 4-Weeks & it will be very fine & fit for Bottling — when you have Bottled off the fine pass the thick thro' a Philtring paper put into a Funnell — that not a drop may be lost.

To obtain the flavour of the Orange Peel paire a few Oranges & put it in Rum for 12 hours—& put that Run into the Cask with the other —

For Punch thought better without the Peel.— Franklin, *On the Art of Eating*, 59.

Oyster Sauce for Boiled Turkey
(Sauce d'huitres pour un dindon bouilli)

Evan Jones remarks on the ubiquity of oysters in nineteenth-century American cuisine: "It is doubtful that any country ever went as crazy over oysters as the United States."[2] Root and de Rochemont add that they "were eaten raw, baked, fried, fricasseed, in soup, in pies, in stuffings, and riding triumphantly on top of grilled steaks."[3]

Take one Pint of oysters draw out the Liquor which you will set apart, put them in cold water, wash and clean them well, put them in an earthen dish with their Liquor, in which you will put a shred of Nutmeg with a little butter strewed with flour and a quarter of a Lemon; boil them, then, put in a half Pint of Cream and boil slowly, all together; this done take out the Lemon, the Nutmeg, squeeze the Juice of a Lemon in the Sauce, then serve it in a Sauceboat.— Franklin, *On the Art of Eating*, 49.

Puff Paste (Pâte feuilletée)

Take a quarter of a peck of flour, rub fine half a pound of butter, a little salt, make it up into a light paste with cold water, just stiff enough to work it well up; then roll it out, and stick pieces of butter all over, and strew a little flour; roll it up, and roll it out again; and so do nine or ten times, till you have rolled in a pound and a half of butter. This crust is mostly used for all sorts of pies. — Franklin, *On the Art of Eating*, 51.

Rice Pudding Baked
(Pour faire un pudding de riz cuit au pour)

Boil a pound of rice just till it is tender; then drain all the water from it as dry as you can, but don't squeeze it; then stir in a good piece of butter, and sweeten to your palate. Grate a small nutmeg in, stir it all together, butter a pan, and pour it in and bake it. You may add a few currants for change. — Franklin, *On the Art of Eating*, 51.

Roast Pig (Pour rôtir un cochon de lait)

Spit your pig and lay it to the fire, which must be a very good one at each end, or hang a flat iron in the middle of the grate. Before you lay your pig down, take a little sage shred small, a piece of butter as big as a walnut, and a little pepper and salt; put them into the pig and sew it up with coarse thread, then flour it all over very well, and keep flouring it till the eyes drop out, or you find the crackling hard. Be sure to save all the gravy that comes out of it, which you must do by setting basons or pans under the pig in the dripping pan, as soon as you find the gravy begins to run. When the pig is enough, stir the fire up brisk; take a coarse cloth, with about a quarter of a pound of butter in it, and rub the pig all over till the crackling is quite crisp, and then take it up. Lay it in your dish, and with a sharp knife cut off the head, and then cut the pig in two, before you draw out the spit. Cut the ears off the head and lay at each end, and cut the under jaw in two and lay on each side: melt some good butter, take the gravy you saved and put into it, boil it, and pour into the dish with the brains bruised fine, and the sage mixed all together, and then send it to table. — Franklin, *On the Art of Eating*, 53.

Sauce for Boiled Ducks or Rabbits
(Sauce pour des canards ou des lapins bouillis)

> In the inimitable words of Alice B. Toklas, "What is sauce for the goose may be sauce for the gander but is not necessarily sauce for the chicken, the duck, the turkey, or the guinea hen."[4] As if in agreement, Franklin was careful to transcribe a unique sauce recipe:

To boiled ducks or rabbits, you must pour boiled onions over them, which is done thus: take the onions, peel them, and boil them in a great deal of water; shift your water, then let them boil about two hours, take them up and throw them into a cullender to drain, then with a knife chop them on a board; put them into a sauce-pan, just shake a little flour over them, put in a little milk or cream, with a good piece of butter; set them over the fire, and when the butter is melted they are enough. — Franklin, *On the Art of Eating*, 49.

JESSIE BENTON FRÉMONT

> The memoirist and historian Jessie Benton Frémont (1824–1902), wife of John C. Frémont, a war hero, explorer, and Republican nominee for President in 1856, was the author of *The Story of the Guard: A Chronicle of the War* (1863), *A Year of American Travel: Narrative of Personal Experience* (1878), *Souvenirs of My Time* (1887), and *Far-West Sketches* (1890). During the late 1860s she also hosted a salon in San Francisco attended by Bret Harte, Herman Melville, and others.

Ham Bones

"The Funeral of a Ham." This is the startling name the Germans give their final use of the unsightly "hambones"— too good still to be thrown away, but too ugly to bring to table.

The bone itself goes into the soup kettle and from the broth it flavors, they take enough to stew *gently (boiling fast kills flavors and hardens meat)*, the shavings of ham that had remained on the bone.

Put these in the broth with a Chili pepper, a very little garlic, soup-herbs and a laurel leaf— pungent, but sparingly used flavors, and let them assimilate by *slow*, steady heat. Then make mashed potatoes into a lining for a pudding-dish (you can also use boiled macaroni in the same way); and lay in the stewed ham in light layers alternating with potatoes (or macaroni) and bake so it will look light and brown, like a potato soufflé. There may be some baking powder to make the brown top crust and sides, or cream (I really do not know how it is done, but it should be brown and raised like a nice dish of baked mashed potatoes) and sent to the table in the dish in which it was baked. It is simple enough — most excellent and *flavorous*, or only fit for a railway eating-station — according to the intelligent patience of the cook.— *How We Cook in Los Angeles* (Los Angeles: Commercial Printing House, 1895), 143–44.

Horace Howard Furness

Horace Howard Furness (1833–1912), a longtime instructor at the University of Pennsylvania, was the leading Shakespearean scholar of his generation and the editor of the "Furness Variorum" of Shakespeare's major plays.

Cream Cheese

Take 1 quart of good cream, let it stand two days in a moderately warm place, stirring in half a teaspoon of salt. Then put it in a piece of cheese cloth and lay it on a plate on a porcelain lined colander, covering it with another plate, on which put a weight. Leave it for 24 hours, then change the cloth. Do this a third time and it will then be fit to use. It can be made more quickly of sour cream in 3 or 4 days.—*Famous Old Receipts*, 325.

Erle Stanley Gardner

Erle Stanley Gardner (1889–1970) began every title in his Perry Mason series with the phrase "Case of." Predictably, he used the same phrase in the title of a cocktail recipe he contributed to a drink book published two years after the end of Prohibition.

Case of the Caretaker's Cat Cocktail

1 jigger Italian vermouth
1 jigger gin
1 pony rum
½ pony grenadine
4 dashes lime juice

Shake, pour, imbibe, kick the cat and send for the caretaker.— Sterling North et al., *So Red the Nose, or Breath in the Afternoon* (New York: Farrar and Rinehart, 1935), n.p.

CHARLOTTE PERKINS GILMAN

An advocate of "kitchenless homes," Charlotte Perkins Gilman (1860–1935) suggests in what may have been a strategic move that her recipe for synthetic quince was an "accidental discovery." Certainly she did not want to seem too adept at domestic labor.

Synthetic Quince

I put too much water with my rhubarb and had a whole dishful of beautiful pink juice left over, about a quart. In this I cooked some apples, quartered, and stewed till soft, and just as an experiment added a saucerful of strawberries—also "left over." The result, being served, looked and tasted exactly like quince, except that the apple was a little softer.— L. O. Kleber, *Suffrage Cook Book* (Pittsburgh: Equal Franchise Federation of Western Pennsylvania, 1915), 200.

ALLEN GINSBERG

The quintessential Beat poet and countercultural icon Allen Ginsberg (1926–1997) was a type of latter-day Transcendentalist. In "A Supermarket in California" (1956), first published in *Howl and Other Poems*, he imagines walking through a grocery store with Walt Whitman: "We strode down the open corridors together in our solitary fancy tasting artichokes, possessing every frozen delicacy, and never passing the cashier."[1]

Cold Summer Borscht

Ginsberg also was a devotee of borscht.

Dozen beets cleaned & chopped to bite size salad-size Strips
Stems & leaves also chopped like salad lettuce
All boiled together lightly salted to make a bright red soup, with beets now soft—boil an hour or more
Add Sugar & Lemon Juice to make the red liquid sweet & sour like Lemonade
Chill 4 gallon(s) of beet liquid—
Serve with

(1) Sour Cream on table
(2) Boiled small or halved potato on the side i.e. so hot potatoes don't heat the cold soup prematurely
(3) Spring salad on table to put into cold red liquid
   (1) Onions—sliced (spring onions)
   (2) Tomatoes—sliced bite sized
   (3) Lettuce—ditto
   (4) Cucumbers—ditto
   (5) a few radishes.

— The Allen Ginsberg Project, ginsbergblog.blog
spot.com/2011/09/cold-summer-borscht.html

GRACE GREENWOOD

The poet and travel writer Grace Greenwood, aka Sara Jean Lippincott (1823–1904), moved in the same New York literary circles as Poe, Julia Ward Howe, and Horace Greeley, and in 1849 she briefly worked as assistant editor of *Godey's Lady's Book*, the leading American women's magazine of the period.

Prune Pudding

Ingredients: One cupful of suet chopped fine, one cupful of molasses, one cupful of sweet milk, one-half pound of prunes and one-half pound of English currants, one teaspoonful of salt, one small teaspoonful of soda mixed in the molasses, three and a half cupfuls of flour.

Boil in a bag or form three hours; or, better, steam it. It may be steamed in teacups, filling them a little more than half full. Serve with brandy sauce.— Henderson, *Practical Cooking and Dinner Giving*, 271.

SARAH JOSEPHA HALE

As editor of *Godey's Lady's Book* for 40 years, Sarah Josepha Hale (1788–1879) was "continually in a position to influence American attitudes about domestic matters, art, politics, and, especially, food." In 1827, she launched a campaign to make Thanksgiving a national holiday. In a single passage in her domestic romance *Northwood*, published that year, she "offered a bounteous formula for generations of succeeding Thanksgiving dinners, all building on the basic components of turkey, stuffing, and pumpkin pie"[1]:

> The roasted turkey took precedence on this occasion, being placed at the head of the table; and well did it become its lordly station, sending forth the rich odor of its savory stuffing, and finely covered with the froth of its basting. At the foot of the board, a sirloin of beef, flanked on either side by a leg of pork and loin of mutton, seemed placed as a bastion to defend the innumerable bowls of gravy and plates of vegetables disposed in that quarter. A goose and pair of ducklings occupied side stations on the table; the middle being graced, as it always is on such occasions, by the rich burgomaster of the provisions, called a chicken pie. This pie, which is wholly formed of the choicest parts of fowls, enriched and seasoned with a profusion of butter and pepper, and covered with an excellent puff paste, is, like the celebrated pumpkin pie, an indispensable part of a good and true Yankee Thanksgiving; the size of the pie usually denoting the gratitude of the party who prepares the feast.[2]

Hale printed recipes for all of these delicacies in *The Good Housekeeper* (1839).

Chicken Pie

Pick, clean, and singe the chickens; if they are very young, keep them whole; if large, cut them in joints, and take off the skin, wash them well, parboil in a pint of water, season them with salt, white pepper, grated nutmeg and mace mixed, and if whole, put into them a bit of butter rolled in flour, and a little of the mixed spices; lay them into a dish with the livers, gizzards, and hearts well seasoned, add the gravy, and the yolks of five hard boiled eggs; cover with a puff paste, and bake it for an hour.

Slices of cold ham and forcemeat balls may be added to this pie. Or wash in cold water two or three ounces of macaroni, break it into small bits, simmer it for nearly half an hour in milk and water, drain, and put it with the chickens into the dish, and also an ounce of butter.— Hale, *The Good Housekeeper* (Boston: Weeks, Jordan, 1839), 74.

Puff Paste

Weigh an equal quantity of flour and butter, rub rather more than the half of the butter into the flour, then add as much cold water as will make it into a stiff paste; work it until the butter be completely mixed with the flour, make it round, beat it with the rolling-pin, dust it, as also the rolling-pin, with flour, and roll it out towards the opposite side of the slab, or paste-board, making it of an equal thickness; then with the point of a knife put little bits of butter all over it, dust flour over and under it, fold in the sides and roll it up, dust it again with flour, beat it a little, and roll it out, always rubbing the rolling-pin with flour, and throwing some underneath the paste, to prevent its sticking to the board. If the butter is not all easily put in at the second time of rolling out the paste, the remainder may be put in at the third; it should be touched as little as possible with the hands.—Hale, *The Good Housekeeper*, 69.

Pumpkin Pie

Stew the pumpkin dry, and make it like squash pie, only season rather higher. In the country, where this *real yankee pie* is prepared in perfection, ginger is almost always used with other spices. There too, part cream instead of milk, is mixed with the pumpkin, which gives it a richer flavor.

Roll the paste rather thicker than for fruit pies, as there is only one crust. If the pie is large and deep it will require to bake an hour in a brisk oven.—Hale, *The Good Housekeeper*, 71.

Roast Beef

The sirloin is too large for a private family; one weighing fifteen pounds is the best size for roasting; but this may be divided if a small one is required. It should be washed in cold water, then dried with a clean cloth and rubbed over with salt, and the fat covered with a piece of white paper tied on with thread. The spit should be clean as sand and water can make it. Be sure and wipe it dry immediately after it is drawn from the meat, and scour and wash it always before using.

The fire must be bright and clear, but not scorching when the meat is put down. Place it about ten inches from the fire at first and gradually move it nearer. It should be basted with a little clean dripping or lard, put into the roaster or tin-kitchen, as soon as it is down. Be sure this

Roaster is perfectly clean. Continue to baste the meat at intervals, and turn the spit frequently, and when the meat is nearly done — or about half an hour before you take it up — remove the paper from the fat, sprinkle on a little salt and baste it well—then pour off the top of the dripping, which is nearly all liquid fat, and would prove unhealthy if used in the gravy; then take a teacup of boiling water, into which put a salt-spoonful of salt, and drop this by degrees, on the brown parts of the joints (the meat will soon brown again.)—Stir the fire and make it clear; sprinkle a little salt over the roast, baste it with butter and dredge it with flour—very soon the froth will rise; then it must be taken up directly and dished.—Pour the gravy from the roaster, skim it, and give it a boil, then send to table in a boat. Scraped horseradish is used to garnish it, or may be sent up in a plate with vinegar.

The inside of the sirloin is excellent for hash.

Twenty minutes of time to each pound of meat is the rule for roasting. In cold weather, and when the meat is very fat it will require a little more time—in warm weather, and with lean beef fifteen minutes to a pound will be sufficient. Experience and judgment must regulate these things.—Hale, *The Good Housekeeper*, 27–28.

Roasted Goose

Geese seem to bear the same relation to poultry that pork does to the flesh of other domestic quadrupeds; that is, the flesh of goose is not suitable for, or agreeable to, the very delicate in constitution. One reason doubtless is that it is the fashion to bring it to table very rare done; a detestable mode!

Take a young goose, pick, singe, and clean well. Make the stuffing with two ounces of onions (about four common sized), and one ounce of green sage chopped very fine; then add a large coffee cup of stale bread crumbs, a little pepper and salt, a bit of butter as big as a walnut, the yolk of an egg or two; mix these well together and stuff the goose; do not fill it entirely; the stuffing requires room to swell. Spit it; tie the spit at both ends to prevent its swinging round, and to keep the stuffing from coming out. The fire must be brisk. Baste it with salt and water at first — then with its own dripping. It will take two hours or more to roast it thoroughly.

A green goose, that is one under four months old, is seasoned with pepper and salt instead of sage and onions. It will roast in an hour. — Hale, *The Good Housekeeper*, 42.

Roasted Pork

Take a leg of pork, one weighing eight pounds will require full three and a half hours to roast it. Wash it clean, and dry it with a cloth; with a sharp knife score the skin in diamonds about an inch square.

Make a stuffing with grated bread, a little sage, and two small onions chopped fine, seasoned with pepper and salt, and moistened with the yolk of an egg. Put this in under the skin of the knuckle, and in deep incisions made in the thick part of the leg; rub a little fine powdered sage into the skin where it is scored; and then, with a paste brush or goose feather, rub the whole surface of the skin with sweet oil or butter; this makes the crackling crisper and browner than basting it with dripping, it will be perfect in color, and the skin will not blister.

Do not put it too near the fire; and it must be moistened at intervals with sweet oil or butter, tied up in a rag. When it is done, skim the fat from the gravy, which may be thickened with a little butter rolled in flour.

Applesauce is always proper to accompany roasted pork — this, with potatoes, mashed or plain, mashed turnips, and pickles are good. — Hale, *The Good Housekeeper*, 33.

Roasted Turkey

Make a stuffing like that for veal; or take a teacup of sausage meat and add a like quantity of bread crumbs, with the beaten yolks of two eggs — then fill the crop; dredge the turkey over with flour, lay it before the fire, taking care this is most on the stuffed part, as that requires the greatest heat. A strip of paper may be put on the breast bone to prevent its scorching. Baste with a little butter or salt and water at first, then with its own dripping. A little before it is taken up, dredge it again with flour, baste with butter and froth it up. A large turkey requires full three hours roasting — a smaller in proportion.

Ham or tongue is usually eaten with turkey; stewed cranberries also. — Hale, *The Good Housekeeper*, 40.

Stuffed Loin of Mutton

Take the skin off a loin of mutton with the flap on; bone it neatly; make a nice veal stuffing and fill the inside of the loin with it where the bones were removed; roll it up tight, skewer the flap, and tie twine round it to keep it firmly together; put the outside skin over it till nearly roasted, and then remove it that the mutton may brown. Serve with a nice gravy, mashed turnips and potatoes. Currant jelly is eaten with mutton.

Mutton must be boiled the same as other meats—that is, *simmered very slowly*, and the scum carefully removed. Always wash it before cooking and put it in cold water. Only allow water sufficient to cover it, and the liquor makes excellent broth, with a little rice and a few carrots, &c.

Mutton for boiling must not be kept so long as it may be for roasting. Two or three days is sufficient; in warm weather less.—Hale, *The Good Housekeeper*, 36.

GAIL HAMILTON

Gail Hamilton, aka Mary Abigail Dodge (1833–1896), was editor of *Our Young Folks* and a celebrated essayist.

Beaten Biscuit

In 1894 Hamilton contributed to a charity cookbook a recipe for beaten biscuit, a standard table bread during the nineteenth century made without baking soda, with the air bubbles beaten into the dough causing the biscuits to rise.

One quart flour, one heaping tablespoonful lard, water to make stiff dough, a little salt. Beat well with rolling pin; work into flat biscuit; make a few holes in each with a fork. Bake in quick oven.—*Recipes Tried and True* (Marion, Ohio: Kelley Mount, 1894), 159.

Blackberry Jam Cake

One cup coffee or light brown sugar, one-half cup butter, two cups flour, one cup blackberry jam, three eggs, three tablespoons sour cream, one teaspoon soda, two teaspoons cinnamon, one-half a nutmeg. Put in the ingredients in the order given. Bake in layers, and finish with boiled icing.—*Recipes Tried and True*, 99.

Brown Bread Cakes

Hamilton reassured the readers of her *Country Living and Country Thinking* (1862), "If the potato crop fails, 'Boston brown bread,' fresh from the oven, will enable you to bear the loss with philosophical resignation."[1]

Of fine maize flour, yellow as the locks of the lovely Lenore, take — well, take enough — I cannot tell exactly how much; it depends upon circumstances. Of fresh new milk, white as the brow of the charming Arabella, take — I don't know exactly how much of that, either; it depends upon circumstances, particularly on the quantity of meal. If you have not new milk, take blue milk, provided it be sweet; or if you have none that is sweet, sour milk will answer; or if "your folks don't keep a cow," take water, clear and sparkling as the eyes of the peerless Amanda; but whether it be milk or water, let it be scalding as the tears of the outraged Isabel. Of molasses, sweet as the tones of the tuneful Lisette, take — a great deal, if it is summer, in the winter not quite so much. Of various other substances, animal, vegetable, and mineral, which it becomes not me to mention, —first, because I have forgotten what they are; secondly, because I never knew; and, thirdly, because, as the immortal Toots remarks, "it is of no consequence," — take whatever seems good in your sight, and cast them together into the kneading-trough, and knead with all your might and main. Provide yourself, then, with a tin plate, not bright and new, for so will your cakes be heavy, your crust cracked, and your soul sorrowful, but one blackened by fire, and venerable with time, and rough with service. With your own roseate fingers scoop out a portion of the pulpy mass. Fear not to touch it; it is soft, yielding, and plastic, as the heart of the affectionate Clara. Turn it lovingly over in your hands; round it; mould it; caress it; soften down its asperities; smooth off its angularities; repress its bold protuberances; encourage its timid shrinkings; and when it is smooth as the velvet cheek of Ida, and oval as the classic face of Helen, give one "last, long, lingering look," and lay it tenderly in the swart arms of its tutelar plate. Repeat the process, until your cakes shall equal the sands on the seashore or the stars in the sky for multitude, or as long as your meal holds out, or till you are tired. I am prescribing for one only. "Ab uno disce omnes" (from Virgil: "From one know all"). To the Stygian cave that yawns dismally from the kitchen stove, consign it without a murmur. Item: said stove must have a prodigious crack up and down the front. A philosophical reason for this I am unable to give. I refer the curious in cause and effect to Galen's deservedly celebrated *Disquisition on the Relations of Fire and Metals*, passim; also *Debrauche on Dough*, p. 35, Appendix. I only know that the only stove whence I ever saw brown bread cakes issue had an immense crack up and down the front. (Since writing the above, a new stove has been substituted for the old one, and still brown bread cakes are duly marshaled every morning. Consequently, you need not be particular about the crack. Still, I would advise all amateurs to consult the authorities I have mentioned. It will be a good exercise.) When your cake has for a sufficient length of time undergone the ordeal of fire, bring it again to the blessed light of day. If the edge be black and blistered, like a giant tree blasted by the lightning's stroke, or if the crust be rent and torn as by internal convulsions, cast it away. It is worthless. Trample it underfoot. Item: put on your stoutest boots, and provide yourself with cork soles; otherwise, the trampling may prove to be anything but an agreeable pastime. But if the surface be a beautiful auburn brown, crisp, brittle, and unbroken, "Joy, joy, forever! your task is done! The gates are past, and breakfast is won"; or, as the clown said of the apple dumplings, "Them's the jockeys for me."—Hamilton, *Country Living and Country Thinking* (Boston: Ticknor & Fields, 1862), 279–82.

Soft Gingerbread

Hamilton noted in *Gala-Days* (1863) that "gingerbread is always to be had by systematic and intelligent foraging."[2]

One-half cup sugar, one-half cup butter, one cup molasses, two and one-half cups flour, one teaspoonful cinnamon, one teaspoonful ginger, one teaspoonful cloves, two eggs, two teaspoonfuls soda in a cup of boiling water (put this in last).—*Recipes Tried and True*, 111.

MARION HARLAND

Marion Harland, aka Mary Virginia Terhune (1830–1922), may fairly be described as the Henry James of American food writing. As a young Virginia homemaker, as she reminisced in her *Autobiography* (1909), as a young wife and mother she owned a copy of Eliza Leslie's *Directions for Cookery* and once "read up on beefsteak" in it.[1] She became a modestly successful domestic novelist with such tales as *Alone* (1854), *Colonel Floyd's Wards* (1866), and *Phemie's Temptation* (1869) before she "discovered a wider audience" in 1871, as Evan Jones remarks, "when she turned to writing books about food and household management."[2] Not that at the time it seemed a shrewd career move. "My departure from the beaten track of novel-writing," she later conceded, in which I had achieved a moderate degree of success, was in direct opposition to the advice of the friends to whom I mentioned the project. The publishers, in whose hands my first cookbook has reached the million mark, confessed frankly to me, after ten editions had sold in as many months, that they accepted the work solely in the hope that I might give them a novel at some subsequent period.[3]

Her first recipe book, *Common Sense in the Household: A Manual of Practical Housewifery* (1871), was her breakout book, and she followed it with such titles as *Breakfast, Luncheon, and Tea* (1875), *The Cottage Kitchen* (1883), *Cookery for Beginners* (1884), and *Marion Harland's Complete Cookbook* (1903). She continued to write fiction, too, particularly such "cooking novels" as *Jessamine* (1873), *Judith* (1883), *The Distractions of Martha* (1906) — one of the chapters in the last is even entitled "What Can Be Done with a Calf's Head." After the turn of the century her popularity rivaled that of Fanny Farmer of Boston Cooking School fame, and Harland contributed a weekly culinary column syndicated in such newspapers as the *Christian Science Monitor, Los Angeles Times, New York Press, Washington Post, Chicago Tribune,* and *Atlanta Constitution* until 1916. During her career, the versatile and indefatigable Harland published literally thousands of recipes.

Early recipe books typically included a section on medicinal foods for babies and invalids. In her final novel *The Carringtons of High Hill* (1919), dictated to an amanuensis because she was blind, Harland remarks on the "beef tea, chicken jelly, and arrowroot blanc-mange" prepared for a patient. "The doctor nodded hearty approval. 'Nothing could be better. We know that you are a genius in invalid cookery.'"[4]

Arrowroot Blanc-Mange

3 cups of new milk
2½ tablespoonfuls of arrowroot, wet up with cold milk
¾ cup of sugar
Vanilla, lemon, or bitter almond flavoring, with a little white wine

Mix the arrowroot to a smooth batter with one cup of the milk. Heat the remainder to boiling; add the arrowroot, stirring constantly. When it begins to thicken put in the sugar and cook ten minutes longer, still stirring it well from the sides and bottom. Take it off; beat well five minutes; flavor with the essence and a small wineglass of white wine. Give a hard final stir before putting it into a mould wet with cold water.

This is very nourishing for invalids and young children. For the latter you may omit the wine. — Harland, *Common Sense in the Household* (New York: Scribner's, 1884), 421.

Beef Tea

1 pound *lean* beef, cut into small pieces

Put into a jar without a drop of water; cover tightly, and set in a pot of cold water. Heat gradually to a boil, and continue this steadily for three or four hours, until the meat is like white rags and the juice all drawn out. Season with salt to taste, and when cold, skim. The patient will often prefer this ice cold to hot. Serve with Albert biscuit or thin "wafers," unleavened.

Wafers

1 pound of flour
2 tablespoonfuls butter
A little salt

Mix with sweet milk into a stiff dough, roll out very thin, cut into round cakes, and again roll these as thin as they can be handled. Lift them carefully, lay in a pan, and bake very quickly.

These are extremely nice, especially for invalids. They should be hardly thicker than writing paper. Flour the baking pan instead of greasing.— Harland, *Common Sense in the Household*, 498.

Boiled Ham

In addition to writing cookbooks, Harland often depicted festive meals in her narratives. In her *Autobiography*, for example, she remembered a Thanksgiving dinner:

> A boiled ham had the place of honor at one end of the board, built out with loose planks to stretch from the yawning fireplace, bounding the lower end of the big kitchen, to Mammy's room at the other. A shoulder balanced the ham, and side-dishes of sausage, chine, spareribs, fried chicken, huge piles of corn and wheat bread, mince and potato pies, and several varieties of preserves, would fill every spare foot of cloth when the hot things were in place.[5]

In *The Carringtons of High Hill*, Harland similarly described a dinner consisting of "green corn on the cob; new potatoes boiled in their jackets; cymblings and stewed tomatoes; boiled ham and a mammoth chicken pie. For dessert there was boiled blackberry pudding with hard sauce."[6] Not surprisingly, Harland included recipes for many of these dishes in her cookbooks.

Soak in water overnight. Next morning wash hard with a coarse cloth or stiff brush, and put on to boil with plenty of cold water. Allow a quarter of an hour to each pound in cooking, and do not boil too fast. Do not remove the skin until cold; it will come off easily and cleanly then, and the juices are better preserved than when it is stripped hot. Send to table with dots of pepper or dry mustard on the top, a tuft of fringed paper twisted about the shank, and garnish with parsley. Cut very thin in carving.— Harland, *Common Sense in the Household*, 135.

Broiled Chicken

In her novel *Jessamine*, Harland alluded to "broiled chicken — a marvel of juicy tenderness" and "an omelette *aux fines herbes* which was an inspiration."[7]

It is possible to render a tough fowl eatable by boiling or stewing it with care. *Never* broil such! And even when assured that your "broiler" is young, it is wise to make this doubly sure by laying it upon sticks extending from side to side of a dripping pan full of boiling water. Set this in the oven, invert a tin pan over the chicken, and let it steam for half an hour. This process relaxes the muscles and renders supple the joints, beside preserving the juices that would be lost in parboiling. The chicken should be split down the back and wiped perfectly dry before it is steamed. Transfer from the vapor-bath to a buttered gridiron, inside downward. Cover with a tin pan or common plate and broil until tender and brown, turning several times; from half to three-quarters of an hour will be sufficient. Put into a hot chafing dish and butter very well. Send to table smoking hot.— Harland, *Common Sense in the Household*, 76.

Brunswick Stew

In *Judith* (1883), one of Harland's characters prepares a Brunswick stew in a mammoth iron pot. As he explains, "I've worked like a dog, mentally and physically, for three weeks to get the materials together. Fifty squirrels, twenty onions, twenty quarts of butterbeans, five dozen ears of green corn (went thirty miles to find some that was planted late enough to be fit for use now), ten pounds of butter, ten quarts of tomatoes (sent to Richmond for *them*!), sixty potatoes, ten pounds of pork (sweet as a nut!), twenty gallons of water! There ain't another pot in a hundred miles that would hold it all."[8] Harland offered a modified, more modest recipe for the dish in her most successful cookbook.

The large gray squirrel is seldom eaten at the North, but is in great request in Virginia and other Southern States. It is generally barbequed, precisely as are rabbits; broiled, fricasseed, or — most popular of all — made into a Brunswick stew. This is named from Brunswick County, Virginia, and is a famous dish — or was — at the political and social picnics known as barbeques. I am happy to be able to give a receipt for this stew that is genuine and explicit, and for which I am indebted to a Virginia housekeeper.

2 squirrels — 3, if small
1 quart of tomatoes — peeled and sliced
1 pint of butterbeans, or Lima
6 potatoes — parboiled and sliced
6 ears of green corn cut from the cob
½ pound butter
½ fat salt pork
1 teaspoonful ground black pepper
Half a teaspoonful cayenne
1 gallon water
1 tablespoonful salt
2 teaspoonfuls white sugar
1 onion, minced small

Put on the water with the salt in it and boil five minutes. Put in the onion, beans, corn, pork or bacon cut into shreds, potatoes, pepper, and the squirrels, which must first be cut into joints and laid in cold salt and water to draw out the blood. Cover closely and stew two and a half hours very slowly, stirring frequently from the bottom. Then add the tomatoes and sugar, and stew an hour longer. Then minutes before you take it from the fire add the butter, cut into bits the size of a walnut, rolled in flour. Give a final boil, taste to see that it is seasoned to your liking, and turn into a soup tureen. It is eaten from soup plates. Chickens may be substituted for squirrels. — Harland, *Common Sense in the Household*, 160.

Chicken Jelly

Half a raw chicken, pounded with a mallet, bones and meat together
Plenty of cold water to cover it well — *about* a quart

Heat slowly in a covered vessel, and let it simmer until the meat is in white rags and the liquid reduced one half. Strain and press, first through a cullender, then through a coarse cloth. Salt to taste, and pepper, if you think best; return to the fire and simmer five minutes longer. Skim when cool. Give to the patient cold — just from the ice — with unleavened wafers. Keep on the ice. You can make into sandwiches by putting the jelly between thin slices of bread spread lightly with butter. — Harland, *Common Sense in the Household*, 505.

Chicken Pie

Line the bottom and sides of a pot with a good rich paste, reserving enough for a top crust and for the square bits to be scattered through the pie. Butter the pot very lavishly, or your pastry will stick to it and burn. Cut up a fine large fowl, and half a pound of corned ham or salt pork. Put in a layer of the latter, pepper it, and cover with pieces of the chicken, and this with the paste dumplings or squares. If you use potatoes, parboil them before putting them into the pie, as the first water in which they are boiled is rank and unwholesome.

The potatoes should be sliced and laid next the pastry squares; then another layer of pork, and so on until your chicken is used up. Cover with pastry rolled out quite thick, and slit this in the middle. Heat very slowly and boil two hours. Turn into a large dish, the lower crust on top, and the gravy about it.

This is the old-fashioned potpie, dear to the memory of men who were schoolboys thirty and forty years ago. If you are not experienced in such manufactures, you had better omit the lower crust; and, having browned the upper, by putting a hot pot lid or stove-cover on top of the pot for some minutes, remove dexterously without breaking. Pour out the chicken into a dish and set the crust above it.

Veal, beefsteak, lamb (not mutton), hares, &c., may be substituted for the chicken. The pork will salt it sufficiently. — Harland, *Common Sense in the Household*, 77–78.

Country Pork Sausages

Six pounds lean fresh pork, three pounds of chine fat, three tablespoonfuls of salt, two of black pepper, four tablespoonfuls of pounded and sifted sage, two of summer savory. Chop the lean and fat pork finely, mix the seasoning in with your hands, taste to see that it has the right flavor, then put them into cases, either the cleaned intestines of the hog, or make long, narrow bags of stout muslin, large enough to contain each enough sausage for a family dish. Fill these with the meat, dip in melted lard, and hang them in a cool, dry dark place. Some prefer to pack the meat in jars, pouring melted lard over it, covering the top, to be taken out as wanted and made into small round cakes with the hands, then fried brown. Many like spices added to the seasoning—cloves, mace and nutmeg. This is a matter of taste. — Fanny Lemira Gillette, *The White House Cookbook* (Chicago: Peale, 1887), 135.

Fried Chicken

Harland celebrated southern fried chicken in *Judith: A Chronicle of Old Virginia* (1883): "An excellent meal it was, including the conventional boiled ham flanked by cabbage ... and the mountainous side-dish to fried chicken, brown, tender, juicy and savory as fried chicken never is outside of Virginia."[9]

Cut up half a pound of fat salt pork in a frying pan, and fry until the grease is extracted, but not until it browns. Wash and cut up a young chicken (broiling size), soak in salt and water for half an hour; wipe dry, season with pepper, and dredge with flour; then fry in the hot fat until each piece is a rich brown on both sides. Take up, drain, and set aside in a hot covered dish. Pour into the gravy left in the frying pan a cup of milk — half cream is better; thicken with a spoonful of flour and a tablespoonful of butter; add some chopped parsley, boil up, and pour over the hot chicken. This is a standard dish in the Old Dominion, and tastes nowhere else as it does when eaten on Virginia soil. The cream gravy is often omitted, and the chicken served up dry, with bunches of fried parsley dropped upon it. — Harland, *Common Sense in the Household*, 76–77.

Galantine

Cut from a piece of fat fresh pork an oblong of skin five or six inches wide and eight or ten long. Leave a lining of fat on the inside. Lay in vinegar, enough to cover it, for four hours; then spread on platter and cover the fat lining with minced meat or any and all kinds (ham holding an important place) veal, mutton, beef, liver, poultry, etc., seasoned piquantly with pepper, salt, herbs, onion, a touch of spice, and a pinch of grated lemon peel. Moisten with gravy and put in a bit of fat now and then. Fold up the pork, rind on all, bringing the edges together and putting in a stitch or two to hold them in place. Wrap in a single thickness of stout cloth, sewing it closely about it, and put on to boil in plenty of cold water in which is mixed half a cup of vinegar to each quart of water. Boil slowly five hours; let the galantine get nearly cold in the water; take it out and lay under heavy weights all night; undo and remove the cloth, clip the threads and draw them out, trim off the edges and it is ready for the table. Cut clear through skin and stuffing in carving it in neat slices. The "relish" is very fine.— *Washington Post*, June 13, 1886, 3.

Lobster Chowder

Meat of one fine lobster, picked out from the shell and cut into bits, one quart of milk, six Boston crackers split and buttered, one even teaspoonful of salt, one scant quarter-teaspoonful of cayenne, two tablespoonfuls of butter rolled in one of prepared flour, a pinch of soda in the milk. Scald the milk, and stir in seasoning, butter, and flour, cook one minute, add the lobster, and simmer five minutes. Line a tureen with the toasted and buttered crackers, dipping each quickly in boiling water before putting it in place, and pour in the chowder. Send around sliced lemon with it.— Parola et al., *Universal Common Sense Cookery Book*, 25.

Mince Pies

> Harland remembered in her *Autobiography* that mince pies were often "concocted according to the incomparable recipe handed down from mother to daughter,"[10] and she published a recipe for them.

2 pounds lean fresh beef, boiled, and when cold, chopped fine
1 pound beef suet, cleared of strings and minced to powder
5 pounds apples, pared and chopped
2 pounds raisins, seeded and chopped
1 pound sultana raisins, washed and picked over
2 pounds currants, washed and *carefully* picked over
¾ pound citron, cut up fine
2 tablespoons cinnamon
1 teaspoonful powdered nutmeg
2 tablespoonfuls mace
1 tablespoonful cloves
1 tablespoonful allspice
1 tablespoonful fine salt
2½ pounds brown sugar
1 quart brown Sherry
1 pint best brandy

Mince meat made by this receipt will keep all winter in a cool place. Keep in stone jars, tied over with double covers. Add a little more liquor (if it should dry out), when you make up a batch of pies. Let the mixture stand at least twenty-four hours after it is made before it is used.

Lay strips of pastry, notched with a jagging iron, in a crossbar patter, upon the pie, instead of a top crust.— Harland, *Common Sense in the Household*, 341–43.

Mother's Crullers

Harland also recalled in her *Autobiography* her "mother's unsurpassable crullers, superintended by herself at Christmas."[11] She included a recipe for "Mother's Crullers" in *Common Sense in the Household*.

1½ teacup sugar
½ teacup sour cream or milk
⅓ teacup butter
1 egg
1 small teaspoonful soda dissolved in hot water
Flour to roll out a tolerably stiff paste.— Harland, *Common Sense in the Household*, 329.

Omelette aux Fines Herbes

Beat six eggs very light, the whites to a stiff froth that will stand alone, the yolks to a smooth thick batter. Add to the yolks a small cupful of milk, pepper, and salt; lastly stir in the whites lightly. Stir in, with two or three strokes of the spoon or whisk, two tablespoonfuls of chopped parsley, green thyme, and sweet marjoram, with pepper and salt. Have ready in a hot frying pan a good lump of butter. When it hisses, pour in your mixture gently and set over a clear fire. It should cook in ten minutes at most. Do not stir, but contrive, as the eggs "set," to slip a broad-bladed knife under the omelette to guard against burning at the bottom. The instant "hiss" of the butter as it flows to the hottest part of the pan will prove the wisdom and efficacy of the precaution. If your oven is hot, you may put the frying pan into it as soon as the middle of the omelette is set. When done, lay a hot dish bottom upward on the top of the pan, and dexterously upset the latter to bring the browned side of the omelette upper-most. Eat soon, or it will fall.— Harland, *Common Sense in the Household*, 246–48.

Peach Marmalade

In Harland's *The Carringtons of High Hill*, a character "helped herself to another beaten biscuit and buttered it, preparatory to spreading each bit with peach marmalade."[12]

Pare, stone, and weigh the fruit; heat slowly to draw out the juice, stirring up often from the bottom with a wooden spoon. After it is hot, boil quickly, still stirring, three-quarters of an hour. Add, then, the sugar, allowing three-quarters of a pound to each pound of the fruit. Boil up well for five minutes, taking off every particle of scum. Add the juice of a lemon for every three pounds of fruit, and a very little water in which one-fourth of the kernels have been boiled and steeped. Stew all together ten minutes, stirring to a smooth paste, and take from the fire. Put up hot in air-tight cans, or, when cold, in small stone or glass jars, with brandied tissue paper fitted neatly to the surface of the marmalade.

A large, ripe pineapple, pared and cut up fine, and stirred with the peaches, is a fine addition to the flavor.— Harland, *Common Sense in the Household*, 447.

Potted Herrings

Clean the fish and cut off the heads and tails. To a dozen herrings allow two tablespoonfuls of salt, one of allspice and one of saltpetre, one teaspoonful, each, of mace and of paprika.

Powder saltpeter, salt and spices finely and mix well. Rub into the fish, inside and out, and pack them down in it, in a covered dish or crock. Leave thus for twelve hours. Wipe perfectly dry and lay in a buttered bake pan. Dispose among them three bay leaves and half a dozen whole cloves. Cut up two tablespoonfuls of butter and scatter over them, cover closely and bake slowly for one hour. Let them cool in the pan without uncovering. Drain off the liquor, when they are quite cold; pack in jars and cover with melted (not hot) butter.

They will be fit to eat in two days. Keep in a cool, dry place.— *Los Angeles Times*, June 26, 1902, A4.

Pumpkin Pie

> Harland heralded "the genuine New England brand" of pumpkin pie in her *Auto-biography*[13] and, of course, published a recipe for it.

1 quart stewed pumpkin — pressed through a sieve
9 eggs — whites and yolks beaten separately
2 scant quarts milk
1 teaspoon mace
1 teaspoon cinnamon, and the same of nutmeg
1½ cup white sugar, or very light brown
Beat all well together and bake in crust without cover.

— Harland, *Common Sense in the Household*, 347.

Ragout of Liver

Heat three or four spoonfuls of nice dripping in a frying pan; add an onion sliced, a tablespoonful of chopped parsley, and thrice as much minced breakfast bacon; when all are hissing hot, lay in the liver cut in pieces as long and wide as your middle finger, and fry brown, turning often; take out the liver, and keep warm in a covered hot-water dish; strain the gravy, rinse out the frying pan, and return to the fire with the gravy and an even tablespoonful of butter worked up well in two of browned flour. Stir until you have a smooth browned roux; thin gradually with half a cupful of boiling water and the juice of half a lemon, add a teaspoonful of minced pickle and a scant half-teaspoonful of curry powder wet with cold water. Boil sharply, pour over the liver; put fresh boiling water in the pan under the dish, and let all stand closely covered for ten minutes before serving.— Parola et al., *Universal Common Sense Cookery Book*, 34–35.

Roast Chine

A chine is treated precisely as is the sparerib, except that the strip of skin running along the back is scored closely. If you wish, you can omit the bread crumb crust, the onion and sage. In carving, cut thin horizontal slices from the ribs. Chine is best cold. The meat next the ribs is delicious when scraped off and made into sandwiches or laid upon buttered toast.

Or you can wash the chine over with beaten egg, dredge with cracker crumbs, seasoned with salt and pepper, and roast, basting with butter and water once when the meat is heated through, afterward with its own gravy. This is a palatable supper dish when cold. Garnish with cucumber pickles cut in round slices.— Harland, *Common Sense in the Household*, 118.

Roast Duck

Clean, wash, and wipe the ducks very carefully. To the usual dressing add a little sage (powdered or green), and a minced shallot. Stuff, and sew up as usual, reserving the giblets for the gravy. If they are tender, they will not require more than an hour to roast. Baste well. Skim the gravy before putting in the giblets and thickening. The giblets should be stewed in a very little water, then chopped fine and added to the gravy in the dripping pan, with a chopped shallot and a spoonful of browned flour.

Accompany with currant or grape jelly.— Harland, *Common Sense in the Household*, 80.

Roast Pig

> Harland also remembered in her *Autobiography* a Christmas dinner that had featured roasted pig: "the whitest, plumpest, tenderest suckling pig the market could offer lay at length in a platter in the storeroom. Before he could go into the oven, he would be buttered from nose to toes, and coated with bread crumbs. When he appeared on the table, he would be adorned with a necklace of sausages, cranberries would fill out the sunken eyes, and a lemon be thrust into his mouth."[14]

A month-old pig, if it be well-grown and plump, is best for this purpose. It is hardly possible that any lady housekeeper will ever be called upon to do the butcher's work upon the bodies of full-grown hogs, or even "shoat"— a task that requires the use of hatchet or cleaver. It is well that she should know how to clean and dress the baby pig, which is not larger than a Thanksgiving turkey.

As soon as it is really cold, make ready a large boiler of scalding water. Lay the pig in cold water for fifteen minutes; then, holding it by the hindleg, plunge it into the boiling water and shake it about violently until you can pull the hair off by the handful. Take it out, wipe it dry, and with a crash cloth or whisk broom rub the hair off, brushing from the tail to the head until the skin is perfectly clean. Cut it open, take out the entrails, and wash very thoroughly with cold water, then with soda and water, to remove any unpleasant odor; next with salt and water. Rinse with fair water and wipe inside. Then wrap in a wet cloth and keep this saturated with cold water until you are ready to stuff it. If these directions be followed implicitly, the pig will be fair and white, as if entrusted to a professional butcher.

For stuffing, take a cupful of bread crumbs, half a chopped onion, two teaspoonfuls powdered sage, three tablespoonfuls melted butter, a saltspoonful of pepper, half a grated nutmeg, half a teaspoonful of salt, two well-beaten eggs. Mix all these ingredients, except the egg, together, incorporating them well; beat in the eggs, and stuff the pig into his natural size and shape. Sew him up and bend his forefeet backward, his hindfeet forward, under and close to the body, and skewering them into the proper position. Dry it well and dredge with flour. Put it to roast with a little hot water, slightly salted, in the dripping pan. Baste with butter and water three times, as the pig gradually warms, afterward with the dripping. When it begins to smoke or steam, rub it over every five minutes or so with a cloth dipped in melted butter. Do not omit this precaution if you would have the skin tender and soft after it begins to brown. A month-old pig will require about an hour and three-quarters or two hours— sometimes longer — to roast, if the fire be brisk and steady.

Should you or your guests dislike onion, prepare your stuffing without it. The following is a good receipt for rich and savory forcemeat for a pig: —

One cup of bread crumbs, an ounce of suet, a bunch of parsley minced fine, teaspoonful of powdered sage, pepper, salt, and nutmeg, a little thyme, half a glass Madeira or Sherry, juice of a lemon, two tablespoonfuls melted butter, a cup of oyster liquor, and two well-beaten eggs. For a Christmas pig, it is worth one's while to take the trouble to prepare this stuffing.

If your pig is large, you can cut off his head and split him down the back before sending to table. Do this with a sharp knife and lay the backs together. But it is a pity! I have before me now the vision of a pig I once saw served whole on the table of a friend that forbids me ever to mutilate him before the guests have a chance to feast their eyes upon the goodly picture. He was done to a turn — a rich, even brown, without a seam or crack from head to tail, and he knelt in a bed of deep-green parsley, alternately with bunches of whitish-green celery tops (the inner and tender leaves); a garland of the same was about his neck, and in his mouth was a tuft of white cauliflower, surrounded by a setting of curled parsley. Very simple, you see; but I never beheld a more ornamental roast.

Skim your gravy well; add a little hot water, thicken with brown flour, boil up once, strain, and, when you have added half a glass of wine and half the juice of a lemon, serve in a tureen.

In carving the pig, cut off the head first; then split down the back, take off hams and shoulders, and separate the ribs. Serve some of the dressing to each person. — Harland, *Common Sense in the Household*, 118–20.

Roast Spare Rib

When first put down to the fire, cover with a greased paper until it is half-done. Remove it then, and dredge with flour. A few minutes later, baste once with butter, and afterward, every little while, with its own gravy. This is necessary, the sparerib being a very dry piece. Just before you take it up, strew over the surface thickly with fine bread crumbs seasoned with powdered sage, pepper, and salt, and a small onion minced into almost invisible bits. Let it cook five minutes and baste once more with butter. Skim the gravy, add a half cupful of hot water, thicken with brown flour, squeeze in the juice of a lemon, strain, and pour over the meat in the dish.

Send tomato catsup around with it, or if you prefer, put a liberal spoonful in the gravy, after it is strained. — Harland, *Common Sense in the Household*, 117–18.

Roast Turkey

> Another Thanksgiving dinner Harland recalled had featured a "mammoth gobbler, fattened for the occasion."[15]

After drawing the turkey, rinse out with several waters, and in next to the last mix a teaspoonful of soda. The inside of a fowl, especially if purchased in the market, is sometimes very sour and imparts an unpleasant taste to the stuffing, if not to the inner part of the legs and side-bones. The soda will act as a corrective and is moreover very cleansing. Fill the body with this water, shake well, empty it out, and rinse with fair water. Then prepare a dressing of bread crumbs, mixed with butter, pepper, salt, thyme or sweet marjoram. You may, if you like, add the beaten yolks of two eggs. A little chopped sausage is esteemed an improvement when well incorporated with the other ingredients. Or mince a dozen oysters and stir into the dressing. The effect upon the turkey meat, particularly that of the breast, is very pleasant.

Stuff the craw with this and tie a string tightly about the neck to prevent the escape of the stuffing. Then fill the body of the turkey and sew it up with strong thread. This and the neck-string are to be removed when the fowl is dished. In roasting, if your fire is brisk, allow about ten minutes to a pound; but it will depend very much upon the turkey's age whether this rule holds good. Dredge it with flour before roasting and baste often; at first with butter and water, afterward with the gravy in the dripping pan. If you lay the turkey in the pan, put in with it a teacup of hot water. Many roast always upon a grating placed on the top of the pan. In that case the boiling water steams the underpart of the fowl and prevents the skin from drying too fast or cracking. Roast to a fine brown and if it threatens to darken too rapidly, lay a sheet of white paper over it until the lower part is also done.

Stew the chopped giblets in just enough water to cover them, and when the turkey is lifted from the pan, add these, with the water in which they were boiled, to the drippings; thicken with a spoonful of browned flour, wet with cold water to prevent lumping, boil up once, and pour into the gravy boat. If the turkey is fat, skim the drippings well before putting in the giblets.

Serve with cranberry sauce. Some lay fried oysters in the dish around the turkey.— Harland, *Common Sense in the Household*, 71.

Strawberry Shortcake

One cup of powdered sugar, one tablespoonful of butter, three eggs, one rounded cup of prepared flour, two tablespoonfuls of cream, one generous quart of berries. Rub the butter and sugar to a cream, whip in the beaten yolks, the milk, the whites, at last the flour. Bake in three jelly-cake tins, and let the cakes get cold. Cut the berries into halves, and lay between them, sprinkling the strata with sugar. Sift sugar on the topmost layer. Slice, and eat with cream.— Parola et al., *Universal Common Sense Cookery Book*, 170–71.

Sweet Potato Pudding

Harland mentions "another Virginia delicacy"[16] in her novel *Judith*.

1 pound mealy sweet potatoes. The firm yellow ones are best.
½ cup butter
¾ cup white sugar
1 tablespoonful cinnamon
1 teaspoonful nutmeg
4 eggs—whites and yolks beaten separately
1 cup of milk
1 lemon, juice and rind, and glass of brandy

Parboil the potatoes, and grate them when quite cold. If grated hot, they are sticky and heavy. Cream the butter and sugar; add the yolk, the spice, and lemon; beat the potato in by degrees and until all is light; then the milk, then the brandy, and stir in the whites. You may make a pudding of this by baking in a deep dish — well buttered, without paste. Cool before eating.— Harland, *Common Sense in the Household*, 348.

Tomato Aspic and Shrimp Salad

Strain the liquor from a can of tomatoes through coarse muslin. Put over the fire, season with salt and paprika and the strained juice of a small onion. When it boils, skim well and pour over half a box of Coxe's gelatin, which has been soaked three hours in a cup of cold water. Set away to form into a jelly.

When ready to use it line a salad dish with lettuce, arrange the contents of a can of shrimps (strained) upon the leaves and spoonfuls of the tomato jelly upon the shrimps. Send around French salad dressing with it.—*Los Angeles Times*, March 6, 1902, A4.

White (Asparagus) Soup

3 pounds veal. The knuckle is best.
3 bunches asparagus, as well bleached as you can procure
1 gallon water
1 cup milk
1 tablespoonful rice flour
Pepper and salt

Cut off the hard green stem, and put half of the tender heads of the asparagus into the water with the meat. Boil in closely covered pot for three hours, until the meat is in rags and the asparagus dissolved. Strain the liquor and return to the pot, with the remaining half of the asparagus heads. Let this boil for twenty minutes more, and add, before taking up, a cup of sweet milk (cream is better) in which has been stirred a tablespoonful of rice flour, arrow-root, or cornstarch. When it has fairly boiled up, serve without further straining, with small squares of toast in the tureen. Season with salt and pepper.— Harland, *Common Sense in the Household*, 19–20.

HARVARD CLUB OF NEW YORK — DINNER AT DELMONICO'S

The members of the Harvard Club of New York gathered for its annual dinner at Delmonico's on the evening of February 22, 1871, and the menu for the event survives among the Julian Hawthorne Papers in the Bancroft Library at the University of California, Berkeley.[1] The 200 attendees, in addition to Hawthorne, included the Unitarian minister Edward Everett Hale, author of "The Man Without a Country"; the poet William Cullen Bryant; the historian and editor Henry Adams; and E. L. Godkin, founding editor of the *Nation*.[2]

Charlotte Russe

Lay a round sheet of white paper at the bottom of a charlotte mold and line it all around with well-pared lady fingers (**No. 3377**). Boil a pint of milk with half a split vanilla bean; beat up in a vessel six egg yolks with six ounces of sugar and dilute the preparation with the boiling milk; pour it at once into the saucepan and thicken over a moderate fire without letting it come to a boil. Then take out the vanilla and add two leaves of gelatin softened in cold water then melted in a gill of boiling water. Run the whole through a fine Chinese strainer into a vessel and leave to cool until it begins to thicken slightly. Then mix with it the volume of three pints of whipped cream and pouring it at once into the charlotte mold cover with another round of paper and place the mold on ice for an hour and a half. When ready to use invert the charlotte on a cold dish covered with a napkin, remove the upper paper and place on top a cover, made with the same paste as the lady fingers, cut the same dimension as the charlotte, icing it with a white vanilla icing (**No. 102**) and decorate with a handsome design of preserved fruits or with royal icing.

3377. Lady Fingers (Biscuits à la cuiller)

Separate the whites from twenty eggs and pour them into a basin; leave the yolks in another vessel; to these yolks add a pound of powdered sugar, part of it being flavored with vanilla

(**No. 3165**) and beat up to make a very light preparation; then put in one pound of sifted flour and the twenty whites beaten to a stiff froth, stirring the whole lightly together. Pour a part of this preparation into a pocket furnished with a half-inch diameter socket and through it push biscuits four and a half inches in length, keeping them slightly apart and laying them on sheets of paper; bestrew with powdered sugar; put on a baking sheet and leave stand a moment until the sugar begins to dissolve, then push it into a moderate oven. As soon as they are of a light gold color and the crust begins to harden remove at once from the oven and from the baking sheet, then range them on a table till cold.

102. Icing with Syrup for Cakes Flavored with Vanilla, Orange, Lemon or Fruit Juices (Glace au sirop pour gâteaux perfumée soit à la vanille, àl'orange, au citron ou au jus de fruits)

Put one pint of water and a pound of sugar in a saucepan, adding half a vanilla bean or else some orange or lemon peel; stand it on the fire, let boil up a few times to obtain a syrup, then remove the saucepan from the range immediately, suppress the vanilla or peels and incorporate sufficient sugar to form a very smooth flowing paste.

3165. To Filter Fruit Juices, to Flavor Syrups with Zest and to Flavor Sugar with Zest or Vanilla (Pour filtrer les sucs de fruits, pour farfumer les sirops aux zestes, pour parfumer le sucre aux zestes et à la vanille)

To Filter Fruit Juices.— Orange and lemon juices are those most frequently filtered, either through a filtering paper and a glass funnel, or through unsized paper, mashed up, washed and converted into a pulp, then spread in layers on a clean sieve. To filter raspberry and currant juices in large quantities use the felt straining bag, as represented for filtering jellies.

To Flavor Syrup with Zest.— Infusions are made of lemon, orange, mandarin or Seville orange peel. First peel the fruits with a small kitchen knife, being careful not to cut off any of the white part, as this is always bitter. To flavor a syrup with these peels they need only to be macerated for twenty-five minutes in a little tepid water; add this infusion with the zest to some cold syrup; after remaining in the syrup twenty-five minutes strain through a fine sieve.

To Flavor Sugar with Zest.— To flavor sugar with fruit peels, rub the fruits on a piece of loaf sugar, and at once grate off the colored damp parts of the sugar with a knife; put this on sheets of paper, and set it in the air to dry, then crush with a rolling pin and pass through a fine sieve.

To Flavor Sugar with Vanilla.— Cut the vanilla beans into small pieces, pound them with the loaf sugar, using one pound of sugar for two ounces of vanilla; sift the sugar through a fine sieve and put it away in closed glass jars.

226. Chicken Forcemeat

Cut in large pieces two raw chicken breasts, pound them in a mortar, adding the same quantity of bread soaked in milk, a teaspoonful of fresh butter and four eggs yolks, seasoning with half a tablespoonful of salt, a scant teaspoonful of pepper, and a teaspoonful of nutmeg. Mix all together; strain, and put in a bowl with three tablespoonfuls of velouté sauce (**No. 152**).— Ranhofer, *The Epicurean*, passim.

Consommé Impérial (Consommé à l'Imperiale)

Place four tablespoons of chicken forcemeat (**No. 226**) in a paper cornet; cut away the end of the cornet. Butter a pan, and with the contents of the cornet, make eighteen round quenelles; put on top of each quenelle a small slice of truffle; poach them for two minutes in white broth (**No. 99**); then drain through a sieve, and serve in the tureen, after pouring one quart of consommé (**No. 100**) over them and adding a tablespoonful of cooked green peas and six cock's combs.— Filippini, *The Table*, 166.

Potatoes Souffléd (Pommes de terre soufflées)

Good souffléd potatoes can best be made by using those called Holland potatoes. First trim the raw potatoes in ovals of equal size, two and a quarter inches long by one and a quarter wide, and then proceed to slice them lengthwise three-sixteenths of an inch in thickness. As quickly as they are cut throw them into a bowl of cold water, leaving them in for twenty-five minutes. Heat two panfuls of fat, one of fresh beef kidney suet, the other having previously been used for other purposes and therefore its strength being somewhat extracted, it should be clean and white. Wipe the sliced potatoes on a cloth, dry them thoroughly, put them in a basket and plunge them into the oldest fat, leaving them cook until they become soft, but do not let them take color. Remove and place them on a large sieve to drain and cool for a few moments, and just before serving plunge the potatoes into the fresh, hot fat, toss them, remove them that do not soufflé, also those that soufflé badly; set them to cool, and return them again to the hot fat. Should they not soufflé at the second immersion, it is useless to try again. Salt the potatoes before serving, dress around the meat, or on a napkin in a separate dish.— Ranhofer, *The Epicurean*, 838.

Sweetbreads, Parisian Style (Ris de veau à la Parisienne)

Stud one-half of the sweetbreads with truffles, envelop them in thin bardes of fat pork, and lard the other half; braise them as for larded and glazed chicken with gravy (**No. 1575**). Decorate a flat border mold with fanciful cuts of truffles, fill it up with forcemeat (**No. 80**) and poach it in a bain-marie. When ready to serve, invert the mold on a dish, unmold and lay the sweetbreads on the border, filling in the empty space with minced truffles and mushrooms mixed with a brown sauce (**No. 414**) reduced with Madeira and lay around the outside of the border some whole mushrooms and ruffles glazed with meat sauce (**No. 402**). Serve a separate sauce boat of brown sauce reduced with the stock and Madeira wine and the truffle and mushroom parings, strained through a tammy.

1575. Sweetbreads Larded and Glazed with Gravy (Ris de veau piqués et glacés au jus)

Prepare the sweetbreads as explained in **No. 1550**; when blanched and stiffened lard them in two sections as shown, with medium lardons. Line a saucepan with slices of fat pork, cut up onions and carrots, a bunch of parsley garnished with thyme and bay leaf and some veal parings, lay the sweetbreads over and moisten with stock (**No. 194a**); season with salt and whole peppers then cover with a buttered paper. Boil up and finish to cook in a slack oven for forty-five minutes, basting frequently during the time; glaze and let assume a good color. Strain the stock through a fine sieve, skim off its fat and reduce it to the consistency of a light syrup. Dish up the sweetbreads and pour the gravy around.

1550. The Way to Prepare Sweet-breads (Manière de préparer les ris de veau)

Sweet bread is a glandulous substance found below the calf's throat and is considered a most delicate morsel. Separate the throat sweetbreads from the hearts; the throat part is the largest of the two, the heart is whiter, of a round shape and more delicate and tender than the throat. Place them in cold water to disgorge for several hours changing it each hour so as to have them very white; lay them in a saucepan with an abundant supply of cold water, set it on the fire and when the sweetbreads are firm to the touch or poached, or more properly speaking parboiled, then refresh and suppress all the windpipes, fibers and fatty parts, afterward lay them under a very light weight. This blanching is for the purpose of hardening the sweetbreads so as to be able to lard them more easily. Blanched sweetbreads are used for sautéing by cutting them in two through their thickness. For brochettes they are cut in slices and for garnishing in the shape of salpicon.

FIG. 332.

Sweetbreads in preparation, from *The Epicurean*.

80. Foies-Gras and Chicken Forcemeat for Borders, Bottoms of Dishes and Surtouts (Farce de foies-gras et de volaille pour bordures, fonds de plat ou surtouts)

Pound well one pound of raw fat livers; season with salt, pepper and nutmeg, then add eight egg yolks, one at a time, continuing to pound the forcemeat; put in three pounds of chicken quenelle forcemeat (89) and when all is well blended stand it on ice to use as needed. Forcemeat borders are made in special molds of a crown form, lightly hollowed on top, an inch and a half to two inches high. The bottoms of dishes and the surtouts are not as high, being only one inch generally and two inches in diameter narrower than the basin of the dish.

402. Meat Glaze, Plain (Glace de viande simple)

To Prepare Meat Glaze. In the everyday work of a kitchen, the meat glaze is always prepared either with the superfluous stocks or remoistening broths; it is a very easy matter to accomplish this. Skim off the fat from all surplus stocks, and then strain them; should they be troubled, clarify with a little lean beef operating the sauce as for consommé. After the liquid is once strained, set it into one or several saucepans, pouring if off steadily from the sediment, and reduce the liquid quickly, while stirring it in the saucepan with a ladle, until it becomes slightly thick; now pour it into a smaller saucepan, and leave it to boil on one side of the fire, while skimming, until the glaze is quite thick, then pour it into cans and let it get cold in a cool place to use when needed.

89. Chicken Quenelle Forcemeat, with Soubise or Tomato (Farce à quenelle de volaille, soubisée ou tomatée)

Ingredients for these Quenelles.— One pound of chicken, half a pound of pâte à chou panada (**No. 121**); a quarter of a pound of butter, half an ounce of salt and nutmeg, six egg yolks, one whole egg, one pint of chicken cream forcemeat. In order to make chicken or game forcemeats only the breasts are used, having them well pared, cut in pieces and pass through the machine. Put this into a mortar, and pound it to a pulp, rub it through a sieve, pound it once more, and add to it the panada, putting it in gradually, then the butter or udder, without stopping the pounding process, and afterward the egg yolks one by one, season with salt and nutmeg, rub the forcemeat again through the sieve, and then lay it in a thin metal vessel on the ice, and beat it up again for a few minutes so as to render it smooth. Poach a small piece of it, and if found to be too consistent, then thin it with a little cold sauce or raw cream, and keep it in a cool place until needed. Instead of using velouté or cream, one pint of chicken cream forcemeat (**No. 75**) may be added, made of chicken, egg whites and cream. Quenelle forcemeats made of chicken can be used with soubise or tomatoes by mixing in either some soubise (**No. 543**), or fine consistent tomato purée (**No. 730**), instead of the cream or velouté.

121. Panada of Flour and Milk, Bread Crumbs, and Pâte à Choux (Panade de farine et de lait, mie de pain et pâte à choux)

Flour and Milk. — Put in a saucepan half pound of flour, also four eggs and work well together adding some salt, and dilute with six to eight gills of milk; stir it over the fire and remove at the first boil, pour it into a bowl, cover with buttered paper and let get cold.

Bread Crumbs. — Soak four ounces of bread crumbs in a pint of water, squeeze out all the liquid and put it into a saucepan with a little salt and three gills of milk; thicken it on the fire without ceasing to beat, and stir it up with a spoon until it detaches itself from the pan, then set it in a bowl, cover with buttered paper and put away to cool.

Pâte à Choux. — Put one pint of water or broth in a saucepan with two ounces of butter, set it on the fire, remove it aside at the first boil, and incorporate into it three quarters of a pound of sifted flour, mix well and dry on a slow fire till the paste detaches itself from the saucepan and let cool slightly, then stir into it gradually two whole eggs and four yolks, set it away in a cool place with a buttered paper over, for further use.

75. Chicken or Game Cream Forcement (Farce à la crème de volaille ou de gibier)

Have one pound of chicken or game meat (the breast), free of nerves or skin, pass them twice through the machine; or else chop and pound to a pulp, then press through a sieve, return to the mortar and mix in one egg white, half an ounce of salt, red pepper and nutmeg, the equal quantity of six or eight gills of cream, before whipping; mixing it in gradually with a whip and working it well. Should the forcemeat be too thick add cream, and if it lack consistency, more egg white.

543. Soubise Sauce

Cut off the stalks and roots from twelve onions after having divided them in two, throw them into boiling salted water for a few minutes, then drain, refresh, and drain them again. Heat a half a pound of butter in a saucepan, add to it the onions and fry them without coloring until well done, then pour in a pint of velouté (**No. 415**) and half a pint of stock (**No. 422**), some peppercorns and grated nutmeg. When the onions are sufficiently cooked, press them forcibly through a tammy and return the sauce to the saucepan on the fire, and add to it six gills of fresh cream; season properly, and incorporate in at the last moment a small piece of fresh butter.

415. Velouté Sauce (Sauce veloutée)

The velouté like the espagnole is also a leading sauce used for making secondary sauces. Melt three-fourths of a pound of butter in a small saucepan; stir into it three-fourths of a pound of good flour, and let the roux cook for a few minutes, then set the saucepan on a slower fire without letting it color; in order to obtain a well thickened sauce, the flour must be well cooked. When the roux is sufficiently done dilute it gradually with four quarts of good stock (**No. 423**). In case there be no special stock prepared for his sauce then use some good clear chicken stock (**No. 195**). Stir the liquid over the fire until it comes to a boil, then move it aside to let it cook on one side only; despumate the sauce for one hour, skimming off all the white particles arising to the surface; remove all the fat, and strain the velouté through a sieve into a vessel and let it get cool while lifting off the scum that forms on the top.

195. Game, Vegetable, Fish and Chicken Stock, for Thick Soups (Fonds de gibier, légumes, poisson et volaille pour potages lies)

In order to make thick stock use consommé of game, vegetables, fish or chicken before they are clarified. Place half a pound of butter in a saucepan with half a pound of sifted flour of the best quality, let cook well on a slow fire without coloring when needed for vegetables, fish or chicken, but for game make a brown roux; for either one or the other dilute this roux with boiling broth (if the soup should be a chicken soup, chicken broth should be used to dilute the roux, if game soup then game broth should be used, fish with fish broth, for vegetable, vegetable broth). Use a whisk turning it rapidly, so as to avoid having lumps; stocks for soups should be kept rather thin, that is to say but little thickened and should be well despumated, the fat removed before passing through the tammy; return the saucepan to the fire, and stir continuously with a spatula from the bottom until the broth boils. Remove the saucepan and place it so that only one side of the contents cook slowly for one hour; skim and take off all the matter that swims on the surface until the stock be entirely free from fat and other impurities floating on top arising from the clarification, then strain through a tammy or fine sieve, and use this stock for thick soups either of game, vegetables, fish or poultry.

422. Veloute Stock (Fond pour velouté)

Butter the bottom of a sixteen quart saucepan, having a thick bottom, cover it with sliced onions and on top of these lay four pounds of knuckle of veal and shoulder, half of each, four pounds of fowl without the breast, and moisten with one pint of remoistening (**No. 189**), put it on a brisk fire and cover the saucepan, as soon as the liquid is reduced to half, moderate the fire and let the sauce fall slowly to a glaze without browning, then moisten with six quarts more of white broth, skim off the fat and scum and season with salt, crushed whole peppers and a little sugar, add a bunch of parsley and celery green, garnished with two bay leaves and as much thyme, also half an ounce of basil, besides four ounces of mushroom parings or stalks and half a pound of minced carrots, then let cook for six hours, remove all the fat, add from time to time a little remoistening, salt it to taste and strain through a sieve or a napkin. Use when needed.

730. Purée of Tomatoes (Purée de tomates)

Cut in halves and press well, half a pound of tomatoes; fry two ounces of minced onions in two ounces of butter without browning, then add the tomatoes, and cook till done, drain them well on a hair sieve, press them through, and put this purée into a saucepan to heat again, stirring in three ounces of kneaded butter (**No. 579**). Just before serving add two ounces of fresh butter.

579. Kneaded Butter (Beurre manié)

Kneaded butter is frequently used at the last moment to thicken sauces and cooked small vegetables. In order to prepare this auxillary, it is necessary to lay a piece of butter on a plate or in a small vessel, and incorporate into it slowly with a wooden spoon, a sufficient quantity of flour to form a smooth paste, but not too consistent, so that it can easily be dissolved by the heat.— Ranhofer, *The Epicurean*, passim.

Italian Salad (Salade à l'Italienne)

Cook in salted water one pint of green peas, half a pint of string beans, half a pint of carrots and as much turnips, both of these pushed through a tin tube; they should be a quarter of an inch in diameter, and three-eighths of an inch long. First blanch the carrots and turnips, then cook them in broth (**No. 194a**) wih salt and sugar, and when done drain and leave them to get cool. Put into a salad bowl the carrots, green peas, some green peppers, string beans, turnips and finely cut-up chervil, tarragon, chives, and finely chopped parsley; season with salt, pepper, vinegar and oil, mixed well together. Cut some beets and potatoes in an eighth of an inch thick slices, remove some rounds from these with a vegetable cutter three-quarters of an inch in diameter, then season; set the beetroots alternated with the potatoes around the base; near the top place a row of round slices of pickles half an inch in diameter; divide the height between the potatoes and the pickles with fillets of anchovies into six panels; in the center of these place a round slice of mortadelle and on the top lay some small channeled mushrooms (**No. 118**).

118. To Turn, Channel and Flute Mushrooms (Pour tourner et canneler les champignons)

Choose the freshest mushrooms and those of equal size, cut off the stems, wipe well the heads, and take them one by one in the left hand, the hollow side underneath; then with the tip of a small pointed knife cut away the peel in regular rings without destroying the mushroom, and turn from right to left pressing all the time against the tip of the small knife; this must be done quickly and let us observe that it is not on the first trial that a mushroom can be properly turned, it takes practice to accomplish this properly. As quickly as each one is done, throw it into a saucepan containing cold, acidulated water, just sufficient to cover, then drain off the water, and cook the mushrooms for seven or eight minutes with the lid on, adding salt, butter and lemon juice, to keep them as white as possible. As for fluting mushrooms, this art is only learned after long experience. Mushroom fluting has become almost a profession, and the difficulties to be overcome can be better understood on examining those pretty mushroom heads so delicately carved, we see displayed by all preserve manufacturers.— Ranhofer, *The Epicurean*, passim.

NATHANIEL HAWTHORNE

Corned Beef

On May 31, 1844, Nathaniel Hawthorne (1804–1864) boiled a pot of corned beef over an open hearth using a recipe from Hale's *The Good Housekeeper*. As he wrote his wife Sophia, "I get along admirably, and am at this moment superintending the corned beef, which has been on the fire, as it appears to me, ever since the beginning of time, and shows no symptom of being done before the crack of doom. Mrs. Hale says it must boil till it becomes tender; and so it shall, if I can find wood to keep the fire a-going."[1]

The perfection of boiling is that it be done slowly and the pot well skimmed. If the scum be permitted to boil down it sticks to the meat and gives it a dirty appearance. A quart of water to a pound of meat is an old rule; but there must always be water sufficient to cover it well, so that the scum may be taken off easily.

When beef is very salt (which it rarely will be if rightly cured) it must be soaked for half an hour or more in lukewarm water, before it is put on to boil, when the water must be changed.

The Round is the best piece to boil — then the H-Bone.

Take part of a Round of beef — put into your boiler with plenty of cold water to cover it; set the pot on one side of the fire to boil gently, if it boil *quick* at first, no art can make the meat tender. *The slower it boils the tenderer it will be.*

Dining room of Nathaniel Hawthorne's home, the Wayside, in Concord, Massachusetts (Library of Congress).

(How much good fuel is wasted, to say nothing of the hard labor cooks impose on themselves and the injury to their health by heating over a great blaze, through this carelessness in making fires. In the country, especially, and often during summer, a fire is prepared nearly hot enough for Nebuchadnezzar's furnace, merely to boil the pot! Instead of hanging the boiler low, it seems the ambition of the housewife to elevate it as near the stars as possible. Three small sticks of wood or two with chips will boil a large dinner, and if the pot is hung very low, but little inconvenience will be felt from the fire. This, in hot weather, for those who are obliged to be in the kitchen, is a great comfort. But the pot is boiling all the time. So to our receipt.)

Be sure to take off all the scum as it rises. When you take the meat up, if any stray scum sticks to it, wash it off with a paste brush. Garnish the dishes with carrots and turnips. Boiled potatoes, carrots, turnips and greens, on separate plates, are good accompaniments.

If the beef weigh ten pounds it requires to boil, or rather simmer about three hours. In cold weather all meats need to be cooked a longer time than in warm weather. Always cook them till tender.—Hale, *The Good Housekeeper*, 29–30.

LAFCADIO HEARN

Among the dishes Lafcadio Hearn (1850–1904) mentions in his story "The Last of the Voudoos" (1885) are a pair of Creole classics: "On grand occasions Jean used to distribute largess among the colored population of his neighborhood in the shape of food — bowls of *gombo* or dishes of *Jimbalaya*."[1] The name of the former dish, a product of the African diaspora, was etymologically derived from the term *ngombo* or *kingombo*, Bantu for okra. Filé powder made from finely chopped dried sassafras was sometimes substituted for okra. Jambalaya was even more a mélange. As Hearn explains, Creole cooking in general "partakes of the nature of its birthplace — New Orleans — which is cosmopolitan in its nature, blending the characteristics of the American, French, Spanish, Italian, West Indian, and Mexican."[2] According to Harry Haff, Hearn's *La Cuisine Creole* "for the first time set down the culinary traditions and artistry" of the city.[3]

Boston Brown Bread

One and a half pints of Indian meal, half a pint of wheat flour, one cup of sweet milk, one cup of sour milk, with a teaspoonful of soda in it; three tablespoonfuls of molasses, one tablespoonful of yeast, and a pinch of salt. Put it in a warm place to rise, then let it bake steadily for four hours; warm by steaming it when wanted to use.— Hearn, *La Cuisine Creole* (New Orleans: Hansell, 1885), 127.

Bouille-Abaisse

Chop some onions and garlic very fine, fry them in olive oil, and when slightly colored add some fish cut up in slices; also a few tomatoes scalded, peeled and sliced, some salt, black and red pepper, thyme, sweet bay, parsley, and half a bottle of white wine, and enough water to cover the fish. Put it over a brisk fire and boil a quarter of an hour. Put slices of toasted bread in a deep dish, place the fish on a shallow dish with some broth, and pour the balance on the bread and serve hot.— Hearn, *La Cuisine Creole*, 252.

Calves' Feet Jelly

Take two calves' feet, add to them a gallon of water which you must reduce by boiling to a quart; strain it while hot, and set away to get cold. When cold take off the fat, and remove any settlings which may be in the bottom. Melt the jelly in a stew pan, and add to it the whites of six eggs, well beaten, half a pint of wine, half a pound of white sugar, the juice of four lemons, and rind of one grated. Boil this a few minutes, and pass it through a flannel strainer. This is a most delicate and nourishing article of diet for the sick and convalescent. If the jelly is dropped upon a slice peel of a lemon instead of a grated peel, it will look prettier.—Hearn, *La Cuisine Creole*, 184.

Country Fried Chicken

Take a young, fat chicken, cut it up, pepper and salt it, dredge it over with flour, and set it by while you mix a cup of lard, and some slices of fat bacon in a frying pan. Let the lard get very hot, then drop in a few pieces of the chicken, always allowing room in the pan for each piece to be turned without crowding. As fast as you fry the pieces, put them on a dish over hot water to keep the heat in them while you make the gravy. Pour off some of the grease the chicken was fried in, and then dredge into the frying pan some flour, let this brown nicely and then pour into it a cup of sweet milk, little at a time; let it froth up, and then place your chicken back into the gravy for three minutes. If you like the chicken brown and dry, pour the gravy under it on the dish for serving.—Hearn, *La Cuisine Creole*, 66–67.

Crayfish Bisque

Parboil the fish, pick out the meat, and mince or pound it in a mortar until very fine; it will require about fifty crayfish. Add to the fish one-third the quantity of bread soaked in milk, and a quarter of a pound of butter, also salt to taste, a bunch of thyme, two leaves of sage, a small piece of garlic, and a chopped onion. Mix all well and cook ten minutes, stirring all the time to keep it from growing hard. Clean the heads of the fish, throw them in strong salt and water for a few minutes and then drain them. Fill each one with the above stuffing, flour them, and fry a light brown. Set a clean stewpan over a slow fire, put into it three spoonfuls of lard or butter, a slice of ham or bacon, two onions chopped fine; dredge over it enough flour to absorb the grease, then add a pint and a half of boiling water, or better still, plain beef stock. Season this with a bunch of thyme, a bay leaf, and salt and pepper to taste. Let it cook slowly for half an hour, then put the heads of the crayfish in and let them boil fifteen minutes. Serve rice with it.—Hearn, *La Cuisine Creole*, 22–23.

Gelatine Snow Pudding

Take two tablespoonfuls of good gelatin, throw over it two spoonfuls of water, let it soak ten minutes, then pour over it half a pint of boiling water, three-quarters of a pound of white sugar, and the juice of two lemons with the rind thrown in. Let it come to a boil, take it off immediately, strain it, let it cool a little, and when it begins to thicken add the beaten whites of two eggs. Beat all thoroughly, and pour it in a mould on ice to get firm. When cold and firm, send it to table in the middle of a glass basin or dish, and pour around it a custard made from the yolks of the eggs, and a pint of milk sweetened and flavored to taste. Sponge cake should be served with this pudding.— Hearn, *La Cuisine Creole*, 172–73.

Gumbo of Okra or Filee

This is a most excellent form of soup, and is an economical way of using up the remains of any cold roasted chicken, turkey, game, or other meats. Cut up and season the chicken, meat, or other material to make the soup; fry to a light brown in a pot, and add boiling water in proportion to your meat. Two pounds of meat or chicken (bones and all), with a half pound of ham, or less of breakfast bacon, will flavor a gallon of soup, which, when boiled down, will make gumbo for six people. When the boiling water is added to the meat, let it simmer for at least two hours. Take the large bones from the pot, and add okra or a preparation of dried and pounded sassafras leaves, called filee. This makes the difference in gumbo. For gumbo for six people use one quart of sliced okra; if filee be used, put in a coffee-cupful. Either gives the smoothness so desirable in this soup. Oysters, crabs, and shrimp may be added when in season, as all improve the gumbo. Never strain gumbo. Add green corn, tomatoes, etc., etc., if desired. Serve gumbo with plain-boiled rice.— Hearn, *La Cuisine Creole*, 18–19.

Graham Muffins for Dyspeptics

Take a quart of Graham flour, one half cup of brown sugar, one teaspoon of salt, two tablespoonfuls of yeast, warm water or milk enough to soften it sufficiently to stir readily with a spoon. When it is light, stir up again and drop in rings and bake. If made overnight, add a little soda in the morning. Bake soft.— Hearn, *La Cuisine Creole*, 133–34.

Jambalaya of Fowls and Rice

Cut up and stew a fowl; when half done, add a cup of raw rice, a slice of ham minced, and pepper and salt; let all cook together until the rice swells and absorbs all the gravy of the stewed chicken, but it must not be allowed to get hard or dry. Serve in a deep dish. Southern children are very fond of this; it is said to be an Indian dish, and very wholesome as well as palatable; it can be made of many things.— Hearn, *La Cuisine Creole*, 106.

Mint Juleps

According to Root and de Rochemont, "Opinions on the proper way to make mint juleps are defended in the South as fiercely as the honor of women.... You are blessed or damned depending on whether you serve your juleps in a glass or in a mug of silver or aluminum."[4] Or as Eudora Welty once opined, "A collection of recipes from the Old South is no more complete than the Old South itself without that magic ingredient, the mint julep."[5] This volume includes several different recipes for juleps imbibed by Hearn, Welty, Theodore Roosevelt, and Walker Percy.

Made of Whiskey, Brandy, Gin, Etc., Etc.
One-half tablespoonful of powdered sugar, one wineglass of water, one of whiskey, brandy or gin, etc., and one-half dozen sprigs of mint. Use plenty of fine ice, and decorate

with strawberries and pineapples, or any fruit in season.— Hearn, *La Cuisine Creole*, 249.

Pudding

Let a quart of milk be set on to boil; while it is getting hot, mix a cup of maizena or corn starch with enough cold water to form it into a thick batter; add to this a cup of white sugar and the yolks of four eggs; take the milk off and stir eggs, maizena, and sugar, into the milk; beat all together a few minutes, then pour the mixture into a baking dish and bake it lightly about ten minutes, or long enough only to cook the eggs; then take the pudding out, and while hot put over it a layer of jelly or jam; beat up the whites of the eggs with a cup of sugar, put this over the jelly and brown.— Hearn, *La Cuisine Creole*, 205.

Rich Wedding Cake or Black Cake

One pound of flour, nine eggs, the whites and yolks beaten separately, one pound of butter beaten to a cream, one pound of brown sugar, one teacupful of molasses, one ounce of grated nutmeg or ground mace, one teaspoonful of ground allspice, one teaspoonful of cinnamon, and a gill of brandy; beat this mixture well. Having picked, washed, and dried three pounds of currants, stone and cut three pounds of raisins, strew half a pound of flour over them, mix it well through, and stir them with a pound of citron, cut in slips, into the cake. Line tin pans with buttered paper, put the mixture in, and inch and a half or two inches deep, and bake in a moderate oven an hour and a half or two hours. Ice according to directions.— Hearn, *La Cuisine Creole*, 144.

Tomato Catsup

Take enough ripe tomatoes to fill a jar, put them in a moderate oven, and bake them until they are thoroughly soft; then strain them through a coarse cloth or sieve, and to every pint of juice put a pint of vinegar, half an ounce of garlic sliced, a quarter of an ounce of salt, and the same of white pepper finely ground. Boil it for one hour, then rub it through a sieve, boil it again to the consistency of cream; when cold, bottle it, put a teaspoonful of sweet oil in each bottle; cork them tight, and keep in a dry place.— Hearn, *La Cuisine Creole*, 103.

Tomato Soup with Vegetables

Cut small, three carrots, three heads of celery, four onions, and two turnips; put them into a saucepan with a tablespoonful of butter, a slice of ham and a half cup of water; let them simmer gently for an hour; then if a very rich soup is desired add to the vegetables two or three quarts of good soup stock, made by boiling a beef bone in three quarts of water until the meat is tender. Let all boil together for half an hour, and then add ten or twelve ripe tomatoes and a half-dozen whole peppers. It should cook for another hour or so. It must then be strained through a sieve or coarse cloth. Serve with toasted or fried bread cut in bits in the tureen. This is an elegant family soup, particularly nice in summer when the vegetables are fresh.— Hearn, *La Cuisine Creole*, 11.

LILLIAN HELLMAN

A gourmet cook, Lillian Hellman (1905–1984) received a National Book Award for her first book of memoirs, *An Unfinished Woman* (1969). The Campbell Soup Company introduced its cream of mushroom soup in 1934 as a cooking component, and Lipton's Noodle Soup was first marketed in 1939 followed by its dry onion soup mix in 1952. Such kitchen innovations were considered liberating for women at the time.

Pot Roast

Nora Ephron included Hellman's recipe for pot roast, which called for such cheap components, in her novel *Heartburn*.

Lillian Hellman's pot roast is the sort of recipe that makes my reputation in the food world what it is, since it contains all sorts of low-rent ingredients like a package of onion soup mix and a can of cream of mushroom soup. It even has something called Kitchen Bouquet in it, although I always leave it out. You take a nice 4-pound piece of beef, the more expensive the better, and put it into a good pot with 1 can of cream of mushroom soup, an envelope of dried onion soup, 1 large chopped onion, 3 cloves chopped garlic, 2 cups red wine and 2 cups water. Add a crushed bay leaf and 1 teaspoon each thyme and basil. Cover and bake in a 350° oven until tender, 3½ hours or so.—Ephron, *Heartburn*, 133–34

ERNEST HEMINGWAY

The recipient of the Nobel Prize for Literature in 1954, Ernest Hemingway (1899–1961) published a surprising number of recipes during his life—and not only drink recipes (though there are a goodly number of those). Hemingway was a sportsman and connoisseur of fine foods who often prepared his own meals while on camping trips or safaris. He even once published a recipe for "fillet of lion" with a classic first line: "First obtain your lion."[1] He seemed attuned to the language of cooking. The title of his story "A Clean, Well Lighted Place," for example, could have been borrowed from a bread recipe.

Bloody Mary

To make a pitcher of Bloody Marys (any smaller amount is worthless) take a good sized pitcher and put in it as big a lump of ice as it will hold. (This to prevent too rapid melting and watering of our product.) Mix a pint of good Russian vodka and an equal amount of chilled tomato juice. Add a table spoon full of Worcester Sauce. Lea and Perrins is usual but can use A1 or any good beefsteak sauce. Stirr (with two rs). Then add a jigger of fresh squeezed lime juice. Stirr. Then add small amounts of celery salt, cayenne pepper, black pepper. Keep on stirring and taste it to see how it is doing. If you get it too powerful weaken with more tomato juice. If it lacks authority add more vodka. Some people like more lime than others. For combating a really terrific hangover increase the amount of Worcester sauce—but don't lose the lovely color.—*Ernest Hemingway: Selected Letters, 1917–1961*, ed. Carlos Baker (New York: Scribner, 1981), 618–19.

Chop Suey

The lunch which Ernest praised so gaily, one of his favorites, was one of my versions of chop suey eaten with chopsticks, which helps the flavor. That one I made with chicken stock and chicken, pearl-tinted shrimp fresh from the ocean that morning, fresh bean sprouts, bamboo shoots and ginger from Havana's Chinatown, onions, mushrooms and such, of course, and something which the Chinese call, in Spanish, ears. Maybe they are membranes of monkey or pig ears, or maybe they are a vegetable. What we like about them is their slippery smooth texture and delicate flavor, resembling tea. We had finished with a flowery lime ice into which I'd stirred a little gin and a little crème de menthe and then refrozen it. — Mary Hemingway, "Life with Papa," *Flair* 1 (January 1951), 116.

Daiquiri

> The hard-drinking Hemingway claimed he invented the drink he named "Death in the Afternoon" "after having spent seven hours overboard trying to get Capt. Bra Saunders' fishing boat off a bank where she had gone with us in a N.W. gale." He submitted the directions for making it to a collection of celebrity cocktail recipes.[2] His acolyte A. E. Hotchner remembered the components in his favorite daiquiri:

A Papa Doble was compounded of two and a half jiggers of Bacardi White Label rum, the juice of two limes and half a grapefruit, and six drops of maraschino, all placed in an electric mixer over shaved ice, whirled vigorously and served foaming in large goblets. — Hotchner, *Papa Hemingway: A Personal Memoir* (New York: Random House, 1966), 5.

Fried Trout

> Hemingway's early journalism and fiction, including "Big Two-Hearted River" (1924) and *The Sun Also Rises* (1926), were punctuated by stories of trout fishing. Stephen L. Tanner even contends that "trout fishing was important for Hemingway and his characters because it offered a way to avoid the *nada* or emptiness of life."[3]

A pan of fried trout can't be bettered and they don't cost any more than ever. But there is a good and bad way of frying them.

The beginner puts his trout and his bacon in and over a brightly burning fire; the bacon curls up and dries into a dry tasteless cinder and the trout is burned outside while it is still raw inside. He eats them and it is all right if he is only out for the day and going home to a good meal at night. But if he is going to face more trout and bacon the next morning and other equally well-cooked dishes for the remainder of two weeks, he is on the pathway to nervous dyspepsia.

The proper way is to cook over coals. Have several cans of Crisco or Cotosuet or one of the vegetable shortenings along that are as good as lard and excellent for all kinds of shortening. Put the bacon in and when it is about half cooked lay the trout in the hot grease, dipping them in cornmeal first. Then put the bacon on top of the trout and it will baste them as it slowly cooks.

The coffee can be boiling at the same time and in a smaller skillet pancakes being made that are satisfying the other campers while they are waiting for the trout.

With the prepared pancake flours you take a cupful of pancake flour and add a cup of water. Mix the water and flour and as soon as the lumps are out it is ready for cooking. Have the skillet hot and keep it well greased. Drop the batter in and as soon as it is done on one side loosen it in the skillet and flip it over. Apple butter, syrup or cinnamon and sugar go well with the cakes.

While the crowd have taken the edge from their appetites with flapjacks, the trout have been cooked and they and the bacon are ready to serve. The trout are crisp outside and firm and pink inside and the bacon is well done — but not too done. If there is anything better than that combination the writer has yet to taste it in a lifetime devoted largely and studiously to eating.

The stew kettle will cook your dried apricots; when they have resumed their predried plumpness after a night of soaking, it will serve to concoct a mulligan in, and it will cook macaroni. When you are not using it, it should be boiling water for the dishes.

In the baker, mere man comes into his own, for he can make a pie that to his bush appetite will have it all over the product that mother used to make, like a tent. Men have always believed that there was something mysterious and difficult about making a pie. Here is a great secret. There is nothing to it. We've been kidded for years. Any man of average office intelligence can make at least as good a pie as his wife.

All there is to a pie is a cup and a half of flour, one-half teaspoonful of salt, one-half cup of lard and cold water. That will make piecrust that will bring tears of joy into your camping partner's eyes.

Mix the salt with the flour, work the lard into the flour, make it up into a good workmanlike dough with cold water. Spread some flour on the back of a box or something flat, and pat the dough around a while. Then roll it out with whatever kind of round bottle you prefer. Put a little more lard on the surface of the sheet of dough and then slosh a little flour on and roll it up and then roll it out again with the bottle.

Cut out a piece of the rolled-out dough big enough to line a pie tin. I like the kind with holes in the bottom. Then put in your dried apples that have soaked all night and been sweetened, or your apricots, or your blueberries, and then take another sheet of the dough and drape it gracefully over the top, soldering it down at the edges with your fingers. Cut a couple of slits in the top dough sheet and prick it a few times with a fork in an artistic manner.

Put it in the baker with a good slow fire for forty-five minutes and then take it out, and if your pals are Frenchmen they will kiss you. The penalty for knowing how to cook is that the others will make you do all the cooking. — Hemingway, "Camping Out," *Toronto Daily Star,* June 26, 1920; rpt. in Hemingway, *Dateline, Toronto: The Complete Toronto Star Dispatches, 1920–1924,* ed. William White (New York: Scribner, 1985), 45–47.

Picadillo

Its base is ordinary ground beef or the usual hamburger mixture of beef and pork. Any practicing cook ought to know more or less the proportion of things, so I make them only relative:

Slice fine and fry in plenty of butter a medium-sized onion, or more if your family is big and you are using more than a pound of beef, also shredded garlic according to your taste. Stir in the meat with salt, pepper, a big dash of marjoram and a big dash of oregano, and before the meat starts burning or sticking to the pan, add about one-half cup of dry white wine. (Here the Cubans use, instead, tomato paste and water, but I prefer this dish without tomatoes.) Let this simmer for awhile during which you make a platter of fluffy white rice. About five minutes before serving, add to the frying pan mixture a half cup of previously soaked raisins, a cup of fairly finely chopped mango or fresh peach, half a cup of sliced celery, a handful of sliced stuffed olives and, if you wish to be fancy, a handful of blanched, chopped almonds. Pour the frying pan mixture on top of the rice. Very small rivulets of the juice of the meat mixture should appear around the edges of the platter, or you haven't used enough butter, wine or fruit. Garnish it with something dark green and very crisp.— Mary Hemingway, "Life with Papa," *Flair* 1 (January 1951), 117.

JOHN HERSEY

John Hersey (1914–1993) received a Pulitzer Prize for his first novel, *A Bell for Adano* (1945), though he is even better known for his New Journalistic account of the atomic bombing of Japan, "Hiroshima" (1946).

Sliced Steak Sandwich

Peter Feibleman records Barbara Hersey's recipe for Sliced Steak Sandwich.

In order to make Hersey's sliced steak sandwiches, cover the bottom of an iron skillet with ⅛ inch of oil, heat it till it's smoking, and cook the steak about 3 minutes on each side. Take it out and slice it thin. Use thin rye bread for the sandwich.

That's all Barbara does.

There are two tricks: (1) Leap back when you put the steak in the skillet or you will burn any exposed part of your body, as I did, and (2) open all windows and doors in the kitchen or you will die of smoke inhalation.— Lillian Hellman and Peter Feibleman, *Eating Together: Recipes and Recollections* (Boston: Little, Brown, 1984), 104.

ISABELLA BEECHER HOOKER

Another of the Beecher siblings, Isabella Beecher Hooker (1822–1907) was, like her sisters Harriet and Catharine, an abolitionist and an advocate of women's rights. As the title of her best-known book, *Womanhood: Its Sanctities and Fidelities* (1874), may suggest, however, she did not fundamentally challenge gender roles, including cooking and housekeeping.

Soup Regency

The bones and remains of cold fowls, such as turkey and chicken: or game, such as partridges, woodcock, etc.; two carrots; two small onions; one head of celery; one turnip; one-half tea cup pearl barley; the yolks of three eggs, boiled hard; one-quarter pint of cream; salt to taste, and two quarts of common stock.

Mode — Place the bones and remains of the fowls in the stew pan, with the vegetables sliced; pour over the stock and simmer for two hours; skim off all the fat and strain it. Wash the barley and boil it in two waters before adding it to the soup; finish simmering in the soup, and when the barley is done take out half and pound the other half with the yolks of the eggs. When well pounded, rub it through a fine colander, add the cream and the salt, if necessary; let it boil up once more and serve very hot, putting in the barley that was taken out first. Time of cooking, 2½ hours. Seasonable from September to March. Sufficient for eight persons.— Carrie V. Shurman, *Favorite Dishes* (Chicago: R. R. Donnelley, 1893), 37.

Sponge Cake

The recipe I send for Sponge Cake was one constantly in use twenty-five years ago. Ten eggs; one-half pound flour; one pound pulverized sugar; one lemon; small teaspoon salt.

Beat yolks separately and very thoroughly; add sugar, salt, lemon juice and grated peel, and beat again. Beat whites to stiffness and add to the yolks, beating well together. Then cut the flour in slowly with large knife and *avoid beating* after this. Bake in two deep, long, narrow tins, in rather slow oven, but hot on the bottom. The secret of success is in cutting in the flour and the baking. But few people will believe this and cannot reach my standard. I have made this cake for forty years with uniform success.— Shurman, *Favorite Dishes*, 152.

Veal Croquettes

Mince cold roast or boiled veal; add one-fourth as much of minced oysters scalded in their own liquor. Season with a dusting of red pepper, salt, a flavor of onion (two fine cut rounds of onion is sufficient), a tablespoonful of lemon juice. Stir this into a half pint of drawn butter made thick with flour; mould the croquettes; roll them in egg, then in cracker crumbs, salted and peppered; put them where they will be cold; when chilled put them in a frying basket into hot fat; two minutes will brown them.— Shurman, *Favorite Dishes*, 62.

ROBINSON JEFFERS

The poet Robinson Jeffers (1887–1962) is best known for his verse celebrating the rugged beauty of the central California seacoast.

For a Poet's Palate

Peel eight small Bermuda onions. Place them whole in a baking dish. Pour over them a can of cream of mushroom soup; add salt and pepper and butter the size of a walnut. Cover and bake an hour. The last fifteen minutes remove cover and allow to brown on top.— Herbert Cerwin, *Famous Recipes by Famous People* (San Francisco: Lane, 1940), 39.

THOMAS JEFFERSON

Thomas Jefferson (1743–1826), author of the Declaration of Independence and *Notes on the State of Virginia* (1785) and third president of the United States, was the first and perhaps only gourmand ever to reside in the White House. "The culinary artistry of France had captivated him ever since the time when he had served as American minister to the court of Louis XVI," and after his return from Paris he planted tomatoes at Monticello, his estate near Charlottesville, Virginia, from seeds he brought from Europe.[1] He also introduced vanilla and macaroni to the U.S.[2] During his presidency (1801–1809), "he took time when he could to oversee all phases of supply and preparation of White House food." For example, the dinner menu at the Executive Mansion for February 6, 1802, recorded by a Massachusetts Congressman, featured "rice soup, round of beef, turkey, mutton, ham, loin of veal, cutlet of mutton or veal, fried eggs, fried beef, a pie called macaroni [and] other jim-cracks, a great variety of fruit, plenty of wines."[3] If Jefferson was vilified by Patrick Henry for spurning "his native vituals in favor of French cuisine,"[4] he was also a viti-culturist and connoisseur, "the foremost American wine expert of his age."[5] As Root and de Rochemont add, moreover, "for eight years he recorded meticulously the first and last appearances of each of thirty-seven different vegetables on the Washington market."[6]

Apple Toddy

Pour over eighteen pippin apples well roasted (without burning) one gallon of boiling water, and let it stand till cold; then press through a sieve to remove skin and seeds. Add to the mixture two quarts of sugar, one quart of brandy, one quart of rum, one quart of sherry, one pint of madeira, one-half pint of arrack, one-half pint of peach brandy, one-half pint of curacao liqueur, and one grated nutmet. Mix well and serve in punch glasses.— Laura S. Fitchett, *Beverages and Sauces of Colonial Virginia* (New York and Washington: Neale, 1906), 23.

Ice Cream

According to Evan Jones, Jefferson purchased "cream machine for ice" in 1784.[7]

2 bottles of good cream
6 yolks of eggs
½ pound of sugar
mix the yolks and sugar
put the cream on a fire in a casserole first putting in a stick of vanilla
When near boiling take it off and pour it gently into the mixture of eggs and sugar
Stir it well
put it on the fire again stirring it thoroughly with a spoon to prevent it sticking to the casserole.
When near boiling take it off and strain it thro a towel
put it in the sorbetière.
then set it in ice an hour before it is to be served. Put into the ice a handful of salt
put ice all around the sorbetière
i.e. a layer of ice a layer of salt for 3 layers.
Put salt on the coverlid of the sorbetière & cover the whole with ice
leave it still half a quarter of an hour
then turn the S[orbetiere] in the ice 10 min.
Open it to loosen with a spatula the ice from the inner sides of the S[sorbetière].
Open it from time to time to detach the ice from the sides
When well taken (prise) stir it well with the spatula
put it in moulds, jostling it well down on the knee
then put the mould into the same bucket of ice
leave it there to the moment of serving it
to withdraw it, immerse the mould in warm water, tossing it well until it will come out & turn it into a plate.— Library of Congress, "Jefferson's Recipe for Vanilla Ice Cream," www.loc.gov/exhibits/treasures/tri034.html

Persimmon Beer

Gather the persimmons perfectly ripe and free from any roughness, work them into large loaves, with bran enough to make them consistent, bake them so thoroughly that the cake may be brown and dry throughout, but not burnt, they are then fit for use; but if you keep them any time, it will be necessary to dry them frequently in an oven moderately warm. Of these loaves broken into a coarse powder, take 8 bushels, pour on them 40 gallons of cold water; & after two or three days draw it off; boil it as other beer, hop it; this makes a strong beer. By putting 30 gal. of water in the same powder, and letting it stand two or three days longer, you may have a very fine small beer.—*American Farmer*, April 16, 1819, 22.

RONALD JOHNSON

Ronald Johnson (1935–1998) was both a poet and the author of four Southwestern cookbooks.

Green Chile Sauce

½ cup chopped green onions
1 pressed clove of garlic
2 tablespoons olive oil
2 tomatoes, peeled, seeded and chopped (or ½ cup canned tomatoes)
1 tablespoon chopped parsley
¼ cup peeled green chiles, chopped
1 teaspoon ground coriander soaked in 1 tablespoon hot water
Salt to taste
Pinch of black pepper
1 whole clove

Sauté onion and garlic in olive oil until the onion is transparent. Add the tomatoes, chiles, parsley, the water drained from the coriander and the rest of the ingredients. Simmer for 10–15 minutes.— Johnson, *The Aficionado's Southwestern Cooking* (Albuquerque: University of New Mexico, 1968), 98.

Huevos Rancheros

1 cup Chile Meat Sauce, or 1 cup Cooked Green Chile Sauce
6 eggs
6 tortillas
Grated Monterey Jack cheese
Avocado slices (optional)

Heat the sauce until it bubbles. In another pan, fry the eggs, then lightly fry the tortillas until they are softened—*they should not be crisp.* Place an egg on each tortilla, then some of the hot sauce. Sprinkle with grated cheese, and garnish with avocado slices if you wish. Serves 6.— Johnson, *The Aficionado's Southwestern Cooking*, 20.

Mexican Summer Soup

¼ cup chopped green onions
2 cups sliced summer squash (or zucchini)
1 tablespoon olive oil
2 tablespoon tomato paste
2 cups chicken broth
1 cup cooked, diced chicken
1 cup fresh, frozen, or canned corn
½ teaspoon dried oregano

½ teaspoon chili powder
2 avocados peeled, seeded and cubed
1 3-ounces package cream cheese

Sauté onions and squash in olive oil for 5 minutes. Add tomato paste and cook a few minutes longer. Add broth, chicken, corn and herbs. Cook gently 15–20 minutes. Just before serving add the cubed avocados. Place in bowls and garnish with cream cheese cut into cubes. Serve with hot tortillas. Serves 6–8.— Johnson, *The Aficionado's Southwestern Cooking*, 29.

HELEN KELLER

Of Helen Keller (1880–1968), Mark Twain declared, "She will make a fame that will endure in history for centuries. Along her special lines she is the most extraordinary product of all the ages."[1] The deafblind author of *The Story of My Life* (1903), Keller's early life is the subject of the Tony Award–winning play *The Miracle Worker* (1957).

Golden Gate Salad

In contributing her salad recipe to *Famous Recipes of Famous Women* in 1925, Keller commented, "I like this salad very much. I ate it first in California, so I call it Golden Gate salad. It is best made of fresh fruits, but it can be made of canned fruits. At home we often serve it instead of dessert, with a little more whipped cream."

½ pound of fresh marshmallows, cut in halves.
2 nice oranges, carefully peeled and cut in small pieces.
2 bananas, cut in dicelike pieces.
2 thick slices of fresh pineapple, cut in the same way.
1 large tart apple, cut fine.
½ pint bottle of red maraschino cherries, cut in half with juice.
½ pint jar of French marrons, broken up with syrup.
The delicate inner stalks of one head of celery, cut in small pieces.
¼ pound of fresh pecans or English walnuts.
Mix nuts, fruits, celery together in dish, and put in ice box.

Dressing

½ pint of thick mayonnaise.
½ pint of thick cream.

Whip cream and mix with mayonnaise and juice of half a lemon. An hour before serving, mix dressing lightly with salad and sprinkle with plenty of paprika. Serve very cold on crisp lettuce leaves.— Stratton, *Favorite Recipes of Famous Women*, 21–22.

JACK KEROUAC

Best known for his novel *On the Road* (1957), Jack Kerouac (1922–1969), like his friend Allen Ginsberg, lived frugally. He reminisced in *The Dharma Bums* (1958) about a cheap soup made with Lipton's dehydrated peas: "At dusk Japhy lit a good big fire and started supper…. He made a soup that night that I shall never forget….

This was nothing but a couple of envelopes of dry pea soup thrown into a pot of water with fried bacon, fat and all, and stirred till boiling. It was rich, real pea taste, with that smoky bacon and bacon fat, just the thing to drink in the cold gathering darkness by a sparkling fire."[1]

Green Pea Soup

Package Lipton Green Pea Soup
Bacon
Onions
Salt & pepper
Simply fry chopped bacon till the pieces are crisped dark brown, then throw the onions and spiced soupmix into bacon and sizzling fat, and stir. Let simmer a minute for excellent pea soup.—*Selected Letters: Jack Kerouac, 1957–1969*, ed. Ann Charters (New York: Penguin, 1999), 365.

Pâte de Porc Gras

2 pounds of ground Boston pork butt (with all the fat)
2 onions
2 garlics
teaspoon dry mustard
Simply immerse the ground pork butt till water just covers it, in pot, with onions & garlic chopped in, and salt and pepper, and dry mustard. Let simmer slowly (say, 5 hours).
Spoon & level into bowls; chill bowls in ice box.
Next day, use as sandwich spread on crackers (preferably good French Bread).
It has been sensationally received by all non–French Canadians I have made it for.—*Selected Letters: Jack Kerouac, 1957–1969*, 364–65.

CAROLINE KIRKLAND

Caroline Kirkland (1801–1864) moved with her family to Michigan in 1835, the subject of her pioneering realist novel *A New Home— Who'll Follow?* (1839).

Bread

One word as to this and similar modes of making bread, so much practiced throughout this country. It is my opinion that the sin of bewitching snow-white flour by means of either of those abominations, "salt risin'," "milk emptin's," "bran 'east," or any of their odious compounds, ought to be classed with the turning of grain into whiskey, and both made indictable offences. To those who know of no other means of producing the requisite sponginess in bread than the wholesome hop-yeast of the brewer, I may be allowed to explain the mode to which I have alluded with such hearty reprobation. Here follows the recipe:

Take quantum suf[ficient] of good sweet milk—add a teaspoon full of salt, and some water, and set the mixture in a warm place till it ferments, then mix your bread with it; and if you are lucky enough to catch it just in the right moment before the fermentation reaches the putrescent stage, you may make tolerably good rolls, but if you are five minutes

too late, you will have to open your doors and windows while your bread is baking.—
Verbum sap [enough said].

   "Salt risin'" is made with water slightly salted and fermented like the other; and becomes
putrid rather sooner; and "bran 'east" is on the same plan. The consequences of letting
these mixtures stand too long will become known to those whom it may concern, when
they shall travel through the remoter parts of Michigan; so I shall not dwell upon them
here — but I offer my counsel to such of my friends as may be removing westward, to bring
with them some form of portable yeast (the old-fashioned dried cakes which mothers and
aunts can furnish are as good as any) — and also full instructions for perpetuating the same;
and to plant hops as soon as they get a corner to plant them in.— Kirkland, *A New Home —
Who'll Follow?* (Boston: Francis, 1839), 58–59.

TED KOOSER

Ted Kooser (b. 1939) was the thirteenth poet laureate of the United States (2004–
06) and the recipient of the Pulitzer Prize for Poetry in 2005 for his collection *Delights
and Shadows.*

How to Make Rhubarb Wine

Go the patch, some afternoon
in early summer, fuzzy with beer
and sunlight, and pick a sack
of rhubard (red or green will do)
and God knows watch for rattlesnakes
or better, listen: they make a sound
like an old lawnmower rolled downhill.
Wear a hat. A straw hat's best
for the heat but lets the gnats in.
Bunch up the stalks and chop the leaves off
with a buck-knife and be careful.
You need ten pounds; a grocery bag
packed full will do it. Then go home
and sit barefooted in the shade
behind the house with a can of beer.

Spread out the rhubarb in the grass
and wash it with cold water
from the garden hose, washing
your feet as well. Then take a nap.
That evening, dice the rhubarb up
and put it in a crock. Then pour
eight quarts of boiling water in,
cover it up with a checkered cloth
to keep the fruit flies out of it,
and let it stand five days or so.
Take time each day to think of it.

When the time is up, dip out the pulp
with your hands for strainers; leave the juice.
Stir in five pounds of sugar
and an envelope of Red Star yeast.
Ferment ten days, under the cloth,
sniffing of it from time to time,
then siphon it off, swallowing some,
and bottle it. Sit back and watch
the liquid clear to honey-yellow,
bottled and ready for the years,
and smile. You've done it awfully well.

> — Kooser, *Sure Signs: New and Selected Poems*
> (Pittsburgh: University of Pittsburgh Press, 1980).

RING LARDNER

Ring Lardner (1885–1933) was author of the satirical baseball novel *You Know Me, Al* (1916) and a longtime columnist for the *Chicago Tribune*.

Dry Martini

Drop two green olives in a dry well. In a few days let down the bucket. Try to acquire those two (2) olives. By the time you have acquired them they will be distilled into a dry Martini. Drop a raisin into it.—*Chicago Tribune*, April 17, 1919, 20.

HARPER LEE

Harper Lee (b. 1926) received the Pulitzer Prize for Literature in 1961 for her novel *To Kill a Mockingbird*.

Crackling Bread

In the first line of her recipe for Crackling Bread, Lee parodies an apocryphal recipe for rabbit stew that begins "First, catch a rabbit."

First, catch your pig. Then ship it to the *abattoir* nearest you. Bake what they send back. Remove the solid fat and throw the rest away. Fry fat, drain off liquid grease, and combine the residue (called "cracklings") with 1½ cups water-ground white meal, 1 teaspoon salt, 1 teaspoon baking powder, 1 egg, 1 cup milk. Bake in very hot oven until brown (about 15 minutes).

Result: one pan crackling bread serving 6. Total cost: about $250, depending upon size of pig. Some historians say by this recipe alone fell the Confederacy.— Barr and Sachs, *Artists' and Writers' Cookbook*, 251.

URSULA K. LE GUIN

The science fiction writer Ursula K. Le Guin (b. 1929) has received five Hugos and six Nebula awards for such novels as *The Left Hand of Darkness* (1969) and *The Dispossessed* (1974). She resides in Oregon, the reason she specifies Tillamook cheese in her recipe for Crab Nebula.

Crab Nebula

Make a cream sauce with tablespoon butter, 2 tablespoons flour, 1 cup milk. Add about 1½ cup grated Tillamook cheese (or more — or less … if you are unable to obtain Tillamook, you may use any inferior American Cheddar, but the difference will be noticeable unless you have a calloused palate).

Now add about ½ pound? 2 cups? — Well, add enough crab. (If you are unable to obtain Pacific crab, you may use those flabby little Atlantic ones, or even lobster; but if you are reduced to King Crab, forget it.)

Flavor with sherry to taste, salt, pepper, parsley.

Serve on rice, or wild rice if you are J. Paul Getty, or English muffins, or whatever. — *Cooking Out of This World*, 104–05.

> In her novel *Always Coming Home* (1985), Le Guin constructs an anthropological
> record — with recipes of their foods — of the Kesh, a Northern California people who
> "might be going to have lived a long, long time from now."

Líriv Metadí or Valley Succotash

Wash about two cups of small red beans (the Valley metadí is very like the Mexican frijole), and cook till done (a couple of hours) with half an onion, three or four garlic cloves, and a bay leaf.

Simmer about a cup and a half of parched corn until thoroughly cooked, and drain (or in season use fresh corn cut off the cob, uncooked).

Simmer a handful of dried black mushrooms for half an hour or so, and keep them in their cooking broth.

When all these ingredients are done combine them, along with:

the juice and pulp of a lemon, or some preserved tamarind pulp an onion chopped and fried in oil with some finely chopped garlic and a spoonful of cumin seeds

a large, mild green chile of the chile verde type, *or* a small, hot green chile (but *not* bell pepper), seeded and chopped fine

three or four tomatoes peeled and chopped coarsely

add, as seasoning, oregano, winter savory, and more lemon to taste

add dried red chile if you want it hot

To thicken the sauce, one dried tomato-paste ball was added; our equivalent would be two or three tablespoons of thick tomato paste. (If fresh tomatoes are not in season, double or triple the quantity of tomato paste.)

All this simmers for about an hour.

Serve with chopped raw onion to garnish, and a sour sauce or chutney made of green tomatoes or tomatillos, flavored with fresh or dry coriander leaf.

This dish, "too heavy for rice," was accompanied by cornbreads, either of the hoe cake or the tortilla type. — Ursula Le Guin, *Always Coming Home* (New York: Harper and Row, 1985), 438.

Primitive Chocolate Mousse

(Also known as Mousse au chocolat, Chocolate Moose, Brown Mouse, and Please Sir I want some More.)

Included because it is curiously hard to find a good plain responsible recipe for this extremely simple and impressive dish. Serves 4:

2 ounces bitter chocolate

2 tablespoons water

⅓ cup sugar

4 egg whites, beaten stiff

4 egg yolks, well beaten

1 or 2 teaspoon vanilla, brandy, rum, or bourbon

⅓ pint whipping cream, whipped

Melt chocolate, water, and sugar in double boiler. If you can stir fast, forget the double boiler.

Beat egg whites stiff. Beat egg yolks well and add vanilla and liquor. Beat in chocolate mixture (cooked a bit); fold in the egg whites.

At this point the French often stop, but about ⅓ pint whipping cream whipped can also be folded in, making it richer.

Chill at least 4 hours in individual dishes. You can make it the day before, in which case it gets spongy, which is equally pleasant.—*Cooking Out of This World*, 107.

ELMORE LEONARD

Elmore Leonard (1925–2013) was the author of *Hombre* (1961), *Get Shorty* (1990), and more than 40 other novels. He often alluded to the foods enjoyed by his characters, such as baked possum in his novella "Fire in the Hole" (2002).

Elmore's Southron Breakfast Treats

Put two packets of Quaker Minute Grits in a bowl, pour in a cup of boiling water, stir, add a pat of butter, salt to taste, and eat it. Mmmmm. Now open a can of Underwood Deviled Ham — the one with the red devil on the white wrapper. Spread it on a slice of bread of your choice. Next, chop up a stalk of celery and sprinkle it all over the Deviled Ham. Top it off with another slice of bread and you have a delicious sandwich to start your day.

Other nourishing starters are cheese and jelly sandwiches and cold bean sandwiches with chopped onions. If you're over seventy you might want to have a glass of prune juice first. Have a nice day.— *The New Great American Writers' Cookbook*, 63.

ALDO LEOPOLD

The nature writer and environmentalist Aldo Leopold (1887–1948) has been credited with pioneering the field of wildlife management.

Deer Steaks

In his most popular book, *A Sand County Almanac* (1949), Leopold inserted a recipe for Deer Steaks.

Kill a mast-fed buck, not earlier than November, not later than January. Hang him in a live oak tree for seven frosts and seven suns. Then cut out the half-frozen "straps" from their bed of tallow under the saddle, and slice them transversely into steaks. Rub each steak with salt, pepper, and flour. Throw into a Dutch oven containing deep smoking-hot bear fat and standing on live oak coals. Fish out the steaks at the first sign of browning. Throw a little flour into the fat, then ice cold water, then milk. Lay a steak on the summit of a steaming sourdough biscuit and drown both in gravy.—*A Sand County Almanac* (1949; rpt. New York: Oxford University Press, 1968), 151–52.

ELIZA LESLIE

The author of such romances as *Amelia, or a Young Ladies' Vicissitudes* (1848), Eliza Leslie (1787–1858) was best-known for her conduct books and cookbooks, particularly *Directions for Cookery in Its Various Branches* (1837) and *The Lady's Receipt Book* (1846).

Eliza Leslie portrait by Thomas Sully (Library of Congress).

Beefsteak (Broiled)

The best beefsteaks are those cut from the ribs or from the inside of the sirloin. All other parts are for this purpose comparatively hard and tough.

They should be cut about three quarters of an inch thick, and, unless the beef is remarkably fine and tender, the steaks will be much improved by beating them on both sides with a steak mallet, or with a rolling-pin. Do not season them till you take them from the fire.

Have ready on your hearth a fine bed of clear bright coals, entirely free from smoke and ashes. Set the gridiron over the coals in a slanting direction, that the meat may not be smoked by the fat dropping into the fire directly under it. When the gridiron is quite hot, rub the bars with suet, sprinkle a little salt over the coals, and lay on the steaks. Turn them frequently with a pair of steak-tongs, or with a knife and fork. A quarter of an hour is generally sufficient time to broil a beefsteak. For those who like them underdone or rare, ten or twelve minutes will be enough.

When the fat blazes and smokes very much as it drips into the fire, quickly remove the gridiron for a moment, till the blaze has subsided. After they are browned, cover the upper side of the steaks with an inverted plate or dish to prevent the flavour from evaporating. Rub a dish with a shallot, or small onion, and place it near the gridiron and close to the fire, that it may be well heated. In turning the steak drop the gravy that may be standing on it into this dish, to save it from being lost. When the steaks are done, sprinkle them with a little salt and pepper, and lay them in a hot dish, putting on each a piece of fresh butter. Then, if it is liked, season them with a very little raw shallot, minced as finely as possible, and moistened with a spoonful of water; and stir a teaspoonful of catsup into the gravy. Send the steaks to table very hot, in a covered dish. You may serve up with them onion sauce in a small tureen.

Pickles are frequently eaten with beefsteaks.— Eliza Leslie, *Directions for Cookery* (Philadelphia: Carey and Hart, 1840), 74–75.

Beefsteak (Fried)

Beefsteaks for frying should be cut thinner than for broiling. Take them from the ribs or sirloin and remove the bone. Beat them to make them tender. Season them with salt and pepper.

Put some fresh butter, or nice beef-dripping into a frying pan, and hold it over a clear bright fire till it boils and has done hissing. Then put in the steaks, and (if you like them) some sliced onions. Fry them about a quarter of an hour, turning them frequently. Steaks, when fried, should be thoroughly done. After they are browned, cover them with a large plate to keep in the juices.

Have ready a hot dish, and when they are done, take out the steaks and onions and lay them in it with another dish on the top, to keep them hot while you give the gravy in the pan another boil up over the fire. You may add to it a spoonful of mushroom catsup. Pour the gravy over the steaks, and send them to table as hot as possible.

Mutton chops may be fried in this manner.— Leslie, *Directions for Cookery*, 76.

Catfish Soup

Catfish that have been caught near the middle of the river are much nicer than those that are taken near the shore where they have access to impure food. The small white ones are the best. Having cut off their heads, skin the fish, and clean them, and cut them in three. To twelve small catfish allow a pound and a half of ham. Cut the ham into small pieces, or slice it very thin, and scald it two or three times in boiling water, lest it be too salt. Chop together a bunch of parsley and some sweet marjoram stripped from the stalks. Put these ingredients into a soup kettle and season them with pepper: the ham will make it salt enough. Add a head of celery cut small, or a large tablespoonful of celery seed tied up in a bit of clear muslin to prevent its dispersing. Put in two quarts of water, cover the kettle, and let it boil slowly till everything is sufficiently done, add the fish and ham quite tender. Skim it frequently. Boil in another vessel a quart of rich milk, in which you have melted a quarter of a pound of butter divided into small bits and rolled in flour. Pour it hot to the soup, and stir in at the last the beaten yolks of four eggs. Give it another boil, just to take off the rawness of the eggs, and then put it into a tureen, taking out the bag of celery seed before you send the soup to table, and adding some toasted bread cut into small squares. In making toast for soup, cut the bread thick, and pare off all the crust.

This soup will be found very fine.

Eel soup may be made in the same manner: chicken soup also.— Leslie, *Directions for Cookery*, 36–37.

Fine Puff Paste

The heroine of Leslie's novella *Henrietta Harrison* "became such a proficient in housewifery that her uncle pronounced her puff paste to be quite equal to that of her instructress."[1]

To every pound of the best fresh butter allow a pound or a quart of superfine flour. Sift the flour into a deep pan, and then sift on a plate some additional flour to use for sprinkling and rolling. Wash the butter through two cold waters; squeezing out all the salt, and whatever milk may remain in it; and then make it up with your hands into a round lump, and put it in ice till you are ready to use it. Then divide the butter into four equal parts. Cut up one of the quarters into the pan of flour; and divide the remaining three quarters into six pieces, cutting each quarter in half. Mix with a knife the flour and butter that is in the pan, adding by degrees a very little cold water till you have made it into a lump of stiff dough. Then sprinkle some flour on the pasteboard, (you should have a marble slab,) take the dough from the pan by lifting it out with the knife, lay it on the board, and flouring your rolling-pin, roll out the paste into a large thin sheet. Then with the knife, put all over it, at equal distances, one of the six pieces of butter divided into small bits. Fold up the sheet of paste, flour it, roll it out again, and add in the same manner another of the portions of butter. Repeat this process till the butter is all in. Then fold it once more, lay it on a plate, and set it in a cool place till you are ready to use it. Then divide it into as many pieces as you want sheets of paste; roll out each sheet, and put them into buttered plates or patty-pans. In using the rolling-pin, observe always to roll from you. Bake the paste in a moderate oven, but rather quick then slow. No air must be admitted to it while baking.

The edges of paste should always be notched before it goes into the oven. For this purpose, use a sharp penknife, dipping it frequently in flour as it becomes sticky. The notches should be even and regular. If you do them imperfectly at first, they cannot be mended by sticking on additional bits of paste; as, when baked, every patch will be doubly conspicuous. There are various ways of notching; one of the neatest is to fold over one corner of each notch; or you may arrange the notches to sand upright and lie flat, alternately, all round the edge. They should be made small and regular. You may form the edge into leaves with the little tin cutters made for the purpose.

If the above directions for puff paste are carefully followed, and if it is not spoiled in baking, it will rise to a great thickness and appear in flakes or leaves according to the number of times you have put in the butter.

It should be eaten the day it is baked.— Leslie, *Directions for Cookery*, 276–78.

French Mustard

> In Leslie's novel *Amelia*, the hostess at a formal dinner asks a guest about her preferences in condiments: "Will you not take some catsup? Which catsup do you prefer, mushroom or tomato? Do you eat mustard? Here is some French mustard."[2]
> In her cookbook, Leslie described how to prepare all three.

Mix together four ounces of the very best mustard powder, four salt-spoons of salt, a large tablespoonful of minced tarragon leaves, and two cloves of garlic chopped fine. Pour on by degrees sufficient vinegar (tarragon vinegar is best) to dilute it to the proper consistence. It will probably require about four wineglassfuls or half a pint. Mix it well, using for the purpose a wooden spoon. When done, put it into a wide-mouthed bottle or into little white jars. Cork it very closely, and keep it in a dry place. It will not be fit for use in less than two days.

This (used as the common mustard) is a very agreeable condiment for beef or mutton.— Leslie, *Directions for Cookery*, 181–82.

Green Corn Pudding

Take twelve ears of green corn, as it is called, (that is, Indian corn when full grown, but before it begins to harden and turn yellow,) and grate it. Have ready a quart of rich milk, and stir into it by degrees a quarter of a pound of fresh butter, and a quarter of a pound of sugar. Beat four eggs till quite light; and then stir them into the milk, &c. alternately with the grated corn, a little of each at a time. Put the mixture into a large buttered dish, and bake it four hours. It may be eaten either warm or cold. For sauce, beat together butter and white sugar in equal proportions, mixed with grated nutmeg.

To make this pudding, — you may, if more convenient, boil the corn and cut it from the cob; but let it get quite cold before you stir it into the milk. If the corn has been previously boiled, the pudding will require but two hours to bake.— Leslie, *Directions for Cookery*, 290.

Lemon Pudding

> The heroine of *Henrietta Harrison* brags that she had enjoyed a meal of "mock turtle, and maccaroni, and lobster, and lemon pudding, and various other nice things that are unfortunately considered improper to be eaten every day."[3]

Grate the yellow part of the rind, and squeeze the juice of two large, smooth lemons. Stir together to a cream, half a pound of butter, and half a pound of powdered white sugar, and add a wineglass of mixed wine and brandy. Beat very light six eggs, and stir them gradually into the mixture. Put it into a buttered dish with a broad edge, round which lay a powder of puff paste neatly notched. Bake it half an hour, and when cool grate white sugar over it.

You may add to the mixture a Naples biscuit, or two finger biscuits, grated.— Leslie, *Directions for Cookery*, 285.

Lobster

Put a handful of salt into a large kettle or pot of boiling water. When the water boils very hard put in the lobster, having first brushed it, and tied the claws together with a bit of twine. Keep it boiling for half an hour to an hour in proportion to its size. If boiled too long the meat will be hard and stringy. When it is done take it out, lay it on its claws to drain, and then wipe it dry. Send it to table cold, with the body and tail split open, and he claws taken off. Lay the large claws next to the body, and the small one outside. Garnish with double parsley.

It is scarcely necessary to mention that the head of a lobster, and what are called the lady-fingers are not to be eaten.— Leslie, *Directions for Cookery*, 61.

Maccaroni [sic]

Have ready a pot of boiling water. Throw a little salt into it, and then by slow degrees put in a pound of the macaroni, a little at a time. Keep stirring it gently, and continue to do so very often while boiling. Take care to keep it well covered with water. Have ready a kettle of boiling water to replenish the maccaroni pot if it should be in danger of getting too dry. In about twenty minutes it will be done. It must be quite soft, but it must not boil long enough to break.

When the maccaroni has boiled sufficiently, pour in immediately a little cold water, and let it stand a few minutes, keeping it covered.

Grate half a pound of Parmesan cheese into a deep dish, and scatter over it a few small bits of butter. Then with a skimmer that is perforated with holes, commence taking up the maccaroni, (draining it well,) and spread a layer of it over the cheese and butter. Spread over it another layer of grated cheese and butter, and then a layer of maccaroni, and so on till your dish is full; having a layer of maccaroni on the top, over which spread some butter without cheese. Cover the dish, and set it in an oven for half an hour. It will then be ready to send to table.

You may grate some nutmeg over each layer of maccaroni.

Allow half a pound of butter to a pound of maccaroni and half a pound of cheese.—Leslie, *Directions for Cookery*, 210.

Mock Turtle or Calf's Head Soup

This soup will require eight hours to prepare. Take a large calf's head, and having cleaned, washed, and soaked it, put it into a pot with a knuckle of veal, and the hock of a ham, or a few slices of bacon; but previously cut off the reserve enough of the veal to make two dozen small forcemeat balls. Put the head and the other meat into as much water as will cover it very well, so that it may not be necessary to replenish it: this soup being always made very rich. Let it boil slowly four hours, skimming it carefully. As soon as no more scum rises, put in six potatoes, and three turnips, all sliced thin; with equal proportions of parsley, sweet marjoram, and sweet basil, chopped fine; and pepper and salt.

An hour before you send the meat to table, make about two dozen small forcemeat balls of minced veal and beef suet in equal quantities, seasoned with pepper and salt; sweet herbs, grated lemon peel, and powdered nutmeg and mace. Add some beaten yolk of egg to make all these ingredients stick together. Flour the balls very well, and fry them in butter. Before you put them into the soup, take out the head, and the other meat. Cut the meat from the head in small pieces, and return it to the soup. When the soup is nearly done, stir in half a pint of Madeira. Have ready at least a dozen egg balls made of the yolks of hard boiled eggs, grated or pounded in a mortar, and mixed with a little flour and sufficient raw yolk of egg to bind them. Make them up into the form and size of boy's marbles. Throw them into the soup at the last, and also squeeze in the juice of a lemon. Let it get another slow boil, and then put it into the tureen.—Leslie, *Directions for Cookery*, 30.

Mushroom Catsup

Take mushrooms that have been freshly gathered, and examine them carefully to ascertain that they are of the right sort. Pick them nicely, and wipe them clean, but do not wash them. Spread a layer of them at the bottom of a deep earthen pan, and then sprinkle them well with salt; then another layer of mushrooms, and another layer of salt, and so on alternately. Throw a folded cloth over the jar, and set it by the fire or in a very cool oven. Let it remain thus for twenty-four hours, and then mash them well with your hands. Next squeeze and strain them through a bag.

To every quart of strained liquor add an ounce and a half of whole black pepper, and boil it slowly in a covered vessel for half an hour. Then add a quarter of an ounce of allspice, half an ounce of sliced ginger, a few cloves, and three or four blades of mace. Boil it with the spice fifteen minutes longer. When it is done, take it off, and let it stand awhile to settle. Pour it carefully off from the sediment, and put it into small bottles, filling them to the top. Secure them well with corks dipped in melted rosin, and leather caps tied over them.

The longer catsup is boiled, the better it will keep.

You may add cayenne and nutmeg to the spices.

The bottles should be quite small, as it soon spoils after being opened.— Leslie, *Directions for Cookery*, 176.

Pepper Pot

Take four pounds of tripe and four ox feet. Put them into a large pot with as much water as will cover them, some whole pepper, and a little salt. Hang them over the fire early in the morning. Let them boil slowly, keeping the pot closely covered. When the tripe is quite tender, and the ox feet boiled to pieces, take them out, and skim the liquid and strain it. Then cut the tripe into small pieces; put it back into the pot, and pour the soup or liquor over it. Have ready some sweet herbs chopped fine, some sliced onions, and some sliced potatoes. Make some small dumplings with flour and butter. Season the vegetables well with pepper and salt, and put them into the pot. Have ready a kettle of boiling water, and pour on as much as will keep the ingredients covered while boiling, but take care not to weaken the taste by putting too much water. Add a large piece of butter rolled in flour, and lastly put in the dumplings. Let it boil till all the things are thoroughly done, and then serve it up in the tureen.— Leslie, *Directions for Cookery*, 87–88

Pickled Oysters

The heroine of Leslie's *Henrietta Harrison* also partakes at tea of "ice queen cakes, and preserved limes, and pickled oysters."[4]

Take a hundred and fifty fine oysters, and pick off carefully the bits of shell that may be sticking to them. Lay the oysters in a deep dish, and then strain the liquor over them. Put them into an iron skillet that is lined with porcelain, and add salt to your taste. Without salt they will not be firm enough. Set the skillet on hot coals, and allow the oysters to simmer till they are heated all through, but not till they boil. Then take out the oysters and put them into a stone jar, leaving the liquor in the skillet. Add to it a pint of clear strong vinegar, a large teaspoonful of blades of mace, three dozen whole cloves, and three dozen whole pepper corns. Let it come to a boil, and when the oysters are quite cold in the jar, pour the liquor on them.

They are fit for use immediately, but are better the next day. In cold weather they will keep a week.

If you intend sending them a considerable distance you must allow the oysters to boil, and double the proportions of the pickle and spice.— Leslie, *Directions for Cookery*, 57.

Pickled Tomatoes

Take a peck of tomatoes, (the small round ones are best for pickling,) and prick every one with a fork. Put them into a broad stone or earthen vessel, and sprinkle salt between every layer of tomatoes. Cover them, and let them remain three days in the salt. Then put them into vinegar and water mixed in equal quantities, half and half, and keep them in it twenty-four hours to draw out the saltness. There must be sufficient of the liquid to cover the tomatoes well.

To a peck of tomatoes allow a bottle of mustard, half an ounce of cloves, and half an ounce of pepper, with a dozen onions sliced thin. Pack the tomatoes in a stone jar, placing the spices and onions alternately with the layers of tomatoes. Put them in till the jar is two-thirds full. Then fill it up with strong cold vinegar, and stop it closely. The pickles will be fit to eat in a fortnight.

If you do not like onions, substitute for them a larger quantity of spice. — Leslie, *Directions for Cookery*, 223–24.

Pork and Beans

Allow two pounds of pickled pork to two quarts of dried beans. If the meat is very salt put it in soak overnight. Put the beans into a pot with cold water, and let them hang all night over the embers of the fire, or set them in the chimney corner, that they may warm as well as soak. Early in the morning rinse them through a colander. Score the rind of the pork, (which should not be a very fat piece,) and put the meat into a clean pot with the beans, which must be seasoned with pepper. Let them boil slowly together for about two hours, and carefully remove all the scum and fat that rises to the top. Then take them out; lay the pork in a tin pan, and cover the meat with the beans, adding a very little water. Put it into an oven, and bake it four hours.

This is a homely dish, but is by many persons much liked. It is customary to bring it to table in the pan in which it is baked. — Leslie, *Directions for Cookery*, 120.

Roasted Beef's Heart

Cut open the heart, and (having removed the ventricles) soak it in cold water to free it from the blood. Parboil it about ten minutes. Prepare a forcemeat of grated bread crumbs, butter or minced suet, sweet marjoram and parsley chopped fine, a little grated lemon peel, nutmeg, pepper, and salt to your taste, and some yolk of egg to bind the ingredients. Stuff the heart with the forcemeat, and secure the opening by tying a string around it. Put it on a spit, and roast it till it is tender throughout.

Add to the gravy a piece of butter rolled in flour, and a glass of red wine. Serve up the heart very hot in a covered dish. It chills immediately.

Eat currant jelly with it.

Boiled beef's heart is frequently used in mince pies. — Leslie, *Directions for Cookery*, 85.

Stewed Carp

Having cut off the head, tail, and fins, season the carp with salt, pepper, and powdered mace, both inside and out. Rub the seasoning on very well, and let them lay in it an hour. Then put them into a stew pan with a little parsley shred fine, a whole onion, a little sweet marjoram, a teacup of thick cream or very rich milk, and a lump of butter rolled in flour. Pour in sufficient water to cover the carp, and let it stew half an hour.

Perch may be done in the same way.

You may dress a piece of sturgeon in this manner, but you must first boil it for twenty minutes to extract the oil. Take off the skin before you proceed to stew the fish. — Leslie, *Directions for Cookery*, 55.

Tomato Catsup

Gather the tomatoes on a dry day, and when quite ripe. Peel them, and cut them into quarters. Put them into a large earthen pan, and mash and squeeze them till they are reduced to a pulp. Allowing half a pint of fine salt to a hundred tomatoes, put them into a preserving kettle, and boil them gently with the salt for two hours, stirring them frequently to prevent their burning. Then strain them through a fine sieve, pressing them with the back of a silver spoon. Season them to your taste with mace, cinnamon, nutmeg, ginger, and white or red pepper, all powdered fine.

Put the tomatoes again over the fire with the spices, and boil it slowly till very thick, stirring it frequently.

When cold, put it up in small bottles, secure the corks well, and it will keep good a year or two.— Leslie, *Directions for Cookery*, 177.

MERIWETHER LEWIS AND WILLIAM CLARK

> Commissioned by Jefferson to explore the territory acquired by the U.S. from France in 1803, Meriwether Lewis (1774–1809) and William Clark (1770–1838) led an expedition of more than 30 people who explored Louisiana Territory in 1804–1806.

Boudin Blanc (White Buffalo Sausage)

> En route to the Pacific, the group was sometimes reduced to grubbing for roots to eat. On May 9, 1805, however, the camp chef Toussaint Charbonneau prepared a meal of "boudin blanc" or white buffalo sausage. According to Thomas Hallock, "Lewis's recitation of Charbonneau's recipe ... serves not only as documentation of a unique frontier cuisine, but also as an example of the captain's own brand of satire that places him, at least to the extent of this little example, in company with Ebenezer Cooke and Benjamin Franklin."[1]

Capt. C. killed 2 bucks and 2 buffaloe, I also killed one buffaloe which proved to be the best meat, it was in tolerable order; we saved the best of the meat, and from the cow I killed we saved the necessary materials for making what our wrighthand cook Charbono calls the *boudin blanc*, and immediately set him about preparing them for supper; this white pudding we all esteem one of the greatest delacies of the forrest, it may not be amiss therefore to give it a place. About 6 feet of the lower extremity of the large gut of the Buffaloe is the first mosel that the cook makes love to, this he holds fast at one end with the right hand, while with the forefinger and thumb of the left he gently compresses it, and discharges what he says *is not good to eat,* but of which in the squel we get a moderate portion; the mustle lying underneath the shoulder blade next to the back, and filletes are next saught, these are needed up very fine with a good portion of kidney suit [suet]; to this composition is then added a just proportion of pepper and salt and a small quantity of flour; thus far advanced, our skilfull opporater C—o seizes his recepticle, which has never once touched the water, for that would intirely distroy the regular order of the whole procedure; you will not forget that the side you now see is that covered with a good coat of fat provided the anamal be in good order; the operator sceizes the receptacle I say, and tying it fast at one end turns it inwards and begins now with repeated evolutions of the hand and arm, and a brisk motion of the finger and thumb to put in what he says is *bon pour manger;* thus by stuffing and compressing he soon distends the receptacle to the utmost limmits of it's power of expansion, and in the course of it's longtudinal progress it drives from the other end of the receptacle a much larger portion of the [*blank*] than was previously discharged by the finger and thumb of the left hand in a former part of the operation; thus when the sides of the recepticle are skilfully exchanged the outer for the iner, and all is compleatly filled with something good to eat, it is tyed at the other end, but not any cut off, for that would make the pattern too scant; it is then baptised in the missouri with two dips and a flirt, and bobbed into the kettle; from whence after it be well boiled it is taken and fryed with bears oil untill it becomes brown, when it is ready to esswage the pangs of a keen appetite or such as travelers in the wilderness are seldom at a loss for.— *The Journals of the Lewis and Clark Expedition*, ed. Gary E. Moulton (Lincoln: University of Nebraska Press, 1987), IV 130–31.

OLIVE LOGAN

Olive Logan (1839–1909) was an actor, lecturer, playwright, and author of the novel *Get Thee Behind Me Satan!* (1872). For several years in the mid–1870s, she contributed a domestic advice column to *Harper's Bazar* [*sic*], one of the new women's magazines.

Veal Cutlets in Papillottes (Curl-papers)

Trim the cutlets neatly, season them with pepper and salt, and fry them in clarified butter. While they are cooking, chop some mushrooms, parsley, and three shallots, add to them the piece of half a lemon, a tablespoonful of meat jelly, two of white sauce, and a little nutmeg. Simmer the mixture over the first, add two yolks of eggs, toss all together till thoroughly mixed, then let it become cool. Then take as many sheets of large-sized notepaper as there are cutlets, cut each somewhat in the form of a heart, and then let them be oiled. Next, place a cutlet with an equal proportion of the sauce in one of these papers, and with the forefinger and thumb of the right hand, twist the edges of the paper tightly under into very close folds; and repeat this with the remainder. A quarter of an hour before sending to table, put the cutlets in the oven in a Sauta pan, to get warm through; then, with a heated iron skewer, mark the papers so as to make it appear that they have been broiled; dish them up on a napkin with fried parsley in the center.—*Jennie June's American Cookery*, 331.

JACK AND CHARMIAN LONDON

Jack London (1876–1916) is best known for his tales of adventure in the Klondike and the South Seas, such as *The Call of the Wild* (1903) and *The Sea-Wolf* (1904). Though born into poverty and a self-identified socialist, he became the first millionaire American writer. He and his wife Charmian London (1871–1955) published several recipes in charity cookbooks.

Corned Beef and Cabbage

While roughing it in the outback, London's characters in *A Daughter of the Snows* (1902) cook over an open fire: "After opening a can of corned beef with the axe, he fried half a dozen thick slices of bacon, set the frying pan back, and boiled the coffee."[1] Similarly, in *The Valley of the Moon* (1913) the characters dine *al fresco*: "When Saxon had served the beans, and Billy the coffee, she stood still a moment and surveyed the spread meal on the blankets— the canister of sugar, the condensed milk tin, the sliced corned beef, the lettuce salad and sliced tomatoes, the slices of fresh French bread, and the steaming plates of beans and mugs of coffee."[2]

Take a nice piece of lean corned brisket and boil it for three hours. If it is not oversalted, the water need not be changed. Do not take it suddenly out of the boiling water, but let it stand awhile before lifting. Meanwhile, in another container gently boil young cabbages the size of two small fists, first cutting into quarters. Be sure not to boil too long and do not salt until a few moments before taking up. Cabbage treated delicately is as sweet and attractive as green peas. Place the beef upon a platter and set the quarters of cabbages wreathwise about it, each section of the vegetable being buttered at the last minute before serving. The success of the dish depends upon its being served piping hot.— Stratton, *Favorite Recipes of Famous Women*, 38–39.

Hawaiian Salad

This is one of my favorite Hawaiian dishes, and it is much esteemed by the natives as a relish with their poi. It is called by them lomi'd salmon —from lomi-lomi, massage — the salt salmon being pulled to pieces by the fingers with much the same movement used in their famous massaging.

The salt salmon (salmon bellies are of course best) should be soaked for some hours in fresh water to mitigate the saltiness, and afterward thoroughly pulled to pieces with fingers or fork. It is then stirred in with raw sliced tomatoes and onions, and salted to taste. A diversion in this simple recipe can be made by adding sliced cucumber, and a squeeze of lemon, as well as paprika and minced green pepper.— Mary Archer, *Belgian Relief Cook Book* (Reading, Pa.: Reading Eagle, 1915); rpt. jacklondons.net/writings/jackLondonRecipes.html.

Italian Spaghetti

Boil one pound of Italian spaghetti for about half an hour. Be sure that the boiling water is first poured upon the spaghetti, as otherwise it will be disagreeably sticky. Peel and boil three good-sized tomatoes. When they are smooth add the juice from one can of French mushrooms and one tablespoon of cornstarch, already mixed with a little water, a clove of garlic, a pinch of cayenne pepper, a little salt and sage as seasoning. Take the mushrooms from which the juice has already been used, cut each of them once or twice and spread the pieces cold over the spaghetti after it has been placed upon a hot platter. Then pour the tomato sauce over the spaghetti and mushrooms, add a little Parmesan cheese and garnish with parsley.— *San Bernardino Sun*, September 7, 1907; rpt. jacklondons.net/writings/jackLondonRecipes.html.

Roast Duck

Born in Oakland, London remembered in his semi-autobiographical novel *John Barleycorn* (1913) how "wild ducks are cooked in the restaurants of San Francisco, and at once I am transported to the light and clatter of many tables, where I gaze at old friends across the golden brims of long-stemmed Rhine-wine glasses."[3] He later contributed a recipe for roast duck to a suffragist cookbook.

The only way in the world to serve a canvas-back or a mallard, or a sprig, or even the toothsome teal, is as follows: The plucked bird should be stuffed with a tight handful of plain raw celery and, in a piping oven, roasted variously 8, 9, 10, or even 11 minutes, according to size of bird and heat of oven. The blood-rare breast is carved with the leg and the carcass then thoroughly squeezed in a press. The resultant liquid is seasoned with salt, pepper, lemon and paprika, and poured hot over the meat. This method of roasting insures the maximum tenderness and flavor in the bird. The longer the wild duck is roasted, the dryer and tougher it becomes.— Kleber, *Suffrage Cook Book*, 46.

HENRY WADSWORTH LONGFELLOW

The unofficial poet laureate of the U.S., Henry Wadsworth Longfellow (1807–1882) resided for nearly 50 years at Craigie House near Harvard College in Cambridge, Massachusetts, where George Washington had resided while he planned the defense of Boston during the American Revolution. The recipes for some dishes his wife Fanny Longfellow prepared for him survive among his papers.

Veal Cutlets with Tomato Sauce

Prepare the cutlets of veal as usual and put them in a pan to stew with salt, pepper, butter, water enough to make a rich gravy. Let them stew till within half an hour of dinner and then pour over them a good quantity of tomato sauce and continue to stew till dished up — the time must depend on the size of the piece of veal.— Evelyn L. Beilenson, *Early American Cooking: Recipes from America's Historic Sites* (White Plains: Peter Pauper, 1985), 34.

Parlor at Craigie House in Cambridge, Massachusetts (Library of Congress).

Vegetable Soup

Slice 6 large carrots, 6 large onions, 4 large turnips, four beets or more and 3 stalks of celery. Put into the pot a piece of butter; — a piece of sugar as large as half an egg; they must not be allowed to discolor by remaining on the fire. When they begin to color they should be met with the soup made the day before; they must then be strained through a sieve. Do not suffer the soup to be too thick. Salt at discretion.— Beilenson, *Early American Cooking*, 34.

ANITA LOOS

The comic novelist and screenwriter Anita Loos (1888–1981) is best known for *Gentlemen Prefer Blondes* (1926) and *But Gentlemen Marry Brunettes* (1928).

Kitten's Tongue

Take 2 eggs and not quite a cup of sugar. Whip them just a little, then add not quite a cupful of melted butter and a cup of flour. Stir the mixture, spread it on a tin in small quantities, bake them. Roll in nuts and sugar.— Stratton, *Favorite Recipes of Famous Women*, 47.

JAMES RUSSELL LOWELL

James Russell Lowell (1819–1891) was one of the so-called Fireside or Schoolhouse Poets. He is best known today for *A Fable for Critics* (1848) and *The Biglow Papers* (1848, 1862).[1]

Eleanor Makes Macaroons

Light of triumph in her eyes,
Eleanor her apron ties;
As she pushes back her sleeves,
High resolve her bosom heaves.
Hasten, cook! impel the fire
To the pace of her desire;
As you hope to save your soul,
Bring a virgin casserole,
Brightest bring of silver spoons, —
Eleanor makes macaroons!
Almond blossoms, now advance
In the smile of Southern France,
Leave your sport with sun and breeze,
Think of duty, not of ease;
Fashion, 'neath their jerkins brown,
Kernels white as thistle-down,
Tiny cheeses made with cream
From the Galaxy's mid-stream,

Blanched in light of honeymoons, —
Eleanor makes macaroons!

Now for sugar, — nay, our plan
Tolerates no work of man.
Hurry, then, ye golden bees;
Fetch your clearest honey, please,
Garnered on a Yorkshire moor,
While the last larks sing and soar,
From the heather blossoms sweet
Where sea-breeze and sunshine meet,
And the Augusts mask as Junes, —
Eleanor makes macaroons!

Next the pestle and mortar find,
Pure rock-crystal, — these to grind
Into paste more smooth than silk,
Whiter than the milkweed's milk:
Spread it on a rose-leaf, thus,
Cate to please Theocritus;
Then the fire with spices swell,
While, for he'r completer spell,
Mystic canticles she croons, —
Eleanor makes macaroons!

Perfect! and all this to waste
On a graybeard's palsied taste!
Poets so their verses write,
Heap them full of life and light,
And then fling them to the rude
Mumbling of the multitude.
Not so dire her fate as theirs,
Since her friend this gift declares
Choicest of his birthday boons, —
Eleanor's dear macaroons!
—*The Complete Poetical Works of James Russell Lowell*
(New York: Grosset and Dunlap, 1908), 384–85.

CHARLES FLETCHER LUMMIS

Charles Fletcher Lummis (1859–1928) was an activist on behalf of Native American rights; founding editor of the magazine *Land of Sunshine*, later entitled *Out West*; and founder of the Southwest Museum in Los Angeles. Lummis contributed 43 recipes to a cookbook he edited in 1903 for the Landmarks Club, with proceeds from its sale financing the Club's efforts to restore the San Juan Capistrano mission and other crumbling landmarks of the Spanish era in California. He had "learned to cook for myself on the frontiers, and to cook well," he boasted, and his recipes were instrumental in introducing Spanish American cuisine to Anglos in the Southwest. These dishes were, he averred, on the whole simpler than our average United States menu,

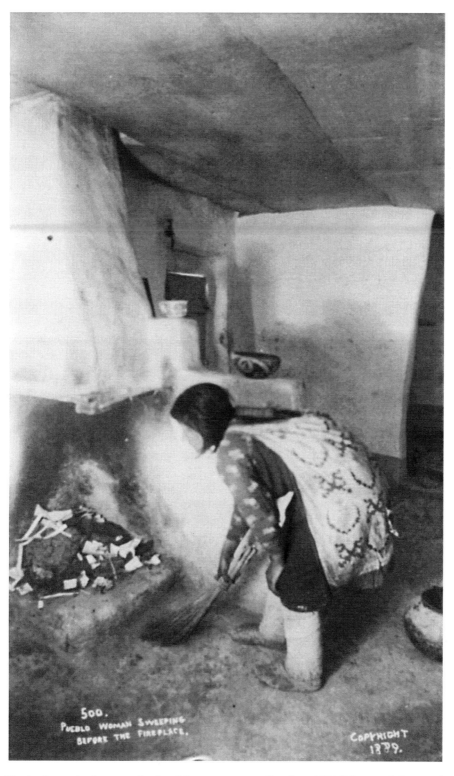

Charles Lummis photograph of an Isleta woman at a fireplace, 1889 (Library of Congress).

with less pastry, less meat, and flummididdle bread. Fruits, vegetables and soups are rather more predominant in it. For anti-bilious reasons it is much more highly seasoned than our own cookery. One of its characteristics is a liberal use of the chile, or native American red pepper, both green and ripe. This is not like the vicious cayenne or the venomous Tabasco, but sweeter, more agreeable and more healthful than either.

He printed recipes for many of these dishes native to "old-time California, New Mexico, Mexico and Peru" for the first time in English in the cookbook.[1]

Atole de Piña (Pineapple Gruel)

The Mexicans prepare the corn for *atole* in much the same way as for *tamales*: but it is very nice made as follows: Into five pints of fast-boiling water besprinkle eleven heaping table-spoons of Indian meal and one teaspoon of salt. Stir well and boil for an hour. Grate one-half of a large pineapple; mix with it one pound of sugar, a small bit of cinnamon, one pint of boiling water, stir well and strain into the boiling meal. Stir the mixture well again, pour into a pitcher and serve hot or cold. If cold, it looks pretty in glass custard cups.— Charles F. Lummis, *Landmarks Club Cookbook: A California Collection of the Choicest Recipes* (Los Angeles: Out West, 1903), 12.

Cajeta de Camote y Piña

Clarify one and one-half pounds of sugar, strain and place again on the fire, and let it boil until when you let it fall from the spoon it is clear and smooth as a mirror. Take it off the fire and add two pounds of *camote* (sweet potatoes) which have been boiled, mashed, and pressed through a sieve. Return to the fire, stir constantly so that it will not stick, and when you can see the bottom of the saucepan add one-quarter of a pineapple which has been grated on a bread grater, and strained. Place again on the fire until you can see bottom once more and it is done. Serve in a preserve dish and eat with a fork or spoon. This makes a delicious dessert, and is well worth any trouble to make.

Instead of pineapples, apples may be used in this recipe with great success, and it is much easier made. Peel, slice, and core one and one-half pounds of apples, stew very soft and add to the mixture in place of the pineapple.— Lummis, *Landmarks Club Cookbook*, 12.

Cajeta de Celaya

Six pints of cow's milk, three pints of goat's milk, mix and boil; allow it to cool, and remove the cream or scum. Burn one and one-half pounds sugar and then stir it into the milk, and add to it four and one-half pounds more of sugar and six ounces of ground rice. Place the mixture on the fire and let it boil until it is thick. One can tell this, if when one takes a little of the paste in a spoon and whirls it around it adheres to the spoon. Then remove from the fire and add half a pint of sherry, stir until it is well mixed, and pour into plates or pretty dishes.— Lummis, *Landmarks Club Cookbook*, 13.

Cajeta de Leche

Take six pints of milk, one and one-half pounds of brown sugar, and a tablespoon of flour. First clarify the sugar; that is, beat up the white of one egg thoroughly with a cup of cold water, and add this to the sugar dissolved with one of water. Heat the whole mixture until a scum appears. Remove from the fire and skim. Repeat until no scum arises. Then put three pints of the milk, the clarified sugar, and the flour (previously mixed with a little milk) in a saucepan on the fire. Stir it constantly, being careful not to remove the spoon, and let it boil until you can see the bottom of the saucepan. Then add another one and one-half pints of milk and repeat the operation; lastly add the remaining one and one-half pints of milk and continue to stir until you can again see the bottom of the saucepan.

Two things of importance are to stir constantly and never to take the spoon with which you are stirring it out of the saucepan until you remove it from the fire; then continue to stir briskly until it is thick. Pour on a plate, let it cool, and it is ready to serve.—Lummis, *Landmarks Club Cookbook*, 12–13.

Candied Peaches

Take twenty-five large peaches and let them lie in water for a little while; then remove the down by rubbing with a cloth. Stone them and put them in a kettle with two lbs granulated sugar—a layer of peaches and a layer of sugar—add one-half pint water and place on a moderate fire. When the syrup is thick, take off the fire, and put peaches and syrup together in a dish. Flatten the peaches with a wooden spoon and turn from time to time, putting them in a place where the sun will shine on them. When they are nearly dry roll in colored sugar. They will keep a long time.—Lummis, *Landmarks Club Cookbook*, 11.

Chile Sauce

The Mexican chile colorado or red pepper is sweeter and less vicious than the Eastern article, and is used in innumerable dishes. It is one of the most healthful condiments in the world, and almost a hygienic necessity in California and other non-humid lands. If an acquired taste, it is certainly one of the last to be given up.

For ordinary sauces, toast lightly your red chiles, dry or fresh, in the oven. Soak in water a few minutes, and grind on a milling-stone or in a mortar to a wet pulp. Strain in a colander to remove bits of skin. The "hotness" can be graduated by leaving or removing the seeds, which contain most of the fire. Add a little salt and a tablespoonful of vinegar and fry all together with a little butter.—Lummis, *Landmarks Club Cookbook*, 7–8.

Chiles Rellenos de Picadillo (Stuffed Green Peppers)

Choose large green peppers with a thick skin. Toast them for a few minutes (the Mexicans put them right on the coals, but they toast nicely on the stove or on a hot pan). Then remove the thin outer skin, the seeds and the veins, which are very hot (or, as the Mexicans say, "*muy bravo*"). Let them soak in salt and water for an hour: this will remove all unpleasant fieriness. Stuff and fry either plain or rolled in egg and bread crumbs; and before removing them from the fire pour over them some tomato sauce. To make the stuffing, chop up some cold meat fine, mix with it an onion, a clove, salt, all chopped fine, and cook; adding, if you wish, a sprinkle of vinegar. To make the sauce, toast the tomatoes in the same manner as the peppers, mash them with a little salt, strain and cook with a little butter.—Lummis, *Landmarks Club Cookbook*, 9.

Gato De Liebre (Hare Pie)

This dish will have a curious sound to many ears; but it is fit for a king, and held in grateful remembrance by those who have ever eaten it cooked by an expert. Even the "udder of a cow" can be procured by pre-arrangement with the butcher. This preparation disputes with the Swiss "Hassen pfeffer" precedence as the most delicious dish ever made from hare or jackrabbit.

Remove all bones, membranes and tendons from a hare (or jackrabbit) roasted beforehand. Pick to pieces roughly, and grind (upon a metate or in a mortar) all the meat, together with the boiled udder of a cow. Mix all, when ground, with bread crumbs moistened in soup, adding salt, pepper, parsley, a bit of garlic, thyme and bay leaves, all chopped very fine. Wet up with yolks of eggs, and give the whole another turn in the mortar. Cover the bottom of a tin pan with thin slices of ham or bacon, putting the preparation on top and covering it with other slices of ham or bacon. Bake in the oven; or cook in a steamer until done, and then fry brown. Remove from pan by putting the latter in boiling water. Remove the slices of bacon and cover the dish with bread crumbs.— Lummis, *Landmarks Club Cookbook*, 5–6.

Guaxolote en Mole Verde (Turkey in Green Sauce)

One of the simpler of scores of ways to prepare the famous Mexican dish of turkey "en mole" (mó-ly) is as follows:

Grind up well (on metate or in mortar) a good quantity of tomatoes with some toasted green chiles— taking the veins out of the latter if it be desired that the "mole" shall not "bite." Grind also one or two branches of green coriander. Fry the turkey raw in medium-sized pieces; and fry the tomatoes, chiles, and coriander by themselves. Then put the pieces of turkey in this sauce, add water, salt it and let it boil till tender; adding a little ground clove, some tiny green chiles, some very small summer-squash (boiled) and some twigs of coriander.— Lummis, *Landmarks Club Cookbook*, 7.

Ostras de la Buena Mujer (Good Woman's Oysters)

Slightly stew the oysters in their own liquor; dry them, and cut them up very fine. Mix up bread moistened in milk (no crusts), with parsley, onion and anchovies, all chopped very fine, salt and a little fresh butter. Knead up the oysters, stirring in several yolks of eggs. This mixture can be laid in cakes upon the shells or in a pan powdered with fine bread crumbs and put into the oven to brown.— Lummis, *Landmarks Club Cookbook*, 7.

Pichones Borrachos (Drunken Pigeons)

Stew your pigeons till nearly done. Toast a number of very red tomatos, remove the skins, and put them to fry with a good slice of bread (broken up) and a handful of almonds. Fry separately a little ground parsley (and a bit of garlic if desired), and add a pint of claret, all the broth in which the pigeons were cooked, a handful of raisins, a few pieces of citron, some ripe olives, a little sugar, cinnamon, pepper and clove. Put the pigeons into this broth and let them cook a few minutes until done.— Lummis, *Landmarks Club Cookbook*, 6.

Pollos de la Bella Mulata
(Chicken à la the Beautiful Mulatto)

For four small chickens, brown in lard half a pound of fresh pork, quarter of a pound of almonds, a piece of bread, four ripe tomatoes. Grind all in a mortar or metate. Fry onions chopped fine, with a little parsley (a bit of garlic if desired). Add the other ingredients and fry all together. Add the chickens, in the broth in which they have been fully cooked with pepper, salt, ground clove and cinnamon. Let come to a boil, add a cup of sherry, and serve.— Lummis, *Landmarks Club Cookbook*, 6–7.

Quesadillas de Prisa (Hurry-up Cheese Cakes)

Upon small and thin pancakes crumble cheese, old or fresh. Double the pancake over, and run a thread through the edges so the cheese cannot fall out. Put them in the oven or in the frying pan until the cheese begins to melt. Then the Quesadillas should be eaten hot — for when cold they lose all their flavor.— Lummis, *Landmarks Club Cookbook*, 7.

Stuffed Potatoes (Peru and Bolivia)

Mashed potato; salt, black pepper, raisins, olives; cloves; beef; hard-boiled egg.

Make a dough of the mashed potato, season with salt, pepper. Mince the cooked lean beef fine, and mold it to egg shape, with raisins— stoned, a little ground clove, minced egg and stoned olives. Cover this with the potato dough, and fry the roll, (which should be the size of a large goose egg), in hot lard, taking care not to burn, but only to give it a bright golden brown.— *How We Cook in Los Angeles*, 273.

JOHN D. MACDONALD

The recipient of a National Book Award in 1980, John D. MacDonald (1916–1986) was the author of the Travis McGee mystery novels. Like Rex Stout's detective Nero Wolfe and Robert B. Parker's Spenser, moreover, MacDonald's hero McGee is a gourmand.

Ceviche de Caracol

Get hold of two or three large, live conchs. Extract animal by punching a hole in the shell as far from the entrance as possible, then pulling animal out of his main entrance to his shell. Cut off digestive system, the dark streaky areas. Place white firm meat on rock and hammer it with a mallet, turning it between blows, so as to break down the tougher fibers.

Put the conch meat on a board and, with a very sharp knife, slice it into squarish morsels no bigger than large garden peas. Place in bowl and submerge completely in half and half lemon and lime juice, with a bit of wine vinegar. Chill for three hours.

While it chills, chop up half a small mild onion, half a fresh tomato, and one half of a small fresh green chili. Chop the chili very very fine. Chop some leaves of cilantro quite coarse. Take the bowl off the ice, pour off most of the juice, and stir in the items you have chopped. Serve in cocktail glasses with a fresh sprig of cilantro on top. Should serve four, but can be a hearty pre-dinner treat for two.— *The Great American Writers' Cookbook*, 127.

Meyer's Superior Cocktail Dip

Dry Chinese mustard moistened to the proper consistency with Tabasco sauce. The unsuspecting have been known to leap four feet straight up into the air after scooping up a tiny portion on a potato chip. Strong men have come down running and gone right through the wall when they missed the open doorway.—*The Dreadful Lemon Sky* (1975; rpt. New York: Ballantine, 1982), 134.

Tolbert's Chili for One Hundred

Tolbert's chili is also featured in MacDonald's *The Dreadful Lemon Sky*: "We three had sat with tears running down our cheeks and told each other in choked voices that the chili was truly delicious."[1]

30 pounds lean stewing beef, in ½ inch cubes
Cooking oil
1 pound kidney suet, rendered
90 red chili peppers, stemmed, seeded, scaled (reserve pepper water), peeled, and ground
1 cup dried oregano, heaping
1 cup crushed cumin seed, heaping
1 cup salt
1 cup powdered cayenne pepper
1 cup Tabasco
20 garlic cloves, chopped
3 level cups Masa Harina (ground Mexican cornmeal)
Unchopped chili pods, stemmed, skinned, and seeded
1 quart "mystery ingredient" (probably Tequila)

Sear beef, a little at a time, in oil. As it browns, remove to large kettle centered over driftwood fire. Add suet and ground chili peppers and enough pepper water to cover meat. When boiling, remove to edge of fire so it will simmer. After 30 minutes, remove from fire, add the next 6 ingredients, and return to center of fire. Bring to a boil and, when boiling, bring kettle to edge of fire and simmer for 45 minutes. Keep kettle covered except for frequent stirrings. Add more pepper water to keep from drying out. (If all pepper water is used, add plain water.) The chili, however, should be thick; so add liquid as sparingly as possible, just sufficient to prevent burning. Remove from fire, skim off fat, stir in cornmeal and return to edge of fire for 30 minutes more. Taste frequently and add some unground chili peppers, about ½ cup at a time, if the chili lacks authority. After last addition of peppers, simmer 30 minutes more. Remove from fire and stir in "mystery ingredient." Yield: 100 servings.—Nancy Webb and Jean Francis Webb, *Plots & Pans: Recipes and Antidotes from the Mystery Writers of America* (New York: Wynword, 1989), 90–91.

MARY PEABODY MANN

Pandowdy

A recipe for pandowdy or apple slump attributed to Louisa May Alcott is widely available on the Internet. It is an obvious fraud, however, because it specifies an oven temperature and rheostats were unknown during Alcott's life. On the other hand, a reliable recipe for the dish appeared in a cookbook compiled by Mary Peabody Mann (1806–1887), the wife of the educational reformer Horace Mann, sister of Elizabeth Palmer Peabody and Sophia Hawthorne, sister-in-law of Nathaniel Hawthorne, and author of *Juanita: A Romance of Real Life in Cuba Fifty Years Ago* (1887). Mary Mann's nephew Julian Hawthorne when well past 80 years old remembered the delicate pastry he had enjoyed during his boyhood: "We are not good enough for the goodness which it incarnated. Nor can I describe it, nor, if I could, could any contemporary cook or housewife concoct it? Yet how simple were the ingredients: apple, breadpaste, a spice or two. A wide and deep bowl of brown crockery held it; after the first baking, the crust had been broken up and mixed in and it was baked again."[1]

Fill a dish with stewed apples, sweetened and flavored. Cover it with a good paste of dough that has been mixed with milk; when this is baked nearly enough, take it off and break it into the apple and replace it in the oven. If the whole has become somewhat dry, pour over it a teacup of rich cream.— Mary Peabody Mann, *Christianity in the Kitchen* (Boston: Ticknor and Fields, 1858), 78–79.

Pigeon Soup

Of eight pigeons, cut up two and put them into four quarts of cold water, with the necks, livers and pinions of the rest; when they have simmered and boiled till the substance is extracted, strain out the soup, then restore it to the kettle with a handful of parsley, a handful of spinach, chopped and mixed with a pint of cream, in which a handful of bread crumbs have been boiled. Truss and season the pigeons with salt and a little mace, and boil them in the soup till they are tender.— Mann, *Christianity in the Kitchen*, 137.

Scalloped Oysters

Take out of the liquor two quarts of oysters, grate a loaf of bread, or eight soft crackers. Wet the pie dish with cream, sprinkle a thick layer of crumbs, and put on them a layer of oysters seasoned to the taste; pour over them a little rich cream, add another layer of crumbs and oysters, and thus alternately till the dish is filled. Turn over the whole as much oyster liquor as will fill the dish, and let it brown twenty or thirty minutes in the oven.— Mann, *Christianity in the Kitchen*, 81.

Sponge Cake

In Mann's *Juanita*, the characters enjoy a "golden panetala (the very ideal of sponge cake).[2]

This cake, if made right, is the least injurious of any form of cake, because it contains no butter. But it is very difficult to make it good. Eggs must be perfectly fresh, in the first place. They should be kept in cold water the night previous, and the whites should be beaten in a cool place, separately, and to a thick broth, with a cork stuck cross-wise upon a fork, and without stopping once. The sugar should be added to the whites after they are so beaten, and then the yolks, after being thoroughly beaten. This order is very important, and care should be taken that no portion of yolk should be mixed with the whites. It should also be done quickly, each ingredient being well prepared previously. Some persons stir the sugar into the yolks, but this is not so surely successful. Others add the whites to the yolks after both are thoroughly beaten, and then mix the flour and sugar, and stir them in. This is better than putting sugar and yolks together, but hardly as sure as to put sugar and whites together. A little rich cream, added to the above ingredients, will keep it moist longer. But too much will make it heavy.

Various proportions of egg, flour, and sugar are used. — Mann, *Christianity in the Kitchen*, 84–85.

Bobbie Ann Mason

The rural Kentucky roots of Bobbie Ann Mason (b. 1940), best known for her novel *In Country* (1985), are evident in the following recipe, which calls for country eggs.

Boiled Custard

4 cups milk
2 or 3 eggs, beaten thoroughly
⅓ cup sugar
2 teaspoons vanilla
Pinch of salt
Nutmeg

Put milk and salt in double boiler on high heat. Stir in sugar until it dissolves. Stir in beaten eggs gradually as milk heats. Begin adding them while milk is warm, not too hot. It's best to pour the eggs in from a measuring cup, slowly, in a thin stream while stirring the milk with the other hand. Cook the mixture, stirring until it coats the spoon. Remove from double boiler and stir in vanilla. Cool. Serve cold, with a sprinkling of grated nutmeg.

Boiled custard is usually served at Christmas, with cake. It is a thick liquid, similar to eggnog, but thicker, and it has a different flavor because the eggs are cooked.

Making the custard will require some trial and error and tasting. Knowing when the mixture coats the spoon is a subtle thing. Tasting it and recognizing when the eggs are cooked will be your best guide. It is best to beat the eggs well, even in a blender, in order to avoid lumps of boiled egg — unless you like it that way. The amount of sugar is also variable, to taste. One tablespoon per cup is fine with me.

This was my grandmother's recipe. She insisted on making it with country eggs, not store-bought eggs. Real country eggs are yellow when cooked, not pale. Boiled custard is a specific for the sick, especially if you are a child.

If you separate the eggs and beat the whites, you can make a floating island. Add the egg whites to the hot liquid at the end, when you're ready to remove the pan from the boiler. You can fold the whites in or spoon them on top and let them float. They should cook in their custard bath. — *The New Great American Writers' Cookbook*, 233.

Mary McCarthy

In her novel *The Group*, set in the 1930s, Mary McCarthy (1912–1989) illustrated changing American cooking customs by incorporating recipes into the text of the novel. Campbell's Condensed Tomato Soup was by the thirties a featured ingredient in hundreds of recipes.

Meat Loaf

Harald was teaching her to cook. His specialties were Italian spaghetti, which any beginner could learn, and those minced sea clams—terribly good—they had the other night, and meat balls cooked in salt in a hot skillet (no fat), and a quick-and-easy meat loaf his mother had taught him: one part beef, one part pork, one part veal; add sliced onions, pour over it a can of Campbell's tomato soup and bake in the oven. Then there was his chile con carne, made with canned kidney beans and tomato soup again and onions and half a pound of hamburger; you served it over rice, and it stretched for six people....

What made a dish, Kay said, was the seasonings. "Listen to how Harald fixes chipped beef. He puts in mustard and Worcestershire sauce and grated cheese — is that right?— and green pepper and an egg; you'd never think it bore any relation to that old milky chipped beef we got at college.... Kay leaned forward. "You ought to get your cook to try the new way of fixing canned beans. You just add catsup and mustard and Worcestershire sauce and sprinkle them with plenty of brown sugar, cover them with bacon, and put them in the oven in a Pyrex dish."— Mary McCarthy, *The Group* (New York: Harcourt, Brace, 1963), 63–64.

HERMAN MELVILLE

Herman Melville (1819–1891) completed *Moby-Dick* in 1851 while living on a farm in western Massachusetts.

Melville's kitchen at Arrowhead near Pittsfield, Massachusetts (Library of Congress).

Clam Chowder

In chapter 15 of *Moby Dick*, Melville described a memorable clam chowder.

It was made of small juicy clams, scarcely bigger than hazel nuts, mixed with pounded ship biscuit, and salted pork cut up into little flakes; the whole enriched with butter, and plentifully seasoned with pepper and salt.—Melville, *Moby-Dick* (New York: Harper and Bros., 1851), 73.

H. L. MENCKEN

Jump Stiddy

The pundit, longtime columnist for the *Baltimore Sun*, and critic of the American "booboisie," H. L. Mencken (1880–1956) was outspoken in his ridicule of Southern philistines. While he once protested that he had "no favorite dish" and knew "nothing whatsoever about cooking,"[1] he reported that on his second day in Tennessee to cover the Scopes "monkey trial" in 1925 he had been offered "a drink made up half of white mule and half of coca cola."[2] A decade later he published a similar recipe for a fictitious cocktail called the "jump stiddy" invented by the "troglodytes of western South Carolina" that consisted of "Coca-Cola and denatured alcohol (usually drawn from automobile radiators)" whose "connoisseurs reputedly preferred the taste of what had been aged in Model-T Fords."—North et al., *So Red the Nose*, n.p.

S. WEIR MITCHELL

S. Weir Mitchell (1829–1914) was a part-time novelist, author of *A Madeira Party* (1895) and the popular historical romance *Hugh Wynne, Free Quaker* (1897), as well as a Philadelphia physician and the leading nerve specialist in the country. He was best-known for pioneering the so-called rest cure, a treatment for nervous diseases such as neuresthenia and hysteria consisting of near-absolute bed rest, daily massages, and a milk-based, fatty diet.

Milk

Mitchell's women patients included Charlotte Perkins Gilman, Edith Wharton, Owen Wister's mother Sarah, and W. D. Howells' daughter Winifred. "It is difficult to treat any of these cases," he explained in his book *Fat and Blood*, "without a resort at some time more or less to the use of milk. In most dyspeptic cases—and few neurasthenic women fail to be obstinately dyspeptic—milk given at the outset, and given alone ... for a fortnight or less, enormously simplifies our treatment. Even after that, milk is the best and most easily managed addition to the general diet."[1] He detailed the ideal medical preparation of milk in his regimen.

Have the utmost care used as to preservation of the milk employed, and as to the perfect cleansing of all vessels in which it is kept. Use well-skimmed milk, as fresh as can be had, and, if possible, let it be obtained from the cow twice a day. At first the skimming should be thorough, and for the treatment of dyspepsia or albuminuria the milk must be as creamless as possible. The milk of the common cow is, for our purposes, preferable to that of the Alderney. It may be used warm or cold, but, except in rare cases of diarrhœa, should not be boiled.

It ought to be given at least every two hours at first, in quantities not to exceed four ounces, and as the amount taken is enlarged, the periods between may be lengthened, but not beyond three hours during the waking day, the last dose to be used at bedtime or near it. If the patient be wakeful, a glass should be left within reach at night, and always its use should be resumed as early as possible in the morning. A little lime-water may be added to the night milk, to preserve it sweet, and it should be kept covered.

The milk given during the day should be taken at set times, and very slowly sipped in mouthfuls; and this is an important rule in many cases. Where it is so disagreeable as to cause great disgust or nausea, the addition of enough of tea or coffee or caramel or salt to merely flavor it may enable us to make its use bearable, and we may by degrees abandon these aids. Another plan, rarely needed, is to use milk with the general diet and lessen the latter until only milk is employed. If these rules be followed, it is rare to find milk causing trouble; but if its use give rise to acidity, the addition of alkalies or lime-water may help us, or these may be used and the milk scalded by adding a fourth of boiling water to the milk, which has been previously put in a warm glass. Some patients digest it best when it has the addition of a teaspoonful of barley- or rice-water to each ounce, the main object being to prevent the formation of large, firm clots in the stomach.— Mitchell, *Fat and Blood* (Philadelphia: Lippincott, 1885), 99–101.

For about a pint of good, rich milk, take one good, fresh egg (if you can get it); while the milk is heating to the boiling point heat the egg in a good-sized bowl very lightly (yolk and white together); pour the boiling milk into the egg, stirring all the time to insure a smooth custard; add a bit of salt, with sugar and nutmeg and brandy, if you like it and need it. The milk is said in this way to cook the egg just enough to render it digestible. We have known and used this recipe in oft-repeated sickness, as well as in health, and can testify to its worth.— Louise E. Hogan, *Children's Diet in Home and School* (New York: Doubleday, Page, 1910), 112.

Raw Soup

At the close of the first week [of the rest cure] I like to add one pound of beef, in the form of raw soup. This is made by chopping up one pound of raw beef and placing it in a bottle with one pint of water and five drops of strong hydrochloric acid. This mixture stands on ice all night, and in the morning the bottle is set in a pan of water at 110° F. and kept two hours at about this temperature. It is then thrown on to a stout cloth and strained until the mass which remains is nearly dry. The filtrate is given in three portions daily. If the raw taste prove very objectionable, the beef to be used is quickly roasted on one side, and then the process is completed in the manner above described. The soup thus made is for the most part raw, but has also the flavor of cooked meat.— Mitchell, *Fat and Blood*, 115–16.

Tea

One pound of lean beef, cut fine; add one pint of cold water and five drops of muriatic acid. Put into a glass jar. Place the jar in a pan of water at 110°, and keep it at that temperature for two hours. Then strain through thick muslin until the meat is dry, or press the juice out by squeezing. The acid makes the tea agreeable to a patient with fever, and also aids in drawing out the juices of the meat.—*Mrs. Lincoln's Boston Cookbook*, 424.

VLADIMIR NABOKOV

"There is always a best way of doing everything, if it be to boil an egg," Ralph Waldo Emerson remarks in *The Conduct of Life* (1860).[1] As if to prove the point, over a century later, on November 18, 1972, the novelist Vladimir Nabokov (1899–1977), author of *Lolita* (1955), *Pale Fire* (1962), and *Ada* (1969), submitted a boiled-egg recipe to Maxime de la Falaise for publication in her book *Seven Centuries of English Cooking: A Collection of Recipes* (1972). However, de la Falaise failed to use it or even acknowledge its receipt. The manuscript survives among Nabokov's papers in the Berg Collection of the New York Public Library.

Eggs à la Nabocoque

Boil water in a saucepan (bubbles mean it is boiling!). Take two eggs (for one person) out of the refrigerator. Hold them under the hot tap water to make them ready for what awaits them.

Place each in a pan, one after the other, and let them slip soundlessly into the (boiling) water. Consult your wristwatch. Stand over them with a spoon preventing them (they are apt to roll) from knocking against the damned side of the pan.

If, however, an egg cracks in the water (now bubbling like mad) and starts to disgorge a cloud of white stuff like a medium in an old-fashioned seance, fish it out and throw it away. Take another and be more careful.

After 200 seconds have passed, or, say, 240 (taking interruptions into account), start scooping the eggs out. Place them, round end up, in two egg cups. With a small spoon tap-tap in a circle and then pry open the lid of the shell. Have some salt and buttered bread (white) ready. Eat.— Vladimir Nabokov Archive, Berg Collection, New York Public Library.

Lorine Niedecker

Lorine Niedecker (1903–1970), an Objectivist poet, lived her entire life in rural Wisconsin.

Bread Pudding

2 cups stale bread crumbs
1 quart scalded milk
⅓ cup sugar,
¼ cup melted butter
2 eggs
½ teaspoon salt
1 teaspoon vanilla or ¼ tsp spice
Soak bread crumbs in warm milk.
Set aside to cool; add sugar, butter, eggs slightly beaten, salt and flavoring;
bake one hr. in buttered pudding dish in slow oven, serve with vanilla sauce.— Hoard Historical Museum.

Chicken Loaf

(½ recipe for 2 people)
2 cups diced chicken
½ cups chopped cooked carrots

1 cup cooked peas
½ cups chopped celery
1 tablespoon minced green pepper
1 cup bread crumbs
½ cup milk
2 egg yolks beaten
1 teaspoon onion juice
1 teaspoon lemon juice
1 teaspoon salt
⅛ teaspoon pepper

—Hoard Historical Museum.

Corn and Cheese Fondue

Makes 4–6 servings
⅔ cup bread cubes
1½ cups cream style corn
2 teaspoons minced onion
2 teaspoons chopped green pepper
¾ cup finely grated cheddar cheese
½ teaspoon salt
2 eggs, well beaten
½ cup hot milk
Preheat oven to 350° F. Combine all ingredients in a bowl. Mix until well blended. Spoon into a greased 9-inch loaf pan. Set in pan of hot water. Bake 1 hour, or until knife inserted in center comes out clean.—Hoard Historical Museum.

Jello Salad

1 pkg. Lemon Jello, 1 pint boiling water (less 2 tablespoons), 2 tablespoon vinegar, ½ teaspoon salt, shake of cayenne pepper, 2 cups cabbage cut fine, 1 cups tart apple cut fine, 8 stuffed olives, cut fine.
Dissolve Jello in boiling water. Add vinegar, salt and pepper. Chill.
When slightly thickened, stir in cabbage, apples, and olives. Put into individual molds. Chill until firm. Serve on lettuce with mayonnaise. Serves 6.—Hoard Historical Museum.

Swedish Meatballs

Serves 4
1 pound ground Beef
¼ pound ground Pork (sausage Meat)
3 teaspoon butter
½ cup crumbs
1 egg slightly beaten
1 teaspoon salt and pepper
¼ teaspoon nutmeg
1 can tomato soup plus

1 can beef bouillon or consommé
Combine meat, seasoning, crumbs & egg into balls. Brown in butter.
Add soup. Simmer for about 1 hour.—Hoard Historical Museum.

CATHERINE OWEN

Catherine Owen, aka Helen Alice Nitsch (d. 1889), was adept at such cookbook novels as *Ten Dollars Enough* (1886) and *Gentle Breadwinners* (1887).

American Walnut Catsup

Take 100 green walnuts while you can run a knitting needle through them. Sprinkle half a pound of salt over them, after bruising them. Let them remain in a wooden vessel six days or eight, beating and mashing them well every day. When they are soft and pulpy, press them well, pile them up on one side the tub, and tilt it so that the juice runs to the other side; take this out from day to day, always pounding the nuts afresh and pressing them to the side till the liquid ceases to flow; simmer the liquid till no more scum rises; then to every three quarts of it add two ounces of best ginger, two ounces of allspice, one of whole pepper, one of cloves, all bruised; boil slowly half an hour; bottle when quite cold, dividing the spice so that each bottle may get its own proportion. They must be quite full, tightly corked and dipped into melted resin, or bottle wax; lay them on their sides in a dry, cool place. It is good in six months, but better in a year.— Owen, *Gentle Breadwinners* (Boston: Houghton Mifflin, 1887), 73–74.

Cigarettes à la Reine

These are the newest development of the rissole and croquette. They require strict attention to details to secure perfect form. Roll puff paste a quarter of an inch thick; prick it all over — this is to deaden it; roll it now till it is no thicker than cartridge paper. Cut it with a sharp knife dipped in flour into strips about two inches and a half wide and about the length of a cigar; lay on each strip a roll of chicken quenelle meat that is very firm, and the roll not thicker than a lady's slender forefinger; be careful that the meat reaches nearly the whole length of the paste, yet leaves a margin for closing, as the least oozing will spoil the appearance. Moisten the edges of the paste all round with white of egg; fold the paste over half an inch; be very careful to see that it adheres thoroughly; then pinch the ends. Roll them gently with a cool hand on the floured board to round them without pressure, taper off the ends cigar fashion. If they are softening, lay them on a floured plate on ice to get firm; then roll them in egg and very finely sifted cracker meal. You may roll or improve the shape, if there is any irregularity, while crumbing them. Remember what you aim to imitate is a cigar. The great danger for the first time is getting them too large; they must therefore be very slender. Fry in deep fat just as rissoles; serve on a napkin, log-house fashion. These dainties, as will have been seen, have a large amount of butter, and soften in a warm room; they must therefore be made in a cold room, and if set on ice some hours before cooking will be much easier to fry without bending or twisting.— Owen, *Choice Cookery* (New York: Harper and Bros., 1889), 135.

Compote of Pigeons

For any dish of pigeons except roast or broiled, wild birds may be used in place of tame. Their flavor is far finer, and if not perfectly young, which is the main objection to the use of wild birds, the preparation remedies the defect. Cut four ounces of lean unsmoked bacon into pieces, and fry five minutes. Split the pigeons in half, skewer each half as neatly as possible with tiny skewers, so that they will not sprawl when dished; flour and season them lightly, and fry a nice brown on both sides; add one small carrot, one small turnip, two sticks of celery, one shallot, six mushrooms— all cut small; add a *bouquet garni* and three gills of rich stock; let them all simmer very slowly in a stew pan for one hour, or longer if the birds are not young. Simmer together a tablespoonful of flour and one of butter; pepper and salt (quantities depend on whether the stock be seasoned); stir constantly, and when they begin to change color pour a gill of brown stock to it, stirring well; remove from the fire. Take up the pigeons, strain the gravy, then stir in the brown thickening you have made; boil up, skim off all fat, then return the birds; let them get thoroughly hot, but not boil. Serve on a border of mashed potatoes, pour the gravy round and over them, and fill the center with peas or spinach.— Owen, *Choice Cookery*, 145–46.

Cutlets Chaudfroid à la Russe

For this cold dish mutton cutlets are used. They must be of the finest quality, and from mutton not newly killed. Cut as many cutlets as required, trim, and scrape the bone. Braise for an hour in a moderate oven till the meat is very tender, remove, and press between two dishes until they are cold. Then trim each cutlet into perfect shape. Boil a quart of strong stock (which already jellies) down to less than half a pint; dip each chop into this glaze once or twice, till they look "varnished." You now require a pint of stiff aspic jelly; turn it out of the bowl, cut one or two slices a quarter of an inch thick from it, to be cut into shapes (or croûtons) with a cutter to garnish the cutlets. Chop the rest of the aspic, lay it round the dish, and the cutlets against it, with the croûtons of aspic to form the outer edge. The center must be filled with a Russian salad, in this case stirred up with very thick mayonnaise, instead of being formally arranged. The mayonnaise must be only sufficient to dress the vegetables, none to run into the other materials, and beet-root must be added last, as it discolors the sauce if stirred up in it.— Owen, *Choice Cookery*, 103.

Genoa Cake

One half pound of shelled almonds
One half pound of citron
One half pound of powdered sugar
One half pound of butter
One half pound of flour
Five eggs
A small wineglass of sherry
One (or two, if not strong) tablespoonfuls of rose-water

Dorothy first separated eggs and beat both whites and yolks, weighed and put to get dry and warm half a pound of flour, weighed butter and sugar and almonds of each half a pound; then she blanched the almonds by pouring boiling water on them; then slipping them out of the skins, which are quite loose when scalded, she laid them between a cloth to dry while she cut the citron, first in thin strips, then in half inch pieces. The almonds were divided into two equal parts, the first chopped as small as peas and put to the citron, the other chopped a little finer and set aside; she dredged a little flour among the citron and large chopped almonds, shook them together and put them to warm, but not get hot. Dorothy had everything she needed round her, and put away everything she did not want before she got her hands into the cake. Mrs. Bevan had contributed a glass of a treasured bottle of sherry, and then the work began.

The butter and sugar (the latter slightly warmed) were put into a bowl, and Dorothy with her right hand at first worked, then beat them back and forth, until they were nearly white and like cream, then the beaten yolks of the eggs were gradually added, beating all the time; the wine was poured in little by little, then the rose-water.... Afer five minutes' more beating, the flour was gently sifted in, and the whites of the eggs. It was now a very stiff batter, which Dorothy beat five minutes more, and then the almonds and citron were added, and just stirred in, but not beaten at all. The whole was now poured into the pan, which was lined with buttered paper, and the remainder of the almonds sprinkled very carefully and evenly over the surface until the batter was nearly hidden by them. The cover of a cardboard box was laid tightly on the cake and it was put into the oven.

"You are sure you want the oven as cool as that, Dora?" asked Mrs. Bevan, who was a deeply interested onlooker.

"Yes, aunt; it must be what you would call a cool bread oven, about 230°, if we had an oven thermometer, which if I do much cooking I shall get. I shall leave the cover on for one hour, then let it brown, or rather become a fine salmonish yellow; it if shows signs of getting darker before the cake is done the cover goes on again, but with a steady oven I don't believe it will."

The cake, after it had been baking an hour and three quarters, was tried by inserting a broom twig, which came forth dry.— Owen, *Gentle Breadwinners*, 38, 42–46.

Mock Haggis

This good dish was made of haslet (or pluck) of pig when she could get it, but at other times of lamb or of sheep, which the butcher always sells for ten cents.

Detach liver and heart from the windpipe, leave the lights on it, wash all well, and put the lights on in a saucepan of salted water; leave the pipe hanging out so that the lights may disgorge. They require at least two hours' boiling, and are better prepared the day before; parboil the liver and heart for twenty minutes, preserve the water; cut the liver, heart, and half the boiled lights into small dice. Use, if possible, a stone pot with a cover; lay at the bottom three or four shaved slices of fat bacon, pork, or the fat of boiled ham (unless you have a pig's haslet, when there is a delicious frilled fat that should be with it). Put a layer of the liver, heart, and lights, and then one of forcemeat made of half a pint of bread crumbs, two teaspoonfuls of sage leaves, dried and rubbed between the hands very fine, and two large onions, parboiled and chopped fine (after boiling), mixed together with a good tea-spoonful of salt and a scant saltspoonful of pepper. After a thin layer of this put another of the liver, lights, and heart, then more forcemeat, and so on until all is in; then pour in a pint of the water the liver was boiled in, put on the cover, and tie stout brown paper over all, or make flour and water paste and lay around the cover to keep in steam; set the jar in the oven, and leave it to cook slowly three hours. When the lid is removed and the dish turned out, the fragrance will remove any doubts as to haslet being acceptable food.— Owen, *Gentle Breadwinners*, 169–70.

WALKER PERCY

Walker Percy (1916–1990) was a southern novelist best known for *The Moviegoer* (1961), for which he received a National Book Award for Fiction, and *Love in the Ruins* (1971).

Cud'n Walker's Uncle Will's Favorite Mint Julep Receipt

You need excellent Bourbon whiskey; rye or Scotch will not do. Put half an inch of sugar in the bottom of the glass and merely dampen it with water. Next, very quickly — and here is the trick in the procedure — crush your ice, actually powder it — preferably in a towel with a wooden mallet, so quickly that it remains dry, and, slipping two sprigs of fresh mint against the inside of the glass, cram the ice in right to the brim, packing it with your hand. Finally, fill the glass, which apparently has no room left for anything else, with Bourbon, the older the better, and grate a bit of nutmeg on the top. The glass will frost immediately. Then settle back in your chair for half an hour of cumulative bliss. — Percy, *Signposts in a Strange Land* (New York: Farrar, Straus and Giroux, 1991), 107.

KATHERINE ANNE PORTER

Katherine Anne Porter (1890–1980) received a Pulitzer Prize and National Book Award in 1966 for her collected stories. She also compiled an extensive private collection of recipes.

Genuine Mole Poblana

In January 1962 Porter transcribed a recipe for "genuine Mole Poblana" given to her by her maid Eufemia while living in Mexico early in the 1930s. The typescript survives in the Southwestern Writers Collection at Texas State University in San Marcos. As Patricia Sharpe allows, "With its recommendation to use canned mole powder, the recipe is hardly a culinary masterpiece."[1]

She, of course, started by frying 7 kinds of dried hot peppers, all sizes and degrees of heat, parching almonds in fat, grinding bitter chocolate, etc. and reducing all to black oily pulp on the grinding stone. We will do as well — but more simply. You will need 1 Pint strong fresh chicken broth made the day before from a bundle of backs and necks. Chill in refrigerator overnight, skim off fat....

1 double square of bitter chocolate — (an ounce, more or less).

4 tablespoons Clemente Jaques Mole Powder.

1 teaspoon each Oregano and Cumin Seed.

4 Ounces Shelled Almonds, parched and ground — Easy way, put in blender with the chicken broth.

Salt to taste.

Grind the almonds and chicken broth together in blender, (together with 4 tablespoons of Mole Powder, the Oregano and Cumin.) Add chocolate. Pour over [previously prepared] chicken — mix well — it will be a rich dark sauce. Cover tightly and put in moderate oven until well cooked and blended. — Patricia Sharpe, "Saucy," *Texas Monthly* 25 (January 1997), 30.

MARJORIE KINNAN RAWLINGS

Recipient of a Pulitzer Prize for her novel *The Yearling* (1938), Marjorie Kinnan Rawlings (1896–1953) followed its success with a memoir of her life in rural Florida entitled *Cross Creek* (1942) and, in the same year, a collection of regional recipes entitled *Cross Creek Cookery*. According to a feature story in the *Saturday Evening Post* at the height of her popularity, "Cooking is author Marjorie Kinnan Rawlings's one vanity, and hunting for her food her chief pastime…. Alligators, turtles, blue ocean crabs, blackbirds, limpkins— long-billed tropical birds— possum, swamp cabbage — heart of palm — wild mustard greens, and a magic salad of pokeweeds dressed with the juice of wild oranges— all of these find a place on her exciting table." In *Cross Creek Cookery* she "tells of her cooking adventures and sets forth her rich and readily edible recipes. Some she inherited from her mother and grandmother."[1]

Alligator-Tail Steak

"Surely we may all be allowed our prejudices," Rawlings allowed in *Cross Creek*, "and I have none against steaks from the tail of an alligator. I can say dispassionately that properly cooked it is a great delicacy. The meat is pink and clean, like veal, and is similar in flavor."[2] She included a recipe for alligator-tail steak in *Cross Creek Cookery*.

Rattlesnake meat is canned commercially in Florida and served as a delicate hors-dœuvre. I have never tried it and do not intend to. It is said to taste much like canned tuna. *Chacun à son gout….*

Steak from the tail of an alligator is another matter. It is truly delicious. It is like liver or veal (which it resembles in texture and coloring) in that it must be cooked very quickly or a very long time. In between, it toughens. Cut strips lengthwise of the tail, four inches long and two inches wide, or cut cross-sections between the vertebræ. Roll in salted and peppered flour and fry quickly in butter. It may also be browned in the butter, hot water and the juice of a lemon added, and simmered for two to two and one-half hours until tender.— Rawlings, *Cross Creek Cookery* (New York: Scribner's, 1942), 111.

Blackbird Pie

"I speak with some trepidation of my blackbird pie," Rawlings admitted in *Cross Creek*,

> for it might have brought down on me Federal dishonor, or roughly speaking, jail. I began the shooting of the blackbirds and the making of the pies in a spirit of innocent experimentalism. I sat in a blind on Orange Lake on my first duck hunt. Around and beyond me the good shots were bringing down their ducks. I had not touched a feather. Nearby, hundreds of red-winged blackbirds were stirring in the tussocks. I thought of the four and twenty blackbirds baked in a pie and wondered if these grain and seed eating birds might not be the edible ones of the rhymed fable. I slipped No. 10 shells into my shotgun, and two shots brought down a dozen birds. I made the dozen very secretly into a pie. It was utterly delicious. For the next few years, when game was scarce, or I had not been to market for meats, I relied on black birds to make a tasty dish…. The blackbirds were exquisite morsels of sweet and tender dark meat. Then I began to be ashamed of shooting the cheerful chirruping things that were so ornamental in the marshes. I decided I would do not more of it. And then I discovered that they were listed on my hunting license, by a name I had not

recognized, among the birds protected by Federal game laws and forbidden to the hunter.[3]

Rawlings advised the readers of *Cross Creek Cookery* to substitute for the red-winged blackbirds "any small birds" such as "ricebirds (legal in season), quail, dove, or one-pound-size chickens."

Brown the whole dressed birds in one tablespoon butter to every bird. Cover with hot water. Add one bay leaf, one teaspoon salt and a dash of pepper. Simmer until tender, tightly covered. Add one carrot cut in strips and two small whole onions to every bird. Simmer fifteen minutes. Add one small raw potato, diced, to every bird. Simmer fifteen minutes more. More hot water may be needed, as gravy should cover mixture. Thicken gravy with one tablespoon flour dissolved in two tablespoons cold water to every cup of gravy. Place mixture in casserole, add two tablespoons chopped parsley, one-quarter cup sherry to every bird, and cover with biscuit crust as for steak and kidney pie. Bake in hot oven twenty minutes or until well browned. Four birds per person are right, so that for six people, one has truly "four and twenty blackbirds baked in a pie."— Rawlings, *Cross Creek Cookery*, 119.

Crab à la Newburg

Rawlings caught fresh crab in the swamps and hammocks near her home. "When we have crab meat to spare," she wrote in *Cross Creek*, "I make a crab Newburg so superlative that I myself taste it in wonder, thinking, 'Can it be I who has brought this noble thing into the world?'"[4]

2 heaping cupfuls of crab meat
½ cup of butter
2 cupfuls of cream
2 tablespoons flour
Juice of 1 lemon
4 eggs
¾ teaspoon salt
Pepper
Dash of clove
½ teaspoon paprika
½ cup dry sherry
1 tablespoon brandy
Serves 4 to 6 according to appetite

Melt the butter in an iron skillet but do not brown. Stir in the crab meat gently. Sauté for one minute. Add lemon juice. Stir in flour. Add cream slowly, stirring constantly and lightly. When sauce is smooth, add salt, pepper, clove and paprika and let mixture bubble five minutes. Have ready the piping hot serving dish, hot plates and toast points. Warn the guests to drink their last cocktail or highball. Stir in the sherry. Beat the eggs just short of foaminess and stir in quickly. Add the brandy. Rush the Newburg, garnished with parsley, and the guests, instantly to table. Serve with any dry white wine and any green salad made with French dressing. Sit back and await compliments.— Rawlings, *Cross Creek Cookery* (New York: Scribner's, 1942), 83–84.

Marjorie Kinnan Rawlings crabbing at Salt Springs (photograph by Jacob Lofman, courtesy Marjorie Kinnan Rawlings Collection, Department of Special and Area Studies Collections, George A. Smathers Libraries, University of Florida, Gainesville).

Okra à la Cross Creek

Despite its reputation as a pedestrian plant, Rawlings insisted, "Okra is a Cinderella among vegetables. It lives a lowly life, stewed stickily with tomatoes, or loss of identity in a Creole gumbo."[5]

Have ready boiling, lightly salted water. Choose only tiny very young fresh okra pods. Wash. Do not cut off the stem end, as you trust me. Drop whole pods in rapidly boiling water and boil exactly seven minutes from the time the water resumes its boiling. Not a moment longer. Drain quickly. Arrange like the spokes of a wheel on hot individual serving dishes. Place individual bowls of Hollandaise in the centers of the dishes. The okra is eaten as one eats unhulled strawberries, lifting with the fingers by the stem end and dipping into the Hollandaise. I recommend this to those who think they don't like okra. It is firm, not slimy, and with the sauce, superb. I usually serve twelve okra pods per person.   Rawlings, *Cross Creek Cookery*, 51–52.

Wild Duck

> Never a devotee of French cooking, Rawlings offered her readers a rustic method of cooking ducks. "I am in violent opposition to the pretendedly Epicurean school of raw bloody duck whisked through a duck press. The advice to 'run your duck through a very hot oven' leaves me shuddering. I prefer my thoroughly done, moist, crumbling duck to any dripping, rubbery slices, fit only for the jaws of a dinosaur."[6]

The ducks must be properly aged — after dressing—from three to five days, without freezing. The flavor needs no embellishment, and I do not even use the conventional onion or celery or apple stuffing. I place them, dressed whole, salted and peppered, breast side up, in a tightly covered roasting pan with an inch of hot water in the pan. The oven is hot, four hundred and fifty degrees, for the first fifteen minutes. The heat is then reduced to three hundred and fifty degrees for the remaining time of cooking. Young ducks will roast in a little over an hour. For old ducks, I allow from two to three hours. They should be based every fifteen minutes with the liquid in the pan. I allow one-half duck per person. An occasional guest can eat a whole duck, but is not encouraged.— Rawlings, *Cross Creek Cookery*, 101–02.

Mary Roberts Rinehart

> Mary Roberts Rinehart (1876–1958) wrote popular murder mystery novels, among them *The Circular Staircase* (1908).

Baked Tomatoes

8 large smooth tomatoes
2 green peppers
1 teaspoon salt
1½ pints milk
1 good sized onion
1½ tablespoon sugar
flour

Wash tomatoes, do not peel, slice piece from top of each and scoop out a little of the tomato. Cut peppers in two lengthwise and remove seeds— place in cold water. Now put onion and peppers through meat chopper, sprinkle a little sugar and a little salt over each tomato and place in good sized baking dish; now put ground onion and ground peppers on top of tomato.

Put butter in skillet and when melted, not brown, stir in flour until a paste is formed, now add gradually the milk as you would for cream dressing, stir constantly.

The dressing must be very thick to allow for the water from the tomatoes. Put *this* sauce around the tomatoes, not on top and place in a moderate oven to bake about one hour slow. Serve if possible in the same dish in which it was baked as it is very attractive.— Kleber, *Suffrage Cook Book*, 80.

KENNETH ROBERTS

Kenneth Roberts (1912–1989) was a popular historical novelist, author of *The Lively Lady* (1931) and *Northwest Passage* (1937).

Beans

My grandmother's beans were prepared like this: Four cupfuls of small white beans were picked over to eliminate the worm-holed specimens and the small stones that so mysteriously intrude among all beans, then covered with water and left to soak overnight. Early the next morning, usually around five o'clock, they were put in a saucepan, covered with cold water and heated until a white scum appeared on the water. They were then taken off the stove, the water thrown away, and the beanpot produced. In the bottom of the beanpot was placed a one-pound piece of salt pork, slashed through the rind at half-inch intervals, together with a large peeled onion; then the beans were poured into the pot on top of the pork and onion. On the beans were put a heaping teaspoon of mustard, half a cup of molasses, and a teaspoon of pepper; the beanpot was filled with boiling water, and the pot put in a slow oven. At the end of two hours, a tablespoon of salt was dissolved in a cup of boiling water and added to the beans. Every hour or so thereafter the cover was removed, and enough boiling water poured in to replace that which had boiled away. An hour before suppertime, the cover was taken off for good, the salt pork pulled to the top, and no more water added. Thus the pork, in the last hour, was crisped and browned, and the top layer of beans crusted and slightly scorched. When the beans were served, the pork was saved and the scorched beans skimmed off and thrown away. The two great tricks of bean-making seemed to be the frequent adding of water up to the final hour of baking, so that no part of the beans had an opportunity to become dry, and the removal of the cover during the last hour.— Kenneth Roberts, *Trending into Maine* (Boston: Little, Brown, 1938), 153–54.

Hot Buttered Rum

Pour one fair-sized drink (or jigger) of rum into an ordinary table tumbler: add one lump of sugar, a pat of butter the size of a single hotel helping, half a teaspoonful of cinnamon, fill up the tumbler with boiling water, stir well and sip thoughtfully. If too sweet, use less sugar in the next attempt. If not sweet enough, add more. If the cinnamon isn't wholly satisfactory, try cloves. If more butter seems desirable, use more.— Roberts, *Trending into Maine*, 162.

Stewed Coot

Place the bird in a kettle of water with a red building-brick free of mortar and blemishes. Parboil the coot and the brick together for three hours. Pour off the water, refill the kettle, and again parboil for three hours. For the third time throw off the water, for the last time add fresh water, and let the coot and the brick simmer together overnight. In the morning throw away the coot and eat the brick.— Roberts, *Trending into Maine*, 159–60.

THEODORE ROOSEVELT

Before he became a national political figure, Theodore Roosevelt (1858–1919) penned *The Naval War of 1812* (1882), *Hunting Trips of a Ranchman* (1885), *Ranch Life and the Hunting Trail* (1888), and the four-volume *The Winning of the West* (1889–1896). He also served as the New York City police commissioner, a colonel in the volunteer cavalry regiment known as the Rough Riders in Cuba during the Spanish-American War, and vice president of the United States before succeeding to the presidency upon William McKinley's assassination in September 1901.

Mint Julep — Kentucky Style

In May 1913, soon after his failed campaign for president on the Progressive Party ticket in 1912, Roosevelt sued George Newett, editor of a Michigan newspaper, for libel and damages in the amount of $10,000 for asserting in print that the former president was a habitual drunk. Roosevelt testified that in the years since he had left the White House in 1909 he had put only two mint juleps to his lips. He had sipped

White House kitchen circa 1902 (Library of Congress).

White House State dining room between 1889 and 1906, photographed by Frances Benjamin Johnston (Library of Congress).

part of one, he said, at the St. Louis Country Club in October 1910.[1] The *St. Louis Post Dispatch* jokingly accused TR of perjury because the juleps blended by Tom Bullock, the club bartender, were too delicious not to finish. "To believe that a red-blooded man, and a true Colonel at that, ever stopped with just a part of one of those refreshments and have made St. Louis hospitality proverbial," the paper editorialized, "is to strain credulity too far."[2] After Roosevelt won his suit and waived damages, Bullock published a bar guide titled *The Ideal Bartender*, which included his recipe for the drink.

Use a large Silver Mug.

Dissolve one lump of Sugar in one-half pony of Water.

Fill mug with Fine Ice.

Two jiggers of Old Bourbon Whiskey.

Stir well; add one boquet of Mint and serve.

Be careful and not bruise the Mint.— Bullock, *The Ideal Bartender* (St. Louis: Buxton and Skinner, 1917), 43.

Spice Cake

Edith Kermit Carow Roosevelt (1861–1948), Roosevelt's second wife and First Lady of the United States from 1901 to 1909, published her recipe for Spice Cake while living in the White House.

One cup butter, 2 cups sugar, 1 cup milk, 4 eggs, 4 cups flour, 2 teaspoonfuls Royal Baking Powder, 1 teaspoonful ground cinnamon, ½ teaspoonful nutmeg.—*Famous Old Receipts*, 285.

Theodore Roosevelt's dining room at Sagamore, Oyster Bay, New York (Library of Congress).

DORI SANDERS

Dori Sanders (b. 1934), the daughter of a South Carolina sharecropper and the author of the novels *Clover* (1990) and *Her Own Place* (1993), continues to farm the family homestead and to sell peaches grown there.

Easy Peach Cobbler

Serves 6 to 8

As this cobbler bakes, the batter bubbles up through the peaches to form a crusty topping. For that reason, some cooks call it "miracle pie." Whatever you call it, it couldn't be easier.

½ cup unsalted butter, melted
1 cup all-purpose flour
2 cups sugar, or to taste
3 teaspoons baking powder
A pinch of salt
1 cup milk
4 cups peeled, pitted and thinly sliced fresh peaches (5 to 6 medium peaches)
1 tablespoon fresh lemon juice
Several dashes ground cinnamon or ground nutmeg (optional)

1. Preheat oven to 375° F.

2. Pour the melted butter into a 13 inch by 9 inch by 2 inch baking dish.

3. In a medium bowl, combine the flour, 1 cup of the sugar, the baking powder, and the salt and mix well. Stir in the milk, mixing until just combined. Pour this batter over the butter but do not stir them together.

4. In a small saucepan, combine the peaches, lemon juice, and remaining cup of sugar and bring to a boil over high heat, stirring constantly. Pour the peaches over the batter but do not stir them together. Sprinkle with cinnamon or nutmeg if desired.

5. Bake in the preheated oven for 40 to 45 minutes or until the top is golden brown. Serve warm or cold.—*Dori Sanders' Country Cooking: Recipes and Stories from the Family Farm Stand* (Chapel Hill: Algonquin, 1995), 78–79.

SATURDAY CLUB OF BOSTON

Founded in 1855, the Saturday Club met the fourth Saturday of every month over dinner at the Parker House in Boston. Among its members were Ralph Waldo Emerson, James Russell Lowell, Henry Wadsworth Longfellow, Nathaniel Hawthorne, Oliver Wendell Holmes, John Greenleaf Whittier, and the publisher James T. Fields. Their meals featured "seven courses at least, with sherry, sauterne, and claret"[1] and, no doubt, Parker House rolls, invented at the hotel in the mid–1860s. According to the chef and food writer James Beard, Parker House rolls are "as much of a tradition in the United States as any bread…. They have been copied by every cookbook author and every baker in the country."[2] The original recipe appears in *The White House Cookbook*.

Parker House Rolls

One pint of milk, boiled and cooled; a piece of butter the size of an egg; one-half cupful of fresh yeast; one tablespoonful of sugar, one pinch of salt, and two quarts of sifted flour.

Melt the butter in the warm milk, then add the sugar, salt and flour, and let it rise overnight. Mix rather soft. In the morning, add to this half of a teaspoonful of soda dissolved in a spoonful of water. Mix in enough flour to make the same stiffness as any biscuit dough; roll out not more than a quarter of an inch thick. Cut with a large round cutter; spread soft butter over the tops and fold one-half over the other by doubling it. Place them apart a little so that there will be room to rise. Cover, and place them near the fire for fifteen or twenty minutes before baking. Bake in rather a quick oven.— Gillette, *The White House Cookbook*, 224–25.

BENJAMIN SHILLABER

The "down East" humorist Benjamin Shillaber (1814–1890), author of *Life and Sayings of Mrs. Partington* (1854) and *Partingtonian Patchwork* (1873), was so well-known among his contemporaries that his wife Lydia published a cookbook.

Boston Baked Beans

In Lydia's cookbook, she featured a recipe for Boston Baked Beans, one of the signature foods of New England. The poet Lucy Larcom explained that the dish was popular as a result of "the Puritanic custom of saving Sunday-work by baking beans on Saturday evening, leaving them in the oven overnight."[1]

Dried pea beans, one quart
Salt pork, half a pound
Granulated sugar or molasses, two tablespoonfuls
Salt and pepper
Put on the beans in plenty of cold water, and let them come to a boil. Parboil until the skins "wrinkle," changing the water two or three times. Drain, and wash thoroughly. Put in a deep "Boston beanpot," and lay the pork, scored, over the top. Add the sugar and salt, and pour over them boiling water enough to cover them. Bake from eight to twelve hours, keeping a cover over the top until an hour before serving. Add more boiling water once or twice. To serve, remove the pork first, then pour out the beans. Do not dip out with a spoon.—*Mrs. Shillaber's Cookbook: A Practical Guide for Housekeepers* (New York: Crowell, 1887), 244–45.

Cucumber Catsup

Cut cucumbers in small pieces, or grate them. Sprinkle them with salt, and let them stand twenty-four hours. Then strain off the water, and add a pinch of black pepper, some black and white mustard seed, and a little celery seed. Add a little chopped onion. Cover all with vinegar, and it is ready for use.—*Mrs. Shillaber's Cookbook*, 87.

LYDIA SIGOURNEY

The popular poet, historian, and romancer Lydia Sigourney (1791–1865), aka "the sweet singer of Hartford," was the author of more than 2000 articles and some 67 books.

Apples with Cream

Sigourney composed her recipe for Apples with Cream in trochaic tetrameter, the same meter as Longfellow's *Hiawatha* (1855), published only three years earlier.

Have you any Greening apples?
If you have not, take some Pippins;
Mark! I do not say they're equal
To the Greenings, for they are not.
Pare and core them very neatly;
Mind you do not waste their substance,
Nor impair their fair proportions;

Poise the household balance nicely:
In one scale, like careful Themis,
Put those flay'd and heartless apples;
In the other strew the product
Of the graceful cane, that yieldeth
Its sweet blood for our refection;
And for every pound of apples,
Weigh three quarters of that sugar,
White, and saccharine, and luscious;
Lay it in a wide-mouth'd kettle,
Cover'd o'er with limpid water.
That same kettle of bell-metal
Set upon your kitchen furnace,
And your stand beside that furnace
Take with lynx-eyed observation;
Still with silver spoon removing
All the feculence that rises
On the eddies, and the bubbles
That within that tossing caldron,
Like a realm in revolution,
The caloric disengages.
When 'tis clarified and perfect,
Plunge your apples in the liquid;
Let it percolate, and enter
Every pore, until they're tender;
Then from the hot bath remove them,
Ere their surface decomposes,
Or their rotund form is broken.
Not in headlong haste remove them,
But with kind consideration,
Cautiously with spoon of silver;
Side by side in dishes place them,
Glass or china, as shall please you.
Cut within the fragrant syrup
Lemons from the sunny tropics;
And when this transparent fluid
With the acid mildly mingles,
Saturates, and coalesces,
Pour it o'er the waiting apples.
Serve them at dessert or tea-time —
Serve them with a smile of greeting,
And each tasteful guest will like them,
For their youth and simple freshness,
Better than the year-old sweetmeats,
Candied, and defunct in flavor.

— Sigourney, *Lucy Howard's Journal*, 100–01.

Beef Soup

A large piece of beef containing a marrow-bone, and which is, I believe, called a hock, was boiled the whole afternoon, carefully taking off whatever rose to the top; then it was poured out to cool. In the morning the oleaginous part was removed, and likewise the sediment at the bottom, in which were small fragments of bone. Returning it to the vessel, which had been nicely cleansed, it was permitted to boil gently and steadily until about an hour before it was to be used. The bones were then taken out, a quantity of carrots, turnips, and potatoes, cut like dice, added, with a little cabbage and celery cut small; some flour, browned at the fire, and mixed evenly without lumps, put in, to thicken and give it color, with salt and pepper sufficient to flavor it.— Sigourney, *Lucy Howard's Journal* (New York: Harper and Bros., 1858), 70.

Calves' Feet Jelly

Cut in pieces four calves' feet
    Put four quarts of water to them,
Make them subject to a heat,
    That to two quarts shall subdue them.
Strain the fluid; let it rest
    All night long from toil and trouble;
Then from foot and forehead take
    Sediment and oily bubble;
Lay it in the pan once more,
    With a pint of wine to boot,
Acid juice of lemons four,
    Sugar that your taste shall suit;
Beat the whites of twice four eggs
    To a snowy froth; and then,
Watchful at your kitchen range,
    Boil for minutes three times ten;
Take it off, and add a cup
    Of cold water to restore it,
Pass it through a flannel bag,
    And in crystal glasses pour it.

Codicil

When you compound this jelly, friend,
    I'd simply hint to you,
From motives of economy,
    To make a custard too,
For there are yolks of eggs, you know,
Which 'twere not well away to throw.
So beat them all with sugar fine,
    A quart of boil'd milk use,
And when 'tis tepid, stir them in,
    With flavoring as you choose;

Then in small cups of china bake it,
Or in deep dish a pudding make it.
                          — Sigourney, *Lucy Howard's Journal*, 87–88.

Cordials

My grandfather said that in the olden time a variety of domestic cordials were compounded for the weak and weary, especially during seasons of severe cold. One of these he mentioned as worthy of a place among my practical recipes, whereupon my mother immediately provided me with the materials, viz., one ounce and a half of white ginger in the root, four pounds of loaf sugar, and two large, fine lemons. It is better to have the ginger unpulverized, that it may leave no sediment, and white rather than yellow, if you wish the cordial colorless. Macerate the root; mix it with the sugar and juice of the lemons; pour upon them six quarts of water; add two large spoonfuls of fresh yeast; stir the whole in some deep vessel, and allow it to stand two days without moving. When the fermentation is complete, pour off the cordial; add enough pure white spirit to prevent its acidulating; strain it through a flannel bag; bottle, and cork it with care. When well made, it is very clear, and has sometimes, at first opening, as much fixed air as Champagne. It is better to put it in pint bottles, as, after being once uncorked, it loses a portion of its life. It is agreeable to the taste, and also a cheap and useful gift to the invalid poor, who frequently, in their convalescence, suffer for the want of a simple restorative, and are thus tempted to the unsafe search of stimulants and the formation of ruinous habits.— Sigourney, *Lucy Howard's Journal*, 75.

Raisin Pudding

It was then rather late, but, hastening to the kitchen, I asked Amy to give me a quart of milk. While it was preparing to boil, I mixed four spoonfuls of flour with some cold milk, taking care that there were no lumps, and at the full boiling-point stirred it in, with a cup of sugar, and half that quantity of butter. When all was well incorporated, I took it off, and, letting it cool, added six eggs well beaten, four drops of essence of lemon, and a cup of raisins, a quantity of which we usually keep stoned, to be ready for any emergency. The pudding was baked in a deep dish, and when it came on the table, well browned, and rising lightly up, the silent look of approving delight from my loved mother more than repaid me.— Sigourney, *Lucy Howard's Journal*, 95–96.

LESLIE MARMON SILKO

Leslie Marmon Silko (b. 1948) of Laguna Pueblo is the author of the novels *Ceremony* (1977) and *Almanac of the Dead* (1991).

Bacardi Golden Rum Cake

Silko writes me, "The rum cake recipe is called the Bacardi Golden Rum Cake. Originally some anonymous person invented the cake and then the Bacardi company who makes Bacardi rum began to give out the recipe for free because the recipe calls for Bacardi dark rum. This was my mother's favorite holiday cake."

Cake ingredients

1 cup chopped walnuts
1 18½ ounce package of yellow cake mix

1 3¾ ounce package of Jell-O Vanilla Instant Pudding and Pie Filling mix
4 eggs
½ cup of cold water
½ cup vegetable oil
½ cup Bacardi dark rum

Glaze ingredients

¼ pound of butter
¼ cup of water
1 cup of sugar
¼ cup of Bacardi dark rum

Melt butter in sauce pan. Stir in water and sugar. Boil 5 minutes, stirring constantly. Remove from heat.

Stir in rum.

Preheat oven to 325 degrees. Grease and flour 10 inch tube or 12 inch Bundt pan. Sprinkle walnuts over bottom of pan.

Mix all cake ingredients together. Pour cake batter over nuts. Bake one hour. Cool. Invert on serving plate. Prick toothpick holes in top of cake. Spoon glaze evenly over top and sides of cake. Allow the cake to absorb glaze. Repeat until the glaze is used up. This cake is best when allowed to soak up the rum glaze overnight or for a day.

UPTON SINCLAIR

The muckraking novel *The Jungle* (1906) by Upton Sinclair (1878–1968) exposed the unsanitary conditions of the packinghouses in Chicago, the city of the "pig" shoulders and hog butcher of the world, and catalyzed the passage of the Pure Food and Drug Act in 1906. Ironically, Sinclair intended the novel not to be an exposé of the meat industry but a political tract, a recruiting tool for the Socialist Party of the United States. As he explained, he "aimed at the public's head and hit them in the stomach."[1] Not surprisingly, Sinclair became a vegetarian.

Apples

My favorite dish is apples. It is prepared in this way: Put some apples in a saucepan with some water and boil for fifteen minutes. I prepared some last night and expect to eat some for supper.—Cerwin, *Famous Recipes by Famous People*, 14.

GARY SNYDER

Gary Snyder (b. 1930) received a Pulitzer Prize for Poetry for *Turtle Island* (1974).

How to Make Stew in the Pinacate
Desert — Recipe for Locke & Drum

A.J. Bayless market bent wire roller basket buy up
parsnips, onion, carrot, rutabaga and potato, bell green pepper,

& nine cuts of dark beef shank.
They run there on their legs, that makes meat tasty.
        Seven at night in Tucson, get some bisquick for the
dumplings. Have some bacon. Go to Hadley's in the
kitchen right beside the frying steak — Diana on the phone —
get a little plastic bag from Drum —
Fill it up with tarragon and chili; four bay leaves;
black pepper corns and basil; powdered oregano, something free,
maybe about two teaspoon worth of salt.
        Now down in Sonora, Pinacate country, build a fire
of Ocotillo, broken twigs and bits of ironweed, in an open
ring of lava: rake some coals aside (and if you're smart) to windward,
keep the other half ablaze for heat and light.
Set Drum's fourteen-inch dutch oven with three legs across the embers.
        Now put in the strips of bacon.
In another pan have all the vegetables cleaned up and peeled and sliced.
Cut the beef shank meat up small and set the bone aside.
Throw in the beef shank meat,
And stir it while it fries hot,
lots of ash and sizzle — singe your brow —
        Like Locke says almost burn it — then add water from
the jeep can —
add the little bag of herbs — cook it all five minutes more —
and then throw in the pan of all the rest.
Cover it up with big hot lid all heavy, sit and wait,
or drink budweiser beer.
        And also mix the dumpling mix aside, some water in some bisquick,
finally drop that off the spoon into the stew.
And let it cook ten minutes more
and lift the black pot off the fire
to set aside another good ten minutes,
Dish it up and eat it with a spoon, sitting on a poncho
in the dark.
                                        — *Critical Quarterly* 7 (Summer 1965), 106.

WILLIAM STAFFORD

William Stafford (1914–1993) received a National Book Award for Poetry for his first collection *Traveling Through the Dark* (1962) and was named the poet laureate of Oregon in 1975.

Gormeh Salzee (Persian Lamb and Parsley Stew)

6 tablespoons butter
3 large bunches parsley, chopped
16 scallions, chopped

3 pounds lean lamb cut into 1-inch cubes

Salt and pepper

Water to cover

3 lemons

5 cups canned kidney beans

1. In a heavy 4 quart pot or Dutch oven, heat 4 tablespoons butter, add parsley and scallions, and cook slowly until parsley is dark green.

2. In a large skillet heat remaining butter, add meat and brown slowly. Season with salt and pepper.

3. Add meat to vegetable mixture, add water to cover, the juice of 2 lemons and quarters of the 3rd. Cover and simmer until meat is almost tender (approx. 1–1½ hours).

Add kidney beans, correct seasoning, and continue cooking until meat is tender.

Serve with Greek style pilaf (rice stirred into melted butter, then broiled in chicken broth with salt to taste).— Victoria McCabe, *John Keats's Porridge: Favorite Recipes of American Poets* (Iowa City: University of Iowa Press, 1975), 92–93.

GERTRUDE STEIN AND ALICE B. TOKLAS

The American expatriates Gertrude Stein (1874–1946) and Alice B. Toklas (1877–1967) lived together in Paris for nearly 40 years. They hosted a Left Bank salon and befriended many of the most important high modernists of the twenties, including Hemingway and Picasso. Stein was a leading literary modernist in her own right, the author of such avant-garde prose-poetry as *Tender Buttons* (1912). After Stein's death, to forestall the sale of more paintings in their art collection, Toklas compiled *The Alice B. Toklas Cook Book* (1954); in its final paragraph Toklas confides to two friends that she was compiling it. "The first one gaily responded, How very amusing. The other asked with no little alarm, But, Alice, have you ever tried to write? As if a cookbook had anything to do with writing."[1] In truth, according to Janet Malcolm, the recipes were "highly involved, expensive and often impractical."[2] As Linda Simon adds, "the recipes seemed too rich and extravagant to be useful to most readers. Eight eggs— set, not scrambled — required no less than one-half pound of butter; a four-egg omelette, appropriately '*sans nom*,' was enriched with three quarters of a cup of heavy cream. Truffles appeared frequently and liqueurs were added freely,' but more than this, the published manuscript was unproofed and untested."[3] Cooking was not really the point, Toklas insisted. It was a "cook book to be read."[4]

Bass for Picasso

One day when Picasso was to lunch with us I decorated a fish in a way that I thought would amuse him. I chose a fine striped bass and cooked it according to a theory of my grandmother who had no experience in cooking and who rarely saw her kitchen but who had endless theories about cooking as well as about many other things. She contended that a fish having lived its life in water, once caught, should have no further contact with the element in which it had born and raised. She recommended that it be roasted or poached in wine or cream or butter. So I made a *court-bouillon* of dry white wine with whole peppers, salt, a laurel leaf,[5] a spring of thyme, a blade of mace, an onion with a clove stuck in it, a carrot, a leek and a bouquet of *fines herbes*. This was gently boiled in the fish-kettle for

Gertrude Stein (left), Alice B. Toklas, and George Platt Lynes in Billignin, June 1931 (Beinecke Library, Yale University, reproduced by permission).

½ hour and then put aside to cool. Then the fish was placed on the rack, the fish kettle covered and slowly brought to a boil and the fish poached for 20 minutes. Taken from the fire it was left to cool in the *court-bouillon*. It was then carefully drained, dried and placed on the fish platter. A short time before serving it I covered the fish with an ordinary mayonnaise and, using a pastry tube, decorated it with a red mayonnaise, not coloured with catsup — horror of horrors — but with tomato paste. Then I made a design with sieved hard-boiled eggs, the whites and the yolks apart, with truffles and with finely chopped *fines herbes*. I was proud of my chef d'oeuvre when it was served and Picasso exclaimed at its beauty. But, said he, should it not rather have been made in honour of Matisse than of me.—*The Alice B. Toklas Cook Book* (New York: Harper and Bros., 1954), 29.

Chowder Alice B. Toklas and Pâte à Beignets

During their summer 1934 visit to the U.S., Stein and Toklas crossed the country and at Del Monte Lodge in Monterey "we ate for the first time abalone, and thought it a delicious food," Toklas recalled. "It was served in a cream sauce in its shell, lightly browned with breadcrumbs without cheese, we gratefully noticed. Abalone has a delicate flavour of its own and requires no barbeque or barbarous adjuncts."[6] On her part, Stein commended "Chowder Alice B. Toklas" in her submission to a celebrity cookbook in 1940. "The best and most favorite dish that I know is the abalone chowder at Del Monte Lodge," she affirmed. "The cooking there is rarely equaled. There's only one place that approaches it in all France, a wee restaurant in an obscure tower, but the cook [Toklas] is a well-known genius."

My other favorite recipe, Pâte à Beignets: one cup sifted pastry flour, one-half cup milk, two eggs, one-half cup powdered sugar, one tablespoon best olive oil, two tablespoons cognac, pinch of salt. Beat the yolks of eggs into flour until light and smooth. Add sugar and stir well; add cognac and beat; add milk and oil. Put away.

Just before using cut in stiffly beaten whites of eggs. Immerse the flowers of the acacia, holding the stems and a few leaves in the hand. The flowers (only) should be completely immersed in one dipping. Drop into iron cocotte into about four inches of boiling oil and quickly fry to golden brown. Lift out with a wire skimmer—drain well. Place on heated dish—sprinkle the flowers with powdered sugar and serve immediately.—Cerwin, *Famous Recipes by Famous People*, 11.

Gougère, a Burgundian Pastry

"Fred Tenevery took Gertrude Stein and me to the Baronne Pierlot's home," Toklas reminisced in 1961,

where the Baronne suggested to Gertrude Stein that we should spend the day in her cellar, where they made the wine, as a quiet place to work. The lunch served there, by the Baronne Pierlot's son, always consisted of a large roast. It was usually preceded by an egg dish. One day we were served a Bougundian gougère. It was made very much like a cream puff. The recipe, which is said to have originated in Lens, France, is found not only in Burgundy, but also in Troyes in the province of Champagne, and in various other parts of France.

The dough: Put in a tick, flat-bottomed casserole 1 cup of water, ¼ pound of butter and a teaspoonful of salt. As soon as the water comes to a boil, withdraw the casserole from the high flame and add 2 cups of sifted flour. Mix, dry out the dough over a high flame, working it with a wooden spoon (like pâté a chou) until well detached from the sides of the casserole. Then, removed from the fire, add 5 whole eggs, one by one, ¼ pound of Gruyère cheese cut into small cubes, and a pinch of white pepper.

The icing: Scoop into a soupspoon the above-described dough and form patties the size of an egg. Deposit these patties one after the other in a buttered baking dish, arranging them side by side in a circle. Adjust the circle both outside and in with the back of a spoon. Glaze with egg yolk, sprinkle with cheese cut in tiny cubes and bake in a slow oven.

Gougère is usually served cold, but can also be served hot as an hors d'oeuvre.— Barr and Sachs, *Artists' and Writers' Cookbook*, n.p.

Haschich Fudge

The most famous recipe in *The Alice B. Toklas Cook Book*—for "haschich fudge" or hash brownies— was sent to her by Brion Gysin. "This is the food of Paradise — of Baudelaire's Artificial Paradise," Gysin observed, tongue in cheek.

> It might provide an entertaining refreshment for a Ladies' Bridge Club or a chapter meeting of the DAR. In Morocco it is thought to be good for warding off the common cold in damp winter weather and is, indeed, more effective if taken with large quantities of hot mint tea. Euphoria and brilliant storms of laughter; ecstatic reveries and extensions of one's personality on several simultaneous planes are to be complacently expected.

According to Traci Marie Kelly, "Toklas claimed that she did not know the meaning of the botanical terms *canabis sativa* when she decided to include the recipe in her collection. Toklas was incensed that the public could have the impression that 'Gertrude had been indulging in haschich all these years.'"[7]

Take 1 teaspoon black peppercorns, 1 whole nutmeg, 4 average sticks of cinnamon, 1 teaspoon coriander. These should all be pulverized in a mortar. About a handful each of stone dates, dried figs, shelled almonds and peanuts: chop these and mix them together. A bunch of *canibus sativa* can be pulverised. This along with the spices should be dusted over the mixed fruit and nuts, kneaded together. About a cup of sugar dissolved in a big pat of butter. Rolled into a cake and cut into pieces or made into balls about the size of a walnut, it should be eaten with care. Two pieces are quite sufficient.

Obtaining the *canibus* may present certain difficulties, but the variety known as *canibus sativa* grows as a common weed, often unrecognised, everywhere in Europe, Asia and parts of Africa; besides being cultivated as a crop for the manufacture of rope. In the Americas, while often discouraged, its cousin, called *canibus indica*, has been observed even in city window boxes. It should be picked and dried as soon as it has gone to seed and while the plant is still green.— *The Alice B. Toklas Cook Book* (London: M. Joseph, 1954).

JOHN STEINBECK

John Steinbeck (1902–1968), recipient of the Nobel Prize for Literature in 1962, is best known for his short novel *Of Mice and Men* (1937) and the Pulitzer Prize winning novel *The Grapes of Wrath* (1939). He was an avid fisherman and set his novella *Cannery Row* (1945) in the sardine packing district of Monterey.

Mysterious Striped Bass

Elaine Steinbeck circulated this recipe, though she allowed she was not sure who invented it. "I think it just growed. John and I used to visit Nathaniel and Marjorie Benchley in Nantucket, and they would pay us back by coming to see us in Sag Harbor. Whenever — we would fish together and cook the catch."[1]

This simple broiled striped bass takes on mystery because nobody can figure out the delicate subtle flavor. It comes from just plain old gin. Maybe one night when we were cooking the gin bottle was handy.

The dried minced onion gives a crunch and the gin gives a punch.

Behead, skin, and fillet fish. If time allows, sprinkle with lemon juice and refrigerate Pre-heat broiler to high. Place fish in a shallow buttered pan. Sprinkle with salt and pepper, melted butter, lemon juice, and dried minced onions. Put under broiler and cook until lightly brown. Then add more melted butter if needed and two to four ounces of gin, depending on the size of the fillets. Put back under broiler to flambé. Cook until brown.—Kay Hillyard, *The Steinbeck House Cookbook* (Salinas, Cal.: Valley Guild, 1964), 105.

Old Fashioned Slaw

1 medium head cabbage
1 small onion
1 large green pepper
18 (approximately) stuffed green olives, sliced
1 tablespoon celery seed
⅔ cup sugar
½ cup salad oil
½ cup cider vinegar
1 teaspoon salt
1 teaspoon prepared mustard

1. Shred or chop cabbage, onion, and green pepper.
2. Sprinkle sliced olives and celery seed over vegetables.
3. In a small saucepan, combine and bring to a boil sugar, oil, vinegar, salt, and mustard.
4. Add hot liquid to vegetables.
5. Mix well, cover, and let stand for 24 hours before serving.— Hillyard, *The Steinbeck House Cookbook*, 81.

HARRIET BEECHER STOWE

Harriet Beecher Stowe contributed her recipe for Bread and Fruit Pudding to *Jennie June's American Cookery Book* (1870). Its editor, Jane Cunningham Croly (1829–1901), was a journalist; co-founder of Sorosis, the first women's club in the U.S.; and mother of the progressive intellectual Herbert Croly.

Bread and Fruit Pudding

Take thin slices of white bread, nearly fill a buttered mould with layers of bread and fruit alternatively; beat four eggs, mix them in a pint of warm milk, and pour it over the bread and fruit. Boil it twenty minutes, and serve with white sauce.—*Jennie June's American Cookery*, 162.

GENE STRATTON-PORTER

Gene Stratton-Porter (1863–1924) was a nature writer and best-selling novelist, author of *The Girl of the Limberlost* (1909) and *Michael O'Halloran* (1915).

Miner's Lettuce Salad

Go to any canyon — I shall not reveal the name of my particular canyon — and locate a bed of miner's lettuce (*Montia perfoliata*). Growing in rank beds beside a cold, clean stream, you will find these pulpy, exquisitely shaped, pungent round leaves from the center of which lifts a tiny head of misty white lace, sending up a palate-teasing, spicy perfume. The crisp, pinkish stems snap in the fingers. Be sure that you wash the leaves carefully so that no lurking germs cling to them. Fill your salad bowl with the crisp leaves, from which the flowerhead has been plucked. For dressing, dice a teacup of the most delicious bacon you can obtain and fry it to a crisp brown together with a small sliced onion. Add to the fat two tablespoons of sugar, half a teaspoon of mustard; salt will scarcely be necessary the bacon will furnish that. Blend the fat, sugar, and mustard, and pour in a measure of the best apple vinegar, diluted to taste. Bring this mixture to the boiling point, and when it has cooled slightly pour it over the lettuce leaves, lightly turning with a silver fork. Garnish the edge of the dish with a deep border of the fresh leaves bearing their lace of white bloom intact, around the edge of the bowl, and sprinkle on top the sifted yolks of two hard-boiled eggs, heaping the diced whites in the center. — Stratton-Porter, *Her Father's Daughter* (New York: Doubleday, Page, 1921), 79–80.

LUCI TAPAHONSO

The Navajo poet Luci Tapahonso (b. 1953) received a Lifetime Achievement Award from the Native Writers' Circle of the Americas in 2006.

Náneeskaadí (Indian Bread or Tortillas)

The process is simple. Take a few handfuls of flour preferably Blue Bird or Navajo Pride.
   Toss with a bit of salt and a palmful of baking powder. Mix well.
   Ponder the next ingredient awhile, but then go ahead and add two fingertips of lard — not too much, just enough to help the texture.
   Mix very well, Then pour in 1½ cups of very hot water (as hot as you can stand) and mix quickly.
   Mix until the dough forms a soft ball and the remaining flour lifts away from the sides of the bowl. Rub olive oil on a griddle and heat it until very warm; then take a ball of dough and pat it into a disk. Stretch it gently, while slapping it back and forth from hand to hand.
   After a few minutes, a rhythm emerges from the soft, muffled slapping combined with the pauses to lay the dough on the griddle, flip it over, its removal from the hot grill, and its quick replacement.
   Soon the kitchen warms, and the fresh scent of náneeskaadí drifts through the house. — Tapahonso, *A Radiant Curve: Poems and Stories* (Tuscon: University of Arizona Press, 2008), 69–70.

IDA TARBELL

The muckraking reporter Ida Tarbell (1857–1944) is best known for her exposé of Big Oil in *The History of the Standard Oil Company* (1904).

How to Mix a Salad

Pinch of salt.
Sprinkle of pepper.
Niggard with the vinegar.
Spendthrift with the oil, and
Devil of a stir.

— Stratton, *Famous Recipes of Famous Women*, 99.

BAYARD TAYLOR

The poet, novelist, and travel writer Bayard Taylor (1825–1878) was one of the most "clubbable" American men of his generation.

Gothic Punch

4 bottle Catawba wine still
1 bottle claret
3 orange
10 tablespoon sugar
1 bottle Champagne
(For a party of ten.)
Four bottles still Catawba; one bottle claret, three oranges, or one pineapple, ten tablespoonfuls of sugar. Let this mixture stand in a very cold place, or in ice, for one hour or more, then add one bottle of champagne.— *The Bar-Tender's Guide* (New York: Dick and Fitzgerald, 1862), 34.

BAYARD TAYLOR — DINNER AT DELMONICO'S

Taylor was appointed U.S. minister to Berlin by President Rutherford B. Hayes in spring 1878. On April 4, exactly a week before his departure for Berlin, he was the guest of honor at a dinner at the Delmonico's located at the corner of Fifth Avenue and 44th Street. Among the attendees were Mark Twain; the poet William Cullen Bryant; the novelists George Parsons Lathrop, Howells, and Charles Dudley Warner; the publishers J. R. Osgood and Ben Ticknor; and the editors George William Curtis, E. L. Godkin, S. S. Conant, Whitelaw Reid, and Richard Watson Gilder.[1]

Bigarade Sauce (Sauce à la bigarade)

A bigarade orange is a sour orange before it changes to an orange color; peel it without touching the white parts, using a peeling knife, cut the pulp up into small fine Julienne, plunge it into boiling water, and cook it until it is tender; drain and inclose it in a covered

AVRIL, 1878.
DÎNER DE 225 COUVERTS.
En l'Honneur de Mr. Bayard Taylor,
Ministre des États Unis à Berlin.

MENU.

Huîtres.

POTAGES.

Consommé Washington.   Tortue verte.

HORS-D'ŒUVRE.

Brissotins à la Richelieu.

RELEVÉS.

Saumon de Kennebeck, sauce crevettes.
Pommes de terre Dauphine.
Filet de bœuf au Madère.
Tomates farcies.

ENTRÉES.

Estomacs de dinde à l'Impératrice.
Petits pois à l'Anglaise.
Escalopes d'agneau à la Chéron.
Haricots flageolets, maître-d'hôtel.
Mignons de canards, sauce bigarade.
Asperges en branches, sauce crème.
Maïs sauté au beurre.

———

Sorbet Young America.

RÔTS.

Chapons.   Pigeonneaux.

Salade de laitue.

ENTREMETS SUCRÉS.

Pouding à la Masséna.

———

Aspic de fruits.   Charlotte Russe.
Corbeille de meringues.   Pain de pêches Chantilly.
Gâteau noisettes.   Gâteau mille feuilles.
Glaces mignonne.   Dame blanche.
Fruits.   Petits fours.   Bonbons.   Devises.

The Bayard Taylor menu from *The Epicurean.*

saucepan with four gills of espagnole (**No. 414**) or velouté (**No. 415**) if needed for a white sauce. Just when ready to serve, finish the sauce with a dash of cayenne pepper, meat glaze, the orange juice and the juice of a lemon; strained through a tammy, adding two ounces of fine butter. The bigarade can be replaced by an orange and a lemon, using the peel and juice of both fruits.— Ranhofer, *The Epicurean*, 294, 298.

Lima Beans, Thickened, Mâitre d'Hôtel
(Haricots flageolets, maitre-d'hotel)

Have a pound of medium-sized, freshly picked lima beans; boil them in salted water in an untinned copper saucepan, then drain. Pour four ounces of butter in a sautoir, heat it well, add the beans and sauté, seasoning with salt and chopped parsley; stir in a little velouté sauce (**No. 415**) and fresh butter, squeeze the juice of a lemon over, then serve.— Ranhofer, *The Epicurean*, passim.

Green Peas, English Style (Petits pois à l'Anglaise)

Boil some green peas in an untinned copper vessel containing boiling salted water and a few mint leaves; when cooked, drain and place them in a sautoir with salt, sugar and fresh butter, divided in small pats, mixing it into the peas without stirring them. Dress in a vegetable dish and lay small bits of butter on top.— Ranhofer, *The Epicurean*, 827.

Potatoes, Dauphine (Pommes de terre Dauphine)

Bake two pounds of potatoes, cut them lengthways in two, remove sufficient pulp to obtain a pound, and mix this with a quarter as much pâte-à-chou (**No. 132**), eggs, a little cream, salt and nutmeg. Divide it to make inch and a half balls, lengthen them to the shape of an egg, roll in butter, then in bread-raspings, and fry in hot frying fat.

132. Cream Cake Paste (Pâte à chou)

Put into a saucepan half a pint of water, a grain of salt, one ounce of sugar and two ounces of butter; set the saucepan on the fire and when the butter floats, remove the pan from off the range, and incorporate into it a quarter of a pound of fine flour, stir vigorously not to have it the least lumpy, and put it back onto a slow fire to dry until it detaches easily from the bottom, then take it off once more, and mix in a tablespoon of orange flower-water; four or five minutes later stir in four or five eggs, adding them one at the time; it must now be more consistent than otherwise, and if a little of it should be dropped from the spoon, it must retain its shape and not spread.— Ranhofer, *The Epicurean*, passim.

Shrimp Sauce (Sauce aux crevettes)

Pour into a flat saucepan about one pint of béchamel sauce (**No. 409**), let it reduce, and incorporate into it six tablespoons of mushroom essence (**No. 392**), and the same quantity of raw cream. When the sauce is very creamy, take it off the fire, and whisk into it gradually with a wire whip three ounces of fresh butter, and at the very last moment two ounces of shrimp butter (**No. 586**). Season and serve it in a separate sauce boat with the shrimp tails, cut up into small pieces if they are large, but if small, leave them whole.

409. Béchamel Sauce (Sauce béchamel)

Alice B. Toklas explains that "*béchamel* is a basic white sauce made with equal quantities of flour and butter, cooked in enough milk to make a creamy mixture."[2] According to Thomas Jefferson Murrey, it was named for "the Marquis de Bechamel, a worthless court-lounger and steward under Louis XIV. Why his unsavory memory has been perpetuated by a gastronomic monument of worth is one of those inexplicable historical facts that students of the art of cookery are continually stumbling upon."[3]

This is made by preparing a roux of butter and flour, and letting it cook for a few minutes while stirring, not allowing it to color in the slightest; remove it to a slower fire and leave it to continue cooking for a quarter of an hour, then dilute it gradually with half boiled milk, and half veal blond (**No. 423**). Stir the liquid on the fire until it boils, then mingle in with it a mirepoix of roots and onions (**No. 419**), fried separately in butter, some mushroom peelings and a bunch of parsley; set it on a slower fire and let cook for twenty-five minutes without ceasing to stir so as to avoid its adhering to the bottom; it must be rather more consistent than light. Strain it through a fine sieve then through a tammy into a vessel, and allow it to cool off while continuing to stir; set it aside for further use.

392. Mushroom Essence (Essence de champignons)
Put one pound of mushrooms previously washed and cut in four into a saucepan with the juice of half a lemon, salt, and a pint of broth; let boil together for ten minutes; cover the saucepan hermetically and let stand till cold; strain through a fine sieve.

586. Shrimp Butter (Beurre de crevettes)
Pound one pound of shrimps without removing their skins, also two ounces of lobster coral; add to this one pound of fresh buter, some salt, cayenne pepper and the juice of a lemon, then press the whole through a sieve.— Ranhofer, *The Epicurean*, passim.

Tenderloin Steak with Madeira, Half-Glaze
(Filet de bœuf au madère, demi-glace)

Have the tenderloin prepared exactly as for plain (**No. 1423**), seasoning it with salt. Put some clarified butter in a sauté pan, when very hot add the tenderloin to cook it slowly, turning it over six minutes after it has been on the fire, then finish cooking, which will take about twelve minutes in all; drain off the fat and pur into the bottom of the saucepan, half a gill of half-glaze sauce (**No. 413**), and a quarter of a gill of good Madeira wine. Reduce quickly, turning the meat over, then dress the tenderloin. Pour into the stewpan a quarter of a gill more Madeira wine, reduce the whole to half, strain the gravy, put it back into a saucepan, stir in some very good butter, then pour the whole over the steak.

1423. Tenderloin — Steak of Ten Ounces, Plain, Broiled or Sautéd
(Filet de bœuf de dix onces grillé ou sauté nature)
Select the tenderloin of a good red color and nicely streaked with fat. Pare it carefully, remove all the fibrous parts, cut it into slices, each weighing eleven ounces, and beat lightly to flatten them to an inch and a quarter in thickness. Trim well in order to give them a round-shaped appearance. Each tenderloin after being trimmed should weigh ten ounces.

413. Half-Glaze Sauce, Thickened (Sauce demi-glace liée)
A half-glaze sauce only differs from an espagnole by its lightness. This sauce is generally made in large quantities at the time, so as not to begin it so frequently, as it requires the utmost care in its preparation. Heat in a saucepan one pound of clarified butter, and when it is very hot fill it up with flour so as to obtain a paste rather too light than otherwise; thicken it well while stirring for a few minutes on the fire, and then set it aside in a warm

part to cook and brown very slowly, without adhering to the bottom of the pan, and without letting it get black. Five or six hours after, pour it into a vessel, cover it with paper, and let this roux stand to get cool.

To make the sauce: dilute the roux very slowly, with some beef stock (**No. 194a**), having it only slightly warm, and prepared for this purpose, and finish it exactly like the espagnole; it must be as clear as possible and of a light color; strain and skim it well. Stir the liquid over the fire to thicken the sauce, managing not to have any lumps in it, and should it not be perfectly smooth, then strain it through a fine colander. Put four ounces of butter in a saucepan, add to it four ounces each of sliced carrots, onions and celery root; the same quantity of lean ham cut in quarter inch squares, a bunch of parsley garnished with bay leaves, thyme and allspice, fry without coloring, pour the sauce over the whole, add four gills of good white, dry wine, and a quarter of a pound of mushroom parings, and let all boil while stirring, then remove it at once to the side of the range, and continue boiling on one side only, so as to be able to despumate it properly for several hours. Strain and put as much of this as is needed into a reducing saucepan with two gills of meat glaze (**No. 401**); boil, reduce it to the necessary degree, using a spatula to stir it from the bottom, without leaving it for one instant, incorporate slowly into it a little good veal blond (**No. 423**) and a small quantity of good white wine. When the sauce is succulent without being too thick, strain it through a tammy and pour it into a vessel, or else into a saucepan to keep warm in a bain-marie.

401. Meat Glaze, Clear (Glace de viande claire)

Have a stockpot sufficiently large to contain four pounds of knuckle of veal, eight pounds of shoulder of veal, six pounds of shin or leg of beef, and add to these sixteen quarts of water and a very little salt; boil, skim, and garnish with a pound and a half of onions, one of them containing four cloves, two pounds of carrots cut in quarters, a bunch of eight medium sized leeks, with a few branches of celery, and a bouquet made of two ounces of parsley leaves, three bay leaves and as much thyme; bring to a boil, skim as fast as the fat and white particles rise to the surface, and boil in this manner for eight hours, then strain it through a sieve, and reduce down to two quarts. Put this into a tin can having a tube half an inch in diameter, a quarter of its height from the bottom, and plugged with a tight cork; cork well and tie it firmly down, then put it on to boil in water for one hour, remove it from the water, and keep it in a warm place for three days to settle, then take out the top, then the lower cork, and receive the glaze as it falls in an earthen vessel. This glaze should be very clear; suppress the bottom, and use it in sauces etc., or else add it to the spanish sauce stocks.—Ranhofer, *The Epicurean*, passim.

Tomatoes Stuffed with Fresh Mushrooms
(Tomates farcies aux champignons frais)

Chop up some clean fresh mushrooms, fry a chopped onion, and add it to these, and continue to fry until all the moisture is evaporated, then season and remove from the fire. Bind it with a little sauce, then with an equal quantity of bread crumbs soaked and pressed a few raw egg yolks, adding some chopped parsley. Select fine, sound tomatoes, smooth and round, of even size, but not too large nor too ripe; cut out a piece from the top in order to open and empty out partially, then salt and drain them for a quarter of an hour, filling them afterward with the mushroom preparation, and smoothing the tops nicely. Range the tomatoes in a small bordered baking pan, bestrew them with bread crumbs and pour over some oil; cook for three-quarters of an hour in a slow stove.— Ranhofer, *The Epicurean*, 844.

Young America Sherbet (Sorbet jeune Amérique)

Imitate a boat in gum paste standing it on a thin board; fasten an American flag at the stern and fill the empty boat with the following sherbet: Place in a vessel one quart of thirty-two degree syrup, one quart of syrup of pears and currants and one gill of lemon juice, the juice of four oranges, half an orange peel and a little vanilla. Infuse for one hour, then bring it to thirty-two degrees; pass through a fine sieve and freeze. Just when prepared to serve incorporate one gill of kirsch, one gill of rum and a quarter of a bottle of champagne.— Ranhofer, *The Epicurean*, 1005.

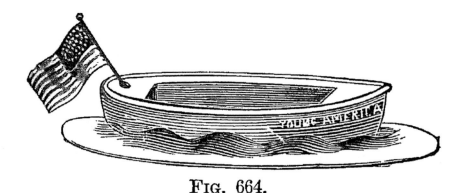

FIG. 664.

A sherbet boat from *The Epicurean*.

ALBERT PAYSON TERHUNE

Albert Payson Terhune (1872–1942), the son of Edward Payson Terhune and Mary Virginia Hawes Terhune (aka Marion Harland), was the author of *Lad: A Dog* (1919). He moved with his wife Anice to the family summer home Sunnybank, near Pompton, New Jersey, in 1912.

Sunnybank Guava Salad

The foundation is crabapple jelly, made just like all crabapple jellies one finds in any cook book, except that one cooks the apples with just one-half the usual quantity of water. After this is done and they have been strained through cheesecloth, add the same quantity of strong Orange-Pekoe tea to the mixture that you had of water, thus making the usual quantity of liquid added to the crab apples; only in this case half the liquid is water and the other half strong tea.

When the jelly is finished it is almost impossible to tell it from guava, except that Sunnybank guava is a bit less heavy than real guava, and even more delicious. For guava salad, I place a round slice of the jelly, about three-quarters of an inch high, on a lettuce leaf. Cover the jelly mounds with a coating of cream cheese (softened in a tiny bit of cream if the cheese is at all crumbly), split two dates and lay the four halves on the cream cheese, and in the middle put a stuffed olive. With this I use a simple French dressing, making it with lemon juice instead of vinegar.— Stratton, *Favorite Recipes of Famous Women*, 94–95.

OCTAVE THANET

Octave Thanet, aka Alice French (1850–1934), wrote Midwestern local-color fiction for popular parlor magazines.

Christmas Plum Pudding

One heaping pint of biscuit crumbs; one quart of fruits—cherries, lemon and orange peel, citron, currants, and raisins; one cup of sugar and molasses; one large wine glass of brandy; one teaspoonful of allspice; one teaspoonful of cinnamon; one-half teaspoonful of cloves; nutmeg to taste; four eggs; milk to moderately soften the dough.

I am bound to confess that this hit-or-miss pudding has never missed in my experience. It should be served with a little brandy poured around it and set on fire just as it enters the dining room. Alcohol will make a more brilliant display than brandy, but the flavor of the pudding is not so good by a long, long distance. A hard sauce flavored with lemon and brandy is the conventional accompaniment. People of sentiment sometimes stick a sprig of holly in the pudding, but when the liquid about it is afire the holly is apt to blaze and the children may have more fun than is good for them.

A plum pudding has a costly sound, but it really need not be expensive. A family of moderate means who eat bread three times a day will accumulate in a few days enough crusts and stale pieces to dry in the oven afterward to be rolled into crumbs and soaked in a quart of milk. A cup of beef suet from the last roast of beef (you may trust the butcher to help the weight along with plenty of trimmings), a cup of molasses, about three teaspoonfuls of spice, a cup of currants, and one of seeded and cut raisins, will with some good sauce make a very toothsome pudding. Eggs make it lighter and better, but eggs may be omitted when they are forty cents a dozen.—*Atlanta Constitution*, December 18, 1892, 30.

Rich Dark Pudding

One pint of flour; four eggs, whites and yolks beaten separately; two tablespoonfuls of baking powder stirred into the flour and the flour sifted four times; one cup of sugar and a scant half cup of butter beaten to a cream; one liquor glass of chatreuse cordial; one liquor glass of maraschino; spice to taste, about three teaspoonfuls or more; one pint of mixed fruits, well floured; milk to make a batter stiff enough to hold up the fruit.

This is a very rich pudding, and can be darkened to absolute blackness by the addition of liquid chocolate—that is, chocolate melted and thinned by hot water.—*Atlanta Constitution*, December 18, 1892, 30.

Salmi of Prairie Chicken (Grouse)

Take the remains of two nice, roasted prairie chickens that served, we will say, for yesterday's dinner, and that the thrifty housewife designed for tomorrow's breakfast; but we think we can do better. Take these; cut the meat off the bones; it is always surprising how much more meat there is on bones than appears to the eye of the casual observer. Break the bones and put them on to stew. A quart of water will not be too much liquid. Simmer them for an hour or so—the time is not of vital importance. Stew the invariable two tablespoonfuls of butter and two tablespoonfuls of flour together until they boil. Attention here is of vital importance. Flavor in any fashion that you like. To keep up the fiction of aristocracy, wine and a dash of lemon are usually added.

Here is a very high-toned Virginian receipt for a salmi gravy:

Flavor the gravy with one small onion chopped fine, one-half teaspoonful curry, one-half teaspoonful chutney sauce, juice of one lemon, one teaspoonful of currant jelly, one teaspoonful chopped parsley, one-half teaspoonful mixed sage and sweet marjoram, one large wineglass full of claret wine.

Having stewed the cut-up chicken in this gravy dispose the stew on small slices of toast symmetrically about a heap of peas, in your prettiest platter. The result is very enticing.— *Atlanta Constitution*, October 23, 1892, 22.

CELIA THAXTER

> The poet Celia Thaxter (1835–1894) lived most of her life with her father at the Appledore Hotel on the Isle of Shoals, a resort 15 miles off the shore of New Hampshire. Maria Parloa briefly worked as a pastry chef in the kitchen there and later published one of Thaxter's recipes.

Graham Pie

Into a pint of Graham flour, stir one teaspoonful of salt; wet with boiling water enough to make a stiff paste. Roll this very thin, and cut into cakes about three inches in diameter; put into these a spoonful of applesauce and fold them. Bake on tin sheets. These can be eaten by any dyspeptic.— Parloa, *The Appledore Cook Book* (Boston: A. F. Graves, 1880), 210.

Appledore Hotel on the Isle of Shoals, New Hampshire, 1901. Celia Thaxter's home is shown second from left (Library of Congress).

MARK TWAIN

Ash Cake

Take a lot of water and add to it a lot of coarse Indian meal and about a quarter of a lot of salt. Mix well together, knead into the form of a "pone," and let the pone stand awhile — not on its edge, but the other way. Rake away a place among the embers, lay it there, and cover it an inch deep with hot ashes. When it is done, remove it; blow off all the ashes but one layer; butter that one and eat.

N.B.— No household should ever be without this talisman. It has been noticed that tramps never return for another ash cake.— Twain, *A Tramp Abroad* (Hartford: American Publishing, 1880), 575–76.

German Coffee

Take a barrel of water and bring it to a boil; rub a chicory berry against a coffee berry, then convey the former into the water. Continue the boiling and evaporation until the intensity of the flavor and aroma of the coffee and chicory has been diminished to a proper degree; then set aside to cool. Now unharness the remains of a once cow from the plow, insert them in a hydraulic press, and when you shall have acquired a teaspoon of that pale blue juice which a German superstition regards as milk, modify the malignity of its strength in a bucket of tepid water and ring up the breakfast. Mix the beverage in a cold cup, partake with moderation, and keep a wet rag around your head to guard against overexcitement.— Twain, *A Tramp Abroad*, 576.

New English Pie

To make this excellent breakfast dish, proceed as follows: Take a sufficiency of water and a sufficiency of flour, and construct a bullet-proof dough. Work this into the form of a disk, with the edges turned up some three-fourths of an inch. Toughen and kiln-dry in a couple days in a mild but unvarying temperature. Construct a cover for this redoubt in the same way and of the same material. Fill with stewed dried apples; aggravate with cloves, lemon peel, and slabs of citron; add two portions of New Orleans sugars, then solder on the lid and set in a safe place till it petrifies. Serve cold at breakfast and invite your enemy.— Twain, *A Tramp Abroad*, 576.

Whiskey and Bitters

While living in London in the winter of 1873-74, Mark Twain (1835–1910) regularly enjoyed whiskey cocktails, especially after his lectures. According to his private secretary, the poet Charles Warren Stoddard, whom he had known since his San Francisco days,

> a diligent search through London had resulted in the collection of ingredients almost unknown in the England of that day and certainly not generally recognized by the natives of the country.... Mark brought with him two dainty glasses brimming with a delicately-tinted liquid. The glasses were equally divided between us. We drank in silence and were supremely happy for some moments. Then Mark, arousing from a revery, would turn to me and say in

that mellow, slowly-flowing voice of his: "Now you make one, Charlie." With genuine embarrassment I would protest. I used to say: "Mark, you know that I cannot make one: I never could. It is not an art that can be acquired. It is a gift, a birthright, and there are not many who are so richly endowed as you. There is no recipe in the wide, wide world that even followed religiously would come within a thousand miles of that you lately offered me.

Stoddard remembered for the rest of his life Twain's "mournful refrain, 'Too much bitters! Too much bitters!'"[1] Twain listed the components of the cocktail in a letter to his wife Olivia from London in January 1874: "Livy my darling, I want you to be sure & remember to have, in the bathroom, when I arrive, a bottle of Scotch whisky, a lemon, some crushed sugar, & a bottle of *Angostura bitters*. Ever since I have been in London I have taken in a wine glass what is called a cocktail (made with those ingredients) before breakfast, before dinner, & just before going to bed."[2]

Mark Twain — Dinner at Delmonico's

In the mythology that has accreted around Twain like a pearl around a grain of sand, the great American writer has been portrayed as a down home diner with rustic tastes. Those who claim that he subsisted on simple fare point to the menu of several dozen of his favorite foods in chapter 49 of *A Tramp Abroad* (1880) — a list that includes pumpkin pie, Southern fried chicken, and Virginia bacon. Evan Jones notes approvingly that the menu "mentions no adornments or sauces except 'real cream,' 'clear maple syrup,' and 'American butter.'"[3] In truth, however, Twain married into a genteel New York family, lived for most of his adult life in polite society, and enjoyed comestibles that belonged to his moment and *milieu*. Andrew Beahrs grudgingly concedes that "in later years" the dinner parties Twain hosted in his fashionable Hartford home "owed a great deal to the rich, elevated food served at Delmonico's — considered the finest restaurant in America.... It is, regretfully, necessary to report at one 1887 dinner at Twain's house involved creamed asparagus, creamed sweetbreads, and creamed shad sauce over shad-roe balls."[4] Why "regretfully?"

Certainly Mark Twain was accustomed to dining on French *haute cuisine*. At the dinner he attended in the St. James Hotel in New York on February 23, 1872, to celebrate the appointment of Richard Henry Stoddard as editor of the *Aldine*, the menu featured green turtle soup, lobster bisque, boiled striped bass with Hollandaise sauce, galantin de dinde décoré aux ruffles, langues de boeuf sur socle au beurre de Montpellier, filet de boeuf décoré en Bellevue, petit cochon de lait a la Sègur, and breaded lamb chops à la Jardiniere.[5] When he delivered his (in)famous speech at John Greenleaf Whittier's seventieth birthday celebration at the Brunswick Hotel in Boston in December 1877, he and a few dozen other contributors to the *Atlantic Monthly* dined on halibut à la Navarine, potatoes à la Hollandaise, terrapin stewed Maryland style, canvasback ducks, and Charlotte russe — though the chefs at neither restaurant published cookbooks, so there is no reliable record of how these dishes were prepared.

Twain was so enamored of fine dining that he issued, under the imprint of his own publishing house, a cookbook entitled *The Table* (1889) compiled by Alessandro Filippini, a Delmonico's chef. Not surprisingly, the Delmonico's on Fifth Avenue in New York was the site of Twain's own seventieth birthday celebration on the evening of December 5, 1905. Among the 172 of Twain's closest friends who attended were the authors Edwin Markham, George Ade, John Burroughs, Dorothy Canfield, Brander Matthews, Louise Chandler Moulton, Charles Chesnutt, Willa Cather, Finley Peter Dunn, Charles Eastman, Mary E. Wilkins, W. D. Howells, Julian Hawthorne, Onoto Watanna, and Owen Wister.[6] Howells reported that they comprised "the

Mark Twain and friends at his 70th birthday celebration at Delmonico's on December 5, 1905. Left to right: Kate Douglas Riggs, Twain, Joseph Twichell, Bliss Carman, Ruth McEnery Stuart, Mary E. Wilkins Freeman, Henry Mills Alden, Henry Rogers (*Harper's Weekly*, December 23, 1905).

Dining room of the Mark Twain House, Hartford, Connecticut (Library of Congress).

W. D. Howells with bottle and glass (Library of Congress).

strangest mixture of literary celebrity and social notoriety that I have ever seen. The smart and the chic were both present, and not at separate tables, always." The food had been in "the best Delmonico" style.[7] Fortunately, an original menu for the dinner is preserved in the New York Public Library special collections.[8] It lists such dishes as oysters, consommé souveraine, green turtle soup, timbales périgordine, cucumbers, persillade potatoes, saddle of lamb Colbert, stuffed tomatoes, Baltimore terrapin, mushrooms on toast with cream, quail, red head duck, fried hominy and currant jelly, celery with mayonnaise, and coffee. Many of these dishes have several components, and I record them in full below.

Baltimore Terrapin (Terrapin à la Baltimore)

Take two medium-sized live terrapins, and blanch them in boiling water for two minutes. Remove the skin from the feet, and put them back to cook with some salt in the saucepan until they feel soft to the touch; them put them aside to cool.

Make a pint of mirepoix (**No. 138**), add to it a tablespoonful of flour, let cook for fifteen minutes, then moisten with half a glassful of Madeira wine, and a cupful of strong broth. Stir well, and constantly, then season with half a pinch of salt, and a very little cayenne pepper; reduce to half. Cut the terrapin into small pieces, throwing the ends of the claws away; put them in a stewpan, straining the sauce over, and finish with an ounce of fresh butter, also the juice of a lemon.

138. Mirepoix

Stew in a saucepan two ounces of fat, two carrots, one onion, one sprig of thyme, one bay leaf, six whole peppers, three cloves, and, if handy, a ham bone cut into pieces. Add two sprigs of celery and half a bunch of parsley roots; cook for fifteen minutes, and use when directed in other recipes. Scraps of baked veal may also be added, if at hand.—Ranhofer, *The Epicurean*, passim.

Coffee

If practicable, procure a small family coffee roaster. Have three quarters of a pound of Java, mixed with a quarter of a pound of Mocha, place it in the roaster, and taking one of the lids from off the stove, put the roaster on a moderate fire, and turn the small handle constantly and slowly until the coffee becomes a good brown color; for this it should take about twenty-five minutes; open the cover to see when it is done, then transfer it to an earthen jar, cover it tightly, and use when needed; or, a more simple way, and even more effectual, is to take a tin baking dish, butter well the bottom, and placing the same quantity of coffee therein, put it in a moderate oven to let get a good golden color; twenty minutes will suffice for this, being careful to toss it frequently with a wooden spoon, then remove to an earthen jar, and cover it well.

Take six scant tablespoonfuls of coffee beans from the jar and grind them in a mill. Have a well cleaned French coffee pot; put the coffee on the filter, with the small strainer over, then pour on a pint and a half of boiling water, little by little, recollecting at the same time that too much care cannot be taken to have the water boiling thoroughly. When all the water is consumed, put on the cover and let it infuse slightly, but on no account must it boil. Serve in six after-dinner cups. Coffee should never be prepared more than five minutes before the time to serve.—Filippini, *The Table*, 380–81.

Consommé à la Souveraine

A garnishing of timbales. Make a preparation with one pint of mushroom purée, two gills of éspagnole sauce with essence of game (**No. 414**), ten egg yolks, salt, red pepper, and nutmeg; fill some dome-shaped molds with this, and poach them in a slack oven, placing the molds in a stew pan with boiling water reaching to half their height; when done, which

means firm to the touch, unmold them, and put them into a vegetable dish with some consommé, also some turnips cut into triangles, half an inch by an eighth of an inch thick,
blanched and cooked in consommé, squares of the red part of carrot cut the same thickness,
blanched and cooked in consommé; some artichoke bottoms cut into quarter of an inch
squares, and half inch round pieces of blanched lettuce leaves.— Ranhofer, *The Epicurean*,
passim.

Cucumbers

Take two medium-sized, fine cucumbers, peel neatly, and cut them in thin slices. Place
in a bowl with a good pinch of salt, and put them in a cold place for two hours. Then
drain the liquid off, and season with half a pinch of pepper, a tablespoonful of vinegar,
and the same quantity of oil. Dress nicely in a radish dish.— Ranhofer, *The Epicurean*, 264–
65.

Fried Hominy and Currant Jelly

Wash a quart of very white hominy in fresh water; drain, put in a saucepan with a quart
of cold water, and place it on the fire, adding a pinch of salt. Boil for thirty minutes, stirring
it well, put it to cool, and cut it into six slices. Dip each slice in beaten egg, roll them in
fresh bread crumbs, and fry in very hot fat until of a good golden color, for four minutes.
Serve on a folded napkin, or use for garnishing when required.

Select sixteen pounds of small, old Dutch currants, not too ripe; those are preferable
which are picked at the end of the month of June. Place them in a copper basin on the hot
stove, and begin stirring them immediately from the bottom, using a wooden spatula; when
they begin to scald, pour them into a clean tub, and with a pounder mash them thoroughly.
Strain them through a flannel jelly-bag back into the copper basin, adding to the juice seven
pounds of granulated sugar. Return the pan to the fire, and let boil until reduced to about
half the quantity, then dip in a skimmer, lift it up, and feel the jelly with the two forefingers;
close them, and open them slowly, if the jelly is mucilaginous, then it is done; if not, cook
for a few minutes longer. Take it from the fire, and pour a little into every glass jar ready
to use, as this will prevent them cracking. Afterwards fill them up. When thoroughly cold,
which will be in about two hours, during which time they must not be disturbed, cork them
tightly, and put them in a closet. Currant jelly prepared in this way will keep in good condition for two years.— Ranhofer, *The Epicurean*, passim.

Green Turtle Soup

Place a pint of green turtle, cut into pieces in a saucepan with two pints of broth (**No. 99**);
add a bouquet (**No. 254**), a glassful of Madeira wine, a little bit of red pepper, half a tablespoonful of salt, a little grated nutmeg, a teaspoonful of English sauce, and a cupful of
Espagnole sauce (**No. 151**). Boil for twenty minutes, and serve with six slices of peeled
lemon, after suppressing the bouquet.

151. Sauce Espagnole — for one gallon

Mix one pint of raw, strong mirepoix (**No. 138**) with two ounces of good fat (chicken's
fat is preferable). Mix with the compound four ounces of flour, and moisten with one
gallon of white broth (**No. 99**). Stir well, and then add, if handy, some baked veal and ham

bones. Boil for three hours, and then remove the fat very carefully; rub the sauce through a very fine sieve, and keep it for many purposes in cooking.— Ranhofer, *The Epicurean*, passim.

Mushrooms on Toast with Cream

Choose a pound of fine, sound, large, fresh mushrooms, neatly pare off the ends, clean, and wash them well. Drain, and place them in a sautoire with an ounce of good butter. Season with a pinch of salt and half a pinch of pepper. Cover, and let them cook for ten minutes, tossing them well meanwhile. Squeeze in the juice of half a medium-sized sound lemon; add a pinch of chopped parsley, nicely sprinkled over. Place six pieces of toasted bread on a hot dish, dress the mushrooms over the toasts, and serve.

Mushrooms Sautés à la Crème

Prepare a pound of fine, fresh mushrooms exactly the same as above, and if very large cut them in two. Place them in a sautoire with an ounce of good butter. Season with a pinch of salt and half a pinch of pepper, then put the lid on, and cook on a moderate fire for six minutes; then add two tablespoonfuls of velouté sauce (**No. 152**), and half a cupful of sweet cream. Cook again for four minutes, and serve them in a very hot dish with six heart-shaped bread croûtons (**No. 133**) around it.

133. Croûtons for Soups
Cut some dice-shaped pieces of bread, and fry them in a pan with clarified butter; when a rich golden color, drain, and add to the soup when needed.— Ranhofer, *The Epicurean*, passim.

Oysters

Put thirty medium-sized oysters in their own water, with half a pint of water added, in a saucepan, with a tablespoonful of salt and half a teaspoonful of pepper, and one ounce of good butter. Let it boil once only; then serve, adding half a pint of cold milk.— Filippini, *The Table*, 154.

Périgordine Timbales

Prepare a very consistent chestnut purée (**No. 712**), adding to it a little meat glaze (**No. 402**), some fresh butter and raw egg yolks; let this get thoroughly cold. Garnish the bottom of the timbale molds with a thin slice of truffle, cut out the center with a half inch vegetable cutter, and replace the piece with a round cut of tongue exactly the same size; fill up the bottom and sides with a chicken and cream forcemeat (**No. 75**), and set in the center a half inch ball of the chestnut purée; cover over with more forcemeat and finish the same as for timbales (**No. 959**). Have a separate sauce boat of half-glaze sauce (**No. 413**), finished with essence of truffles (**No. 395**).

712. Purée of Chestnuts (Purée de marrons)
Peel one pound of chestnuts, plunge them into boiling water so as to remove the inner skin, then lay them in a saucepan, and moisten them to their height with white broth (**No. 189**),

adding a stalk of celery. Cook them with the lid on over a moderate fire, and when soft, and the broth entirely reduced, pound them in a mortar with two ounces of butter, seasoning with a little salt and sugar; pass this purée through a hair or tinned brass sieve (iron sieve should not be used for passing purées) and return it to the saucepan to heat without ceasing to stir, but at the same time watching that it does not boil, beat in a little velouté (**No. 415**) and cream.

959. Timbales, Remarks on (Observations sur les timbales)

There are several kinds of timbales; those made with a very thin timbale paste; those of quenelle forcemeat and those of cream forcemeat, either of chicken, game or fish. The name timbale should only be applied to those made of paste cylindrical-shaped like a footless goblet, or a silver mug, or else half spherical-shaped in imitation of the kettle drum used in an orchestra and filled with a garnishing of some kind. A "bung" would better represent the idea of what is commonly called timbale, and I would suggest the adoption of the French of bung "bondon," for I scarcely believe that the elegance of the bill of fare would be marred by reading: "Bondons of Pickerel à la Walton," or "Bondons of Chicken à la Reine," or "Bondons of Woodcock à la Diane," or "Bondons of Pheasants à la Benois." I have not the slightest intention of changing the conventional name. I only suggest an idea that might be advantageously followed if so desired. For making timbales cylindrical, molds two and five-eighths inches wide by two and one-eighth inches high are generally used; butter the insides with fresh unmelted butter and decorate with fanciful cuts of truffles, tongue, pistachios, etc. They may also be strewn with truffles, tongue, lobster coral and pistachios, all these being chopped up finely and separately, then dried in the air. Fill the forcemeat either with or without a salpicon, then poach; for this consult Elementary Methods (**No. 152**). Invert onto a dish containing a little consommé and serve the sauce that accompanies the timbales separately.

152. To Poach Small Timbales (Pour pocher les petites timbales)

Range the timbales in a sautoire; fifteen minutes before serving fill it to half the height of the molds with boiling water, and set the sautoire on the fire; when the water is ready to boil, remove and place it in a slack oven for ten or fifteen minutes; after a lapse of ten minutes touch the forcemeat in the center, and if firm, take them out, let stand for a little and invert the molds into a cloth to drain off all the liquid. Unmold.

395. Truffle Essence (Essence de truffles)

Brush and peel two pounds of fresh truffles; put them into a saucepan with half a bottle of Madeira wine and a pint of broth (**No. 187**); add two ounces of celery, as much carrots and as much onions, all minced up very fine, a bunch of parsley, thyme, bay leaf, salt and ground pepper. Cover the saucepan and allow the truffles to boil slowly for twenty minutes. Then let them get cold in their broth, keeping the cover hermetically closed. Strain through a napkin or fine sieve.— Ranhofer, *The Epicurean*, passim.

Potatoes English Style, Persillade Balls
(Pommes à l'Anglaise, en boules persillade)

Boiled English Style— Peel some raw potatoes; pare them in the shape of large olives, and put them in a saucepan with salt and water; cover and let the liquid boil until the potatoes are done, then drain off the water and cover over with a cloth. Close the saucepan and set it in the oven for a few moments to dry them well; pour a little melted salt butter over and dress in a vegetable dish.

Persillade Balls are potatoes formed into balls three-quarters of an inch to one inch in diameter with a vegetable spoon and cooked the same as the English. Serve them in a vegetable dish, pour salted butter and chopped parsley over.— Ranhofer, *The Epicurean*, 833.

Quail Roasted, Plain

Pick six fine, tender, fat quails, singe, draw, and wipe them well; truss them, laying a thin layer of lard on the breasts. Put them in a roasting pan, spreading a very little butter on top of each quail; then pour half a cupful of water in the pan. Season with a pinch of salt, and let cook in the oven for eighteen minutes. Place on a hot dish six heart-shaped pieces of toast; untruss the quails, and arrange them on top, decorating with a little watercress. Strain the gravy into a sauce bowl, and serve it separately.— Filippini, *The Table*, 276.

Red Head Duck, Roasted
(Canards sauvages à tête rouge rôtis)

Select two fine redhead ducks, pick them as far up as one inch from the head, being very careful not to tear the skin; singe and draw. In order to accomplish this, the skin must be cut the whole length of the neck from its beginning until the back of the head is reached, remove the pouch and windpipe, stick the finger in the neck far down in the inside to detach the lights from the bones and all adhering to the breast, make an incision above the rump and take out the gizzard drawing up the whole of the insides; cut the neck where it begins at the carcass, cutting the skin as far up as it is picked. Wipe the duck carefully, thrust the feet inside and season it interiorly with salt and mignonette. Should the duck be gamy it must have the inside washed out. Pick the feathers from the head and separate it where the neck finishes; pick out the eyes and place the head in the opening that was used for drawing the bird; truss the duck bringing the feet toward the front and passing the trussing needle threaded with string near the first joint of the thigh next to the feet. Run the needle through the duck under the breast and then across the other thigh, pressing the duck down well so as to round well the breast, bring the neck skin down on the back and run the needle on the bias through the pinion bone at the same time through the neck skin to pass it through the other pinion and return from whence it started, pull the string tight and push the rump inward, running the needle through to keep it in place, and bringing it back to one inch from its starting point, passing it through the skin and through the head by the eyes, fasten the two ends of string together tying them firmly.

Lay them on the spit to roast for fourteen to eighteen minutes, more or less according to their weight; salt over, remove them from the spit and untruss and serve on a very hot dish, or they can be roasted in the oven, putting them into a baking pan; pour a little fat over and set them in a hot oven; they will take a few minutes longer to cook this way, then serve on a very hot dish. Four slices can be taken from each duck, two on each fillet and one or two of these served to one guest.— Ranhofer, *The Epicurean*, 641.

Saddle of Lamb, Sauce Colbert

Pare and trim a fine saddle of mutton, weighing about six pounds (if possible). Lift off the upper skin, make one slight incision in the middle, also three on each side; tie it firmly together with three strings, so that it retains its shape, season it with a good pinch of salt, and it will then be ready to roast. Place the saddle in a roasting pan, adding a gill of cold water; put it in a moderate oven, and let cook for forty-five minutes. Baste it frequently with its own gravy, and serve on a very hot dish. Skim off all the fat, strain the gravy into a sauce bowl, and serve with half a pint of Colbert sauce (**No. 190**) in a bowl.

N.B. Should the saddle be of heavier weight, say twelve to fourteen pounds, one hour and a quarter will be necessary to cook it.

190. Sauce Colbert [named after Jean-Baptiste Colbert, the chief minister of finances during the reign of Louis XIV]

Put in a saucepan half a pint of very thick Madeira sauce (**No. 185**); add to it very gradually one ounce of good, fresh butter, also two tablespoonfuls of meat glaze (**No. 141**). Mix well together without boiling; then squeeze in the juice of half a sound lemon, and add one teaspoonful of chopped parsley when serving.

185. Sauce Demi-Glace, or Madeira

Add one small glassful of mushroom liquor to one pint of good Espagnole sauce (**No. 151**); also a small glassful of Madeira wine, a bouquet (**No. 254**), and a scant teaspoonful of pepper. Remove the fat carefully and cook for thirty minutes, leaving the sauce in a rather liquid state; then strain and use when needed. This takes the place of all Madeira sauces.

141. Meat Glaze — Glace de Viande

As this meat glaze, when properly made, will keep in perfect condition for any length of time, I would advise that half a pint be made at a time in the following manner. Place in a large saucepan ten quarts of white broth (**No. 99**), or nine quarts of consommé (**No. 100**), and reduce it on a moderate fire for fully four hours, at which time it should be reduced to half a pint. Transfer it in a stone jar or bowl; put a cover on, and keep in a cool place for general use. — Ranhofer, *The Epicurean*, passim.

Salad: Celery Mayonnaise

If the heads of celery be large and white, use two; if they should be small, use three. Pare off the green stalks, trim the roots nicely, and cut it into short shreds; wash thoroughly in cold water, lift it up with the hands, and drain in a cloth. When well drained, place the celery in a salad bowl, and season with a pinch of salt, half a pinch of pepper, and three tablespoonfuls of mayonnaise dressing (**No. 206**). Mix well just before serving.

206. Sauce Mayonnaise

Place two fresh egg yolks into an earthen bowl, with half a teaspoonful of ground English mustard, half a pinch of salt, half a saltspoonful of red pepper; sharply stir with a wooden spoon for two or three minutes without ceasing. Pour in, drop by drop, one and a half cupfuls of the best olive oil. Should it become too thick, add, drop by drop, the equivalent of a teaspoonful of very good vinegar, stirring vigorously with the wooden spoon meanwhile. Taste, and if found a little too acid, gradually add a tablespoonful of oil, stirring continually until all added. The whole operation to prepare the above sauce will take from ten to twelve minutes. To avoid spoiling the sauce, the sweet oil should be always be kept in a place of moderate temperature, say, from 70° to 75° Fahrenheit. — Ranhofer, *The Epicurean*, passim.

Stuffed Tomatoes

Wash and dry well six fine, sound red tomatoes. Cut the top of each up, without detaching, so that it will serve as a cover. Scoop out the inside of each with a vegetable scoop; and place on a plate for further action. Season the inside of the six emptied tomatoes with one pinch of salt and half a pinch of pepper, equally divided. Chop very fine one medium-sized, sound, peeled onion; place it in a saucepan with half an ounce of butter; and cook for three minutes on a brisk fire, being careful not to let get brown. Add six chopped mushrooms and one ounce of sausage meat. Season with one pinch of salt and half a pinch of pepper; cook for three minutes, stirring once in a while. Add now the tomatoes which were scooped out, with half a cupful of fresh bread crumbs and a teaspoonful of fresh chopped parsley. Mix well together, and cook for two minutes longer, or until it comes to a boil; then place in a bowl to cool. Stuff the emptied tomatoes with the above preparation, close down the covers, gently lay them on a tin plate (dish), cover them with a buttered paper, and cook in a moderate oven for eighteen minutes, then serve.

Stuffed tomatoes are served as a garnishing in various ways.— Filippini, *The Table*, 308.

CARL VAN VECHTEN

Carl Van Vechten (1880–1964), photographer and novelist, was one of the major proponents of the Harlem Renaissance. In his novel *The Merry-Go-Round* (1918) he imagines a member of the Metropolitan Opera Company who owns a restaurant: "Have you seen Bernard Bégué standing before his cook stove preparing food for his patrons? His huge form, clad in white, viewed through the open doorway connecting the dining room with the kitchen, almost conceals the great stove, but occasionally you can catch sight of the pots and pans, the *casseroles* of *pot-au-feu*, the roasting chicken, the filets of sole, all the ingredients of a dinner, *cuisine bourgeoise* … and after dining, you can hear Bégué sing the Uncle-priest in *Madama Butterfly* at the Opera House."[1]

Garlic Ice Cream (a dressing for salad)

This was invented by the silent film star Theda Bara, who shared it with Van Vechten in 1927.

4 small potatoes, chopped to pulp
1 tablespoon Worcestershire sauce
1 teaspoon Tabasco
½ teaspoon salt
1 teaspoon onion juice
1 cup mayonnaise
2 spoons Cowboy's Delight (may be procured from Old Smoky Sales Co., 124 West 4th Street, Los Angeles, California)

Beat till ingredients are well mixed. Freeze in icebox. DO NOT STIR WHILE FREEZING. Serve in avocados (cut in half)— Barr and Sachs, *Artists' and Writers' Cookbook*, n.p.

Viennese Cheese Pancakes

2 yolks of eggs.
2 teaspoons sugar.

½ teaspoon salt.

2 cups milk.

½ cup, or more, flour.

Beat the yolks of the eggs and pour all together in large bowl. Make THIN pancakes and fill them with: pot cheese, raisins, yellow of one egg, vanilla, sugar. Bake for 10 minutes in rich butter.—Barr and Sachs, *Artists' and Writers' Cookbook*, n.p.

METTA VICTOR

Metta Victor, aka Metta Victoria Fuller (1831–1885), wrote more than 100 dime novels as well as crime fiction.

Green Tomato Pickles

Take any size, but those ready to ripen are the best, place them in a vessel, and throw on a handful of salt; cover with boiling water, and let them stand till cold; then slice them through transversely, once or twice, according to the size; then lay them in a crock with thin-sliced onions. Prepare the vinegar with cloves, cinnamon, and allspice, and pour on hot. Cover and set away for a few days. They will be found very delicious, and will keep all winter. Those who dislike onions may omit them.—Victor, *Beadle's Dime Novel Cook Book* (New York: Beadle and Adams, 1868), 77.

Head Cheese

Thoroughly clean the hog's head, split it in two, take out the eyes and brains, cut off the nose and ears, and pour scalding water over the latter and the head, and scrape them clean. Then rinse all in old water, and put it into water to cover it; let it boil gently, taking off the scum as it rises; when boiled so that the bones leave the meat readily, take it from the water into a large wooden bowl or tray; take from it every particle of bone; chop the meat small, and season to taste with salt and pepper, and if like, a little chopped sage or thyme; spread a cloth in a colander or sieve; set it in a deep dish, and put the meat in, then fold the cloth closely over it, lay a plate on, which may press equally the whole surface. Let the weight be more or less heavy, according as you may wish the cheese to be fat or lean; a heavy weight by pressing out the fat will of course leave the cheese lean.

When cold, scrape off whatever fat may be found on the outside of the cloth, and keep the cheese in the cloth in a cool place. To be eaten sliced then, with or without mustard and vinegar, or catsup.—Victor, *Beadle's Dime Novel Cook Book*, 35.

Oyster Catsup

Take fine fresh oysters; wash them in their own liquor, skim it, pound them in a marble mortar; to a pint of oysters add a pint of sherry; boil them up, and add an ounce of salt, two drachms of pounded mace, and one of cayenne; let it just boil up again, skim it, and rub it through a sieve, and when cold bottle it; then cork it well, and seal it down.—Victor, *Beadle's Dime Novel Cook Book*, 84.

Tomato Chowder

Soak a peck of green tomatoes for twenty-four hours in salt and water, chop them up quite fine in the chopping bowl, adding three or four onions, mix with them a teacupful of white mustard seed; scald sufficient good vinegar to cover them, spicing it with pepper-corns, cloves, and allspice, tied loosely in a thin muslin beg; pour the vinegar upon the tomatoes, tie up the mouths of the jars in which it is put away. One of the best pickles ever made.— Victor, *Beadle's Dime Novel Cook Book*, 80.

GERALD VIZENOR

> A member of the Minnesota Chippewa Tribe, White Earth Reservation, the poet and novelist Gerald Vizenor (b. 1934) has taught at UC-Santa Cruz, UC-Berkeley, the University of Oklahoma, and the University of New Mexico. He received American Book Awards in 1988 and 2011.

Banquet Français

Messy Fairbanks, the famous native *chef de cuisine*, chopped, stirred, stewed, seasoned, baked, and prepared with incredible concentration the Banquet Français at the Hotel Leecy on the White Earth Reservation in Minnesota. The actual menu for the special dinner was selected from a country cookbook published in Paris. Messy converted the weights and measures and Catherine Heady, the government schoolteacher, translated the recipes into English.

John Leecy told me that he had conceived of the banquet when he read my recent stories about the Café du Dôme and the cubist painter Marie Vassilieff in Paris. So, he decided to arrange a memorable banquet at the Hotel Leecy on the reservation to celebrate our return, to respect the native casualties of the war, to praise our ancestors of the fur trade, and to honor the courage of Corporal Lawrence Vizenor who had received the Distinguished Service Cross in the First World War in France.

The Banquet Français menu was printed on deckle edge paper in fancy calligraphy. The title, *Soldiers of the Fur Trade*, and four names, Lawrence Vizenor, Basile Hudon Beaulieu, Aloysius Hudon Beaulieu, Patch Zhimagaanish were printed on the cover, and inside with the actual menu were the names of the invited guests and banquet storiers.

The first course was *Soupe de Poissons*, or puréed fish soup with sunfish, perch, and crappies, and stewed with fennel, tomatoes, garlic, orange peel, and black pepper. The soup was served with fresh butter and warm baguettes. Animosh caught the fish that very day at Bad Boy Lake.

Messy told the first story that night about the federal agent as she poured more wine, and as the waiters removed the soup bowls. Foamy had tracked the scent of prohibited alcohol that morning to the kitchen of the Hotel Leecy. The agent had an acute nose for the wine in the *Coq au Beaulieu*, the main course of the banquet. The red wine, sliced onions, celery, carrots, garlic, smoked thick bacon, and peppercorns were simmered with two chickens. Later the chickens were garnished with baby onions, mushrooms, and parsley.

Messy raised a cleaver and shouted at the agent that she would chop his skinny *niinag* right down to the short hairs and throw it to the dogs if he ever came sniffing around the kitchen again. Foamy protected his crotch with both hands, turned and hurried back to the government house. Only a rabid dog would eat a federal pecker.

Messy and the waiters served *Coq au Beaulieu*, the main course, and with salads and fresh vegetables. The *Truffade*, a potato cake with cheese and bacon, *Poireaux Vinaigrette*, leeks with shallots, chopped boiled eggs, cider vinegar, mustard, and parsley, *Petits Pois à la Française*, sweet, fresh green peas with butter and sugar, and *Fèves à la Tourangelle*, baby lima beans, bacon, butter, baby onions, chives, and parsley, were so distinctive and delicious that each vegetable on the menu could have been the third, fourth, fifth and other courses at the Banquet Français. Lima beans were a substitute for the *fèves*, fava or broad beans, because no one of the reservation had ever heard of fava beans or the country recipe.

John Leecy poured out Wiser's rye whiskey, his favorite from Ontario, Canada, in thick glasses with the third course of cheese, a special selection as usual from the Marin French Cheese Company in California.

Odysseus, Catherine Heady, and Doctor Mendor were heavy whiskey drinkers. John Leecy was a connoisseur of singular white lightning, and later the moonshine drinkers were extremely pleased to savor Cape Breton Silver, a special raw moonshine distilled from potato skins in Nova Scotia, Canada. The moonshine was served from a mason jar and with no label. My tongue hurt, eyes smarted, a torture taste with no name that could have been distilled in a rain bucket on the reservation.

Wine was my choice, a palatable drink with a culture and memory. Whiskey and moonshine were too strong for me, and the outcome was risky in the best of company. My choice of wine was a serious deviation on the reservation. The big boasters about white lightning were scored as more manly, an ancient pretense, and wine drinkers were pompous outsiders. I was only an outsider among the hard drinkers. Yes, the fur trade created a new culture of outsiders with traces of a wine culture. France and the First World War only increased my deviation from the reservation of white lightning drinkers.

Odysseus cut thick wedges of Camembert and slowly savored the Cape Breton Silver. French cheese, white lightning, and ironic stories were worthy courses of the trader, or the marvelous dance moves of a respected outsider. Odysseus, as usual, told a perfect story about a moonshiner with crazy hair that night between the banquet courses of cheese and dessert.—"Banquet Français" is a selection from Gerald Vizenor's historical novel, *Blue Ravens: Native American Indians in the First World War*, forthcoming from Wesleyan University Press.

SAM WARD

Perhaps the greatest gourmand of his generation, Sam Ward (1814–1884), the brother of the author of "The Battle Hymn of the Republic," was a poet by avocation and a political lobbyist by vocation. His biographer asserts that he "happily shared his knowledge of cookery and offered advice on menus for all sorts of occasions."[1]

Grouse, Roasted à la Sam Ward

Take two fine fat grouse; pick, singe, draw, and dry them well; then truss them nicely. Place them in a roasting pan, putting inside of each bird a piece of broiled toast four inches long and two wide. Drip in on each toast, with a spoon, a small glassful of good Madeira wine or sherry; season the grouse with a pinch of salt; spread a little butter over. Put them in a brisk oven, and let cook for eighteen minutes, taking care to baste them frequently. Lay them on a hot dish, untruss, strain the gravy over, and decorate with a little watercress.

Serve with a little red currant jelly separately.—*Mrs. Shillaber's Cookbook* 280; rpt. George Augustus Sala, *The Thorough Cookbook* (New York: Brentano's, 1896), 275.

Ham

I soak it for four days in water, changing it four times a day; then boil it five hours in cider, with a wisp of new hay; then I baste it with brandy, sherry, or claret, according to the weather; and when they have tasted a slice of that ham, why, they will pass anything I want in Congress.—*Chicago Tribune*, May 15, 1875, 2.

Sam Ward Hashed Fillet of Beef

Victor Hirtzler, chef at the Hotel St. Francis in San Francisco for more than 20 years, "went to California in 1904 where he was the opening chef for the splendid new St. Francis Hotel," the only "truly first-class hotel west of Chicago."[2] There he named a signature dish after Sam Ward.

Take the unused portions of roasted or larded tenderloin of beef and cut in small squares. Also an equal amount of boiled potatoes cut in the same way. In a sauté pan put one chopped onion and two green peppers cut in small dices, with two ounces of butter. Simmer until soft, then add the potato and meat, one cup of bouillon, or two cups, if necessary, season with salt, cover, put in oven and cook for thirty minutes. Serve on platter with chopped parsley on top, and garnished with small pieces of toast.— Hirtzler, *The Hotel St. Francis Cook Book* (Chicago: Hotel Monthly, 1919), 120.

Verses for the Kitchen

Always have lobster sauce with salmon,
And put mint sauce your roasted lamb on.
In dressing salad mind this law —
With two hard yolks use one that's raw.
Roast veal with rich stock gravy serve;
And pickled mushrooms, too, observe.
Roast *pork*, sans apple sauce, past doubt
Is "Hamlet" with the *Prince* left out.
Your mutton chops with paper cover
And make them amber brown all over.
Broil lightly your beefsteak — to fry it
Argues contempt of Christian diet.
To roast spring chickens is to spoil 'em —
Just split 'em down the back and broil 'em.
It gives true epicures the vapors
To see boiled mutton minus capers.
The cook deserves a hearty cuffing
Who serves roast fowls with tasteless stuffing.
Smelts require egg and biscuit powder —
Don't put fat pork in your clam chowder.
Egg sauce — few make it right, alas!
Is good with bluefish or with bass.

Nice oyster sauce gives zest to cod —
A fish, when fresh, to feast a god.
But one might rhyme for weeks this way,
And still have lots of things to say.
And so I'll close, for, reader mine,
This is about the hour I dine.

— *Cottage Hearth*, 1 March 1876, 72.

ROBERT PENN WARREN

Robert Penn Warren (1905–1989), one of the Fugitive poets and Southern Agrarians, received a Pulitzer Prize for his novel *All the King's Men* (1946) and Pulitzer prizes for Poetry in 1958 and 1979. He was also awarded the Presidential Medal of Freedom in 1980 by Jimmy Carter. Though he protested in *The Great American Writers' Cookbook* (1981) that "the only recipe I know is how to boil water, and I don't think you need that information,"[1] he shared a drink recipe with a friend.

Insidious Punch

Here is the recipe: 1 quart sauterne; 1 quart gin; 1 pint rum; 1 half-pint sherry; 1 pint grapefruit juice; enough pineapple juice to sweeten to taste; 1 large cake of ice. It has the mildest flavor in the world, but, since you know the recipe, it is superfluous for me to point out that it is not for the women and children. — *Selected Letters of Robert Penn Warren*, ed. Randy Hendricks and James A. Perkins (Baton Rouge: Louisiana State University Press, 2006), III 22–23.

BOOKER T. WASHINGTON

Booker T. Washington (1856–1915) founded the Tuskegee Institute and was often considered the "spokesman" for African Americans during his life. He dined with Theodore Roosevelt in the White House, likely in the State Dining Room on the evening of October 16, 1901, only a month after Roosevelt became president. It marked the first time an African American had been entertained at the Executive Mansion, and the event was extremely controversial, especially in the South. Unfortunately, the menu of that meal does not survive. The evening of February 12, 1909, however, Washington joined a group of Republican party elders at the Waldorf-Astoria in New York for the 23 annual Lincoln Dinner, and both the menu and many of the recipes for those dishes are in the public record.

Pommes de Terre Sautees (Sautéd Potato)

Cut up into slices eight medium-sized cold boiled potatoes, place an ounce and a half of butter in a frying pan and add the potatoes, seasoning with half a pinch of salt and pepper, and toss them well in the pan for a couple of minutes, after which form them into the shape of an omelette and allow them to become a golden color, which will require about five minutes' time. With a spoon take up all the butter lying at the bottom of the pan, and slide the potatoes onto a hot dish, and serve. — Oscar Tschirky, *The Cook Book by "Oscar" of the Waldorf* (Chicago and New York: Werner, 1896), 475.

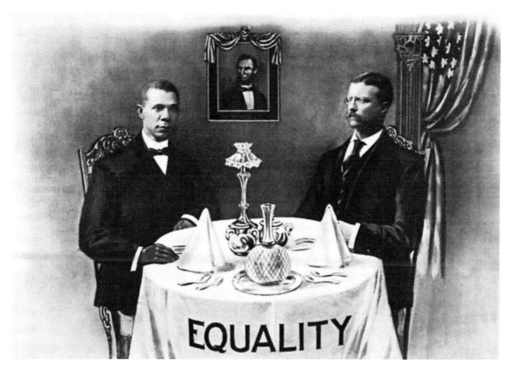

Booker T. Washington and Theodore Roosevelt. Lithograph by C. H. Thomas and P. H. Lacey, published by Royal Picture Gallery Co., Chicago (1903).

In the dining room of the Waldorf-Astoria, New York, circa 1902 (Library of Congress).

Roast Turkey with Sauce Diable

Singe, draw, and truss a turkey, season it interiorly with salt and cayenne pepper, put it in a baking dish with the washed liver and gizzard, and sufficient water to make the gravy, and bake it in a brisk oven, basting frequently. When it begins to brown dredge it over with flour, turning it often so that each part can be equally browned. Cover the breast with a sheet of buttered paper. When cooked, cut the liver and gizzard up, place them in a small saucepan with a lump of butter and one teaspoonful of cream, and stir it over the fire until it is hot. Place the turkey on a hot dish, first removing the paper from the breast. Skim the fat off the gravy into the baking pan, and strain it into the saucepan with the gizzard and liver. Pour the gravy over the turkey, and serve it while very hot.

Put three peeled and chopped shallots into a saucepan, add one clove of garlic, one bay leaf, a bunch of parsley and thyme, one-half teaspoonful of cayenne and coarsely crushed white pepper, one and one-half pint of Spanish sauce, and one-half pint of veal broth. When boiling, move the sauce to the edge of the fire, and let it simmer for half an hour. Skim the sauce, strain it through a fine hair-sieve, and serve.—Tschirky, *The Cook Book by "Oscar" of the Waldorf*, 334, 513.

George Washington

The "Father of His Country," George Washington (1732–1799) served as commander-in-chief of the Continental Army during the American Revolution, presided at the Constitutional Convention in 1787, and served as the first president of the United States before retiring to Mount Vernon, his Virginia estate, in 1797. The definitive

Washington's kitchen at Mt. Vernon (Library of Congress).

edition of Washington's writings, including his Farewell Address and private papers, commenced publication in 1968 and to date comprises 52 volumes. According to Harry Haff, his wife Martha "took pride in her table" at Mount Vernon; "her recipes and methods still appeal to modern readers and her cookbook is still available."[1] Still, the homes of slaveowners, including both Washington and Thomas Jefferson, often featured kitchens and dining rooms far apart: they preferred to inconvenience slaves and servants rather than tolerate the smells of meal preparation. As a result, "food arrived on Washington's table lukewarm."[2]

Small Beer

In 1757, George Washington, then a colonel in the colonial army, scribbled a "small beer" recipe in his private notebook. Little could he have imagined it would spark a *cause célèbre* a century and a half later during Prohibition or "the Dry Blight," as Frank Case termed it.[3] The backstory: In 1926, the officers of the Association Against the Prohibition Amendment asked the U.S. Department of Justice whether it would be legal under the Volstead Act, which forbade even the possession of any "recipe advertised, designed, or intended for use in the unlawful manufacture of intoxicating liquor," to read Washington's notebook entry aloud at its annual Washington's Birthday dinner at the Mayflower Hotel in D.C. The department ignored the inquiry, so

George Washington's beer recipe (*Washington Post*, March 2, 1926, 1).

the association proceeded with its challenge to the law. The reading, by Representative John Phillip Hill of Maryland, the leader of the "wets" in Congress, was "wildly applauded" by an audience of 500.[4] A week later, on March 2, emboldened by the failure of the Justice Department to object, the editors of the *Washington Post* published a facsimile of the recipe in Washington's handwriting on the front page of the newspaper.[5] Its appearance predictably infuriated the "drys" in Congress, who called for the immediate arrest of the *Post* editors.[6] After Representative Emanuel Celler of New York inserted the recipe into the *Congressional Record* in early March,[7] the "wets" argued that, according to the letter of an unreasonable and unenforceable law, the employees in the Government Printing Office were guilty of criminal mischief and the Justice Department ought to confiscate all copies of the *Record*. Thus the "drys" were hoist on their own petard.

Take a large Siffer [Sifter] full of Bran Hops to your Taste. Boil these 3 hours then strain out 30 Gall[ons] into a cooler put in 3 Gall[ons] Molasses while the Beer is Scalding hot or rather draw the Melasses [sic] into the cooler & St[r]ain the Beer on it while boiling Hot. let this stand till it is little more than Blood warm then put in a quart of Yeast if the Weather is very Cold cover it over with a Blank[et] & let it Work in the Cooler 24 hours then put it into the Cask — leave the bung open till it is almost don[e] Working — Bottle it that day Week it was Brewed. — "Washington's Note Book: Selections from a Newly Discovered Manuscript," *Bulletin of the New York Public Library* 24 (August 1920), 435.

OTONO WATANNA

Otono Watanna, aka Winnifred Eaton (1875–1954), and her sister Sui Sin Far, aka Edith Eaton, were the earliest Asian American authors, though Watanna purported to be of Japanese descent to escape the anti–Chinese prejudice experienced by her sister. She collaborated with Sara Bosse on one of the earliest Asian cookbooks in English.

Fried Bamboo Shoots

Take one can of bamboo shoots and drain off all water. Wipe the bamboo shoots dry, and slice in long thin strips. Have ready boiling peanut oil, and toss the shoots into that. Cook until crisp. Delicious. Must be eaten hot. — Sara Bosse and Watanna, *Chinese-Japanese Cook Book* (Chicago and New York: Rand McNally, 1914), 60.

Gai Grun Yung Waa (Bird's-nest Soup)

One half pound of bird's nest; one pint of chicken stock; one quarter pound of cooked breast of chicken; one boiled egg; one quarter pound of minced ham; one teaspoonful of salt.

To make this soup, the bird's nest is first boiled an hour, then drained and put into cold water. Meanwhile, the cooked chicken meat is well-pounded, so as not to be in large or hard pieces, and a cupful of the cold stock is added to it. Next the bird's nest is taken from the cold water and well-drained, and added to the soup stock. Boil for half an hour. Now the chicken meat is added, and also the egg, the latter having previously been finely crumbled. The soup is taken off the fire as it begins to boil again after the last addition. Before serving, the minced ham is sprinkled on top.

Bird's nest is a gelatinous substance, a species of seaweed, with which certain Chinese

Cover of Sara Bosse's and Onoto Watanna's *Chinese-Japanese Cook Book* (1914).

birds, the esculent swallow and the white-backed swallow, build their nests. It is also found in Java. It is one of the most delicious of Chinese foods, and esteemed and praised not alone by the Chinese but by all travelers in the Orient.— Bosse and Watanna, *Chinese-Japanese Cook Book*, 15.

Mushi Kujira (Boiled Whale or Bass)

Two pounds of fish; one half teacupful of syou [soy sauce]; orange and lemon skin; two long, large radishes; two tablespoonfuls of vinegar; salt, and dash of cayenne pepper.

Take off all bones and slice the fish daintily in long slices, and then in half-inch dice. Sprinkle with salt, and leave for about fifteen minutes. Cut radishes in long, even, delicate strips. Boil for a few minutes, strain, then add half a cup of syou sauce and two tablespoonfuls of a fine vinegar. When it boils, drop in the fish slices. Boil up, then push to back of range, and, covered tight, let it simmer for half an hour. Grate the peels of half a lemon and half an orange, and sprinkle over the fish, after having removed it to a hot platter. Serve with boiled rice.

Note. This dish comes from Nagasaki, and is really a Japanized Chinese dish. Japanese cooking of fish greatly resembles that of the Chinese.—Bosse and Watanna, *Chinese-Japanese Cook Book*, 75.

Roast Squab

One plump squab; two chicken livers; one dozen fresh mushrooms; one tablespoonful of Chinese almonds; one tablespoonful of chicken fat; two tablespoonfuls of syou; one teaspoonful of salt; one quarter small onion; one teaspoonful of cornstarch.

Clean and singe a plump squab. Rub inside and out with salt. Stuff it with the following: A dozen mushrooms, peeled and cut small, a tablespoonful of almonds which have been blanched and chopped fine, and a little minced onion. Mix together, and fill the squab. Now sew or skew tight, and melt the tablespoonful of chicken fat and pour it over the squab. Place in a hot oven and roast for half an hour, basting and turning frequently. Make the gravy, meanwhile, by chopping fine two chicken livers and frying them in a teaspoonful of chicken fat. When very brown, stir in a teaspoonful of cornstarch until brown. Now add two tablespoonfuls of syou, and serve with the squab.—Bosse and Watanna, *Chinese-Japanese Cook Book*, 29.

Usagi Amai-Sui (Sweet and Sour Hare)

One good sized-rabbit or hare; one cupful of vinegar; one cupful of syou sauce; one tablespoonful of salt; three tablespoonfuls of sugar; one half cupful of mirin sauce; one tablespoonful of mixed spices; one half pound of fat fresh pork; one dozen red plums; one small lime or lemon.

Take a small hare or large rabbit that has been hanging for at least two days, and after it has been skinned, and the insides removed, wash well in cold water. Cut in quarters and put in a deep dish, covering it well with the vinegar, sugar, salt, and so on, mixed with water. Add the spices also, and a quarter cupful of mirin sauce. Cover it well, and let it pickle in a cool place for two or three days; then remove it from the liquid and cut in small pieces. Have ready the fat pork cut in small pieces, and fry. Toss in the hare, and brown. Now have ready a covered China cook dish or casserole, and place in it the hare and pork, adding the syou sauce, a pinch of salt, pinch of the spices, and the quarter cupful of mirin sauce. Cover up tightly, and cook in a slow oven for one hour. Then prepare a dozen large red plums, removing the stones, and add them. Dissolve one teaspoonful of Kanton (Japanese gelatine) and mix with the gravy, taking care not to break the plums. Cook for another five minutes, then place on a hot platter, decorated with slices of lemon or limes, with a plum placed on top of each slice. This is good served either with white bean cakes or rice.—Bosse and Watanna, *Chinese-Japanese Cook Book*, 83–84.

DANIEL WEBSTER

The *Writings and Speeches* of the statesman and politician Daniel Webster (1782–1852), including "The Plymouth Oration" (1820) and his speech at the Bunker Hill Monument in 1825, were published in 18 volumes in 1903.

Punch

Long after his death, Webster's private recipe for punch circulated in the press. A champion of American commerce and an opponent of the shipping embargoes imposed early in the 19th century, he jocularly called for it to be made with smuggled French brandy.

One bottle of pure old French brandy (smuggled direct preferred), one bottle sherry, one ditto old Jamaica rum, two ditto claret, one ditto champagne, one dozen lemons, one pint strong tea, sugar, strawberries and pineapple to suit the taste, plenty of ice, no water.—*Harrisburg Patriot*, July 19, 1873, 1.

EUDORA WELTY

Recipient of a Pulitzer Prize in 1973 for her novel *The Optimist's Daughter*, Eudora Welty (1909–2001) worked as a photographer for the Works Projects Administration during the Great Depression and was hired by the Federal Writers' Project to record recipes for "America Eats," a culinary history that was never published. Long filed away in the Library of Congress, these files became the basis of the compilation of recipes published under the title *The Food of a Younger Land: From the Lost WPA Files* (2009). Welty assured her readers, "Yankees are welcome to make these dishes."[1]

Barbeque Sauce

1 pint Wesson oil
2 pounds butter
5 bottles barbeque sauce (3½ ounce bottles)
½ pint vinegar
1 cup lemon juice
2 bottles tomato catsup (14 ounce bottles)
1 bottle Worcestershire sauce (10 ounce bottles)
1 tablespoon Tabasco sauce
2 buttons garlic, chopped fine
Salt and pepper to taste

This will barbeque eight chickens weighing from 2½ to 3 pounds. In barbecuing, keep a slow fire and have live coals to add during the process of cooking, which takes about two hours. The secret lies in the slow cooking and the constant mopping of the meat with the sauce. Keep the chickens wet at all times and turn often. If hotter sauce is desired, add red pepper and more Tabasco sauce.—Manuscript Division, Library of Congress.

Beaten Biscuit

4 cups flour, measured before sifting
¾ cup lard

1 teaspoon salt
4 teaspoons sugar
enough ice water and milk to make a stiff dough (about ½ cup)
Break 150 times until the dough pops. Roll out and cut, and prick with a fork. Bake in a 400-degree oven. When biscuits are a light brown, turn off the heat and leave them in the oven with the door open until they sink well, to make them done in the middle.—Manuscript Division, Library of Congress.

> "Vicksburg, in the old steamboat days Mississippi's wicked, wide-open town, lived high with all the trimmings," Welty noted during the Depression. "Perched on the bluffs overlooking the Mississippi, it is famous still for its excellent catfish."[2]

Catfish

Take a catfish weighing ½ pound. Season well with salt and pepper, and roll in cornmeal. Use a pot of deep fat with temperature of 360 degrees. Place the fish in the pot and fry until done. Serve very hot.—Manuscript Division, Library of Congress.

Fish Court Bouillon

5 or 6 onions
1 bunch parsley
2 or 4 pieces celery
4 pieces garlic
6 small cans tomatoes
1 or 2 bay leaves
Hot peppers to taste
Cut up fine, fry brown, and let simmer for about an hour, slowly. Prepare the fish, and put into the gravy. Do not stir. Cook until fish is done.

This will serve 8 to 10 people, for 10 or more double the ingredients.

To prepare fish, fry without cornmeal, and put in a plate or pan. Pour a portion of the gravy over it, and let it set for a while. Just before serving, pour the rest of the hot gravy over the fish.—Manuscript Division, Library of Congress.

Jellied Apples

Pare and core one dozen apples of a variety which will jell successfully. Winesap and Jonathan are both good.

To each dozen apples moisten well two and one-half cups of sugar. Allow this to boil for about five minutes. Then immerse apples in this syrup, allowing plenty of room about each apple. Add the juice of one-half lemon, cover closely, and allow to cook slowly until apples appear somewhat clear. Close watching and frequent turning is necessary to prevent them from falling apart.

Remove from stove and fill centers with a mixture of chopped raisins, pecans, and crystallized ginger, the latter adding very much to the flavor of the finished dish. Sprinkle each apple with granulated sugar and baste several times with the thickening syrup, then place in a 350-degree oven to glaze without cover on vessel. Baste several times during this last process.—Manuscript Division, Library of Congress.

Lye Hominy

1 gallon shelled corn
½ quart oak ashes
Salt to taste
Boil corn about three hours, or until the husk comes off, with oak ashes which must be tied in a bag — a small sugar sack will answer. Then wash in three waters. Cook a second time about four hours, or until tender. — Manuscript Division, Library of Congress.

Mint Julep

Have silver goblet thoroughly chilled.
Take half lump sugar and dissolve in tablespoon water.
Take single leaf mint and bruise it between fingers, dropping it into dissolved sugar.
Strain after stirring.
Fill the goblet with crushed ice, to capacity.
Pour in all the bourbon whiskey the goblet will hold.
Put a sprig of mint in the top of the goblet, for bouquet.
Let goblet stand until FROSTED.
Serve rapidly. — Manuscript Division, Library of Congress.

Okra Gumbo

2 or 3 onions
½ bunch parsley
5 or 6 pieces celery
1 small piece garlic
4 cans of okra, or a dozen fresh pieces
1 can tomatoes
1 pound veal stew, or 1 slice raw ham
Cut all ingredients in small pieces and fry brown. Let simmer for a while. If shrimp are desired, pick and parboil them and add to the ingredients the shrimp and the water in which they were boiled. If oysters or crab meat is desired, add to gumbo about twenty minutes before done. Add as much water as desired. — Manuscript Division, Library of Congress.

Seafood Gumbo

2 quarts okra, sliced
2 large green peppers
1 large stalk celery
6 medium sized onions
1 bunch parsley
½ quart diced ham
2 cans #2 tomatoes
2 cans tomato paste
3 pounds cleaned shrimp
2 dozen hard crabs, cleaned and broken into bits
100 oysters and juice

½ cup bacon drippings
1 cup flour
Small bundle of bay leaf and thyme
Salt and pepper to taste
1 teaspoon Lea & Perrins Sauce
1½ gallons chicken or ham stock

Put ham in pot and smother until done. Then add sliced okra, and also celery, peppers, onions, and parsley all ground together. Cover and cook until well done. Then add tomatoes and tomato paste.

Next put in the shrimp, crabs, crab meat and oysters. Make brown roux of bacon dripping and flour and add to the above. Add the soup stock, and throw into pot bay leaves and thyme, salt and pepper, and Lea & Perrins Sauce.

This makes three gallons of gumbo. Add one tablespoon of steamed rice to each serving.— Manuscript Division, Library of Congress.

Spanish Rice

4 tablespoons oil
1 cup rice
1 onion sliced
1 green pepper, chopped
1 quart canned tomatoes
2 teaspoons salt
a little less than ¼ teaspoon pepper

Heat 2 teaspoons oil in large frying pan and add rice. Cook until brown, stirring constantly. Cook remaining 2 tablespoons oil with onion and green pepper until the onion is yellow and tender. Combine with rice. Add tomatoes and let it simmer until the rice is tender, stirring constantly. Add a little hot tomato juice if the rice seems dry. Add seasonings. Serves 6.— Manuscript Division, Library of Congress.

Stuffed Eggs

12 eggs
1 pound can of spinach or equal amount of fresh spinach
1 small onion, cut fine
Salt and pepper to taste
Juice of 1 lemon or ½ cup vinegar
½ cup melted butter or oil
1 large can mushroom soup

Boil eggs hard, peel, and cut lengthwise. Mash yolks fine. Add butter, seasoning, and spinach. Stuff each half egg, press together, and pour over them mushroom soup thickened with cornstarch, and chopped pimento for color.— Manuscript Division, Library of Congress.

WALT WHITMAN

Walt Whitman (1819–1892). When Oscar Wilde visited Whitman at his home in Camden, New Jersey, in January 1882, Wilde remembered, "There was a big chair for

Walt Whitman at home in Camden, New Jersey (Library of Congress).

him and a little stool for me, a pine table on which was a copy of Shakespeare, a translation of Dante, and a cruse of water."[1] Among Whitman's daybooks in the Library of Congress are two recipes he preserved around the same time, one for doughnuts and another for coffee cake. Neither has ever before been published.

Coffee Cake

Pour one cup of boiling hot, strong coffee on one cup of lard or pork fat; add one cup of molasses, one cup of brown sugar, three well-beaten eggs, one teaspoonful each of cloves, cinnamon, allspice, one-half teaspoon nutmeg, one teaspoonful of soda dissolved in a little warm water, flour enough to make a stiff batter. Bake in a sheet-iron pan one hour and a half in a slow oven.— Commonplace Books 1876–1891, Walt Whitman Papers, Charles E. Feinberg Collection (Library of Congress).

Doughnuts

2¼ pounds of flour, ¾ of sugar, 1 teaspoon baker's yeast, 1½ pints of milk, 3 cups of butter, a little salt and cinnamon. Warm the butter and milk together. It should make a soft dough. W[ith a rolling pin] very light roll out and cut in any sh[ape to suit your] fancy; fry in lard at blue-smoke point.— Commonplace Books 1876–1891, Walt Whitman Papers, Charles E. Feinberg Collection (Library of Congress).

A. D. T. Whitney

The popular domestic novelist A. D. T. Whitney (1824–1906) was avidly read by, among other young women, Charlotte Perkins Gilman, who allowed that Whitney helped set the standards for the behavior of "nice girls."[1]

Brown Bread

In Whitney's novel *The Other Girls* (1873) the dutiful heroine stops at a local bakery to buy one of the "fresh big loaves of real brown bread for her father's tea."[2] Not surprisingly, Whitney later contributed a recipe for brown bread to Maria Parola's *Universal Common Sense Cookery Book* (1892).

Make ready: one even cup of Indian meal; two heaping cups of rye meal; one teaspoonful of salt, and one of soda, mixed together with the sifted meal in a large bowl; one cupful of molasses, in a quart measure or small bowl, with spoon; a large beating spoon; palette knife, to scrape your mixture from the bowl; a tin bread or pudding boiler, well buttered.

Stir the meal, salt, and soda, dry, until thoroughly mingled. Pour one pint of hot water to the molasses, and stir it up. Pour the molasses and water into the middle of your meal, stirring to a smooth batter as in previous directions; beat all quickly and well for several minutes; it should be of a consistence to stir easily, and break in pouring, but not to run. With some qualities of molasses, you may need to add from a spoonful or two to half a cup more of warm water, to make it right.

Put into your tin boiler, cover tight, and put this into an iron kettle with boiling water in it. Cover the kettle also. Boil steadily for three hours, looking from time to time to see if the water in the kettle is boiling away. Keep it replenished, always from boiling water. Take the bread boiler out at the end of the three hours, and set it into the oven for about ten minutes; longer if the oven is not quick. This is to dry the outside steam off, and form a tender crust. Put hot upon the table; cut and help hot.—Parola et al., *Universal Common Sense Cookery Book*, 155–56.

One-Two-Three-Four Cookies

1 cup butter
2 cups sugar
3 cups flour
4 eggs
½ teaspoonful soda
1 teaspoonful cream of tartar
½ teasponful salt
1 teaspoonful spice, or 2 tablespoonfuls caraway seed, or 2 teaspoonfuls yellow ginger

Cream the butter, and add half the sugar. Beat the yolks, add the remaining half of the sugar, and beat them with the butter, then add the beaten whites. Mix the soda, cream of tartar, spice, and salt with the flour, and stir into the butter mixture. Take a teaspoonful of the dough, make it into a ball with floured hands, place the balls in the pan some distance apart, then press or flatten into a round cake, and bake about ten minutes.—*Mrs. Lincoln's Boston Cookbook*, 386.

KATE DOUGLAS WIGGIN

Kate Douglas Wiggin (1856–1923) was the author of the best-selling children's book *Rebecca of Sunnybrook Farm* (1903), the editor of *A Book of Dorcas Dishes* (1911), and the occasional target of highbrow critics.

Large Family Bread

A little soda measured in a silver spoon; two-thirds and a half as much again cream of tartar. If the weather is hot simply reverse the quantities and say nothing to the neighbors.

One quart of Graham flour.

One quart of white flour.

One quart of Indian meal, in the order named.

One cup new milch cow's milk.

One cup farrow cow's milk.

One cup ordinary milk; sweet if sweet, sour if it has turned.

Bathe the hands carefully and plunge them into the mixture, kneading it vigorously for an hour, being careful to stand in the draught of an open window all the time.

Grease the pans well with cocoa butter or beeswax.

Pour in the mixture if soft enough; crowd or push it in if it resists force, as it sometimes does with an inexperienced cook.

Never allow the fire to go out when bread is baking, as it often spoils it.

Remove the pans when, according to your best judgment, the bread is done, and never ask advice, as it is always unsettling.

Keep the loaves in a tin cake box under the spare room bed, where the children can run and get a slice whenever disposed.

This recipe sometimes cures the bad habit of eating between meals.—Wiggin, "Three Literary Recipes," *Harper's Bazar* [*sic*] 46 (September 1912), 435.

Novelty Cake

Three Plymouth Rock hen's eggs.

Three turkey's eggs.

Three duck's eggs.

Beat separately, and never under any circumstances allow them to come together. Beat them earnestly, until they can stand alone or you cannot.

Butter size of a gold thimble.

One cup of lard.

One cup of suet.

One cup of buttermilk.

One cup of maple syrup (the kind procured from trees)

One cup of self-raising buckwheat flour.

One cup of oatmeal.

One and one-half cups of talcum powder.

Enough soda to insure that golden brown color so often secured by young housekeepers, but not enough to settle in dark spots. You have already a substantial novelty here, but if you will add a dust of catnip and a dash of peppermint, vanilla, and witch-hazel, you will have a cake that can be distinguished from any other, even with the eyes closed. Set this mixture (which is either a thin batter or a stiff dough, as it happens) well out of reach of the cat, until it has thoroughly made up its mind what it will be. Meanwhile, take a white lisle-thread glove or the top of a baby's stocking; wash and boil. When thoroughly dry, butter with it a dozen popover cups. Give the mixture an extra stir at the last moment. In cold weather the maple syrup sometimes refuses to mix with the talcum powder, and the suet does not combine easily with the oatmeal. The last thing, add six tablespoonfuls of watermelon seeds, which give a handsome finish. They are not edible, but when eating the cake each person can dispose of his seeds in some genteel and unostentatious way.— *Harper's Bazar* [*sic*] 46 (September 1912), 435.

Substitute Washington Pie

Beat twenty-five eggs twenty-five minutes in a quick oven, but reserve the whites of twenty-three. Remove gently and set the pan in the sink, adding two-thirds of a gill of old-fashioned homemade yeast. (If you have neither gill nor yeast in the house substitute a plain china cup without handle and a tablespoonful of washing soda.) When passing through the kitchen subsequently, remember the mixture and place it on the ice. (If you have no ice, in the cellar.) Stir in a blue bowl (or a yellow bowl if more convenient) a package of cornstarch and two boxes of gelatin. (If that cannot easily be procured, use flour and Irish moss.) If the cake still seems too thin to roll out, add a quart of lightly sifted flour. (Indian meal will answer if the flour barrel is low.) Bake slowly, trying every five minutes with a clean broom straw. (In case you are out of broom straws the little finger of the right hand will do.)

Vegetable filling for same

Beat the whites of your twenty-five eggs until you can turn the platter upside down and count ten. Remove the eggs from the floor and stir in:

One clove of garlic (one ring of onion will produce about the same effect).
One-eighth of an ounce minced string beans (or pea pods).
One saltspoon of horseradish (or ginger).
Two tablespoons of Infant's Food (or malted milk).
One-half cup grated cheese (apple sauce is a good substitute).

Split the cake as many times as its height seems to suggest and insert the filling between the layers. This recipe keeps well and lasts a long time.— *Harper's Bazar* [*sic*] 46 (September 1912), 435.

TENNESSEE WILLIAMS

Tennessee Williams (1911–1983) wrote *The Glass Menagerie* (1944) and received Pulitzer prizes for *A Streetcar Named Desire* (1948) and *Cat on a Hot Tin Roof* (1955). He was awarded the Presidential Medal of Freedom by Jimmy Carter in 1980.

Grits

I use quick grits. If there's a secret to their cooking it's continual stirring and taking them off the burner at just the right thickness. I stir in "Bacos" or bits of real bacon, cheddar cheese and oleo-margarine. I use substitute salt, so I salt mine separately.

Yankee dinner guests remain recalcitrant, but now and then a Southerner comes along who enjoys them as much as I.— *The Great American Writers' Cookbook*, 173.

OWEN WISTER

Born to a privileged Philadelphia family, Owen Wister expressed his taste for fine dining in each of his two novels. In *The Virginian* (1902), the original formulaic Western novel, the hero outduels the villain Trampas by relating a tall tale about California ranches that raise frogs for eastern restaurants, specifically Augustin's in Philadelphia and Delmonico's in New York. While the chefs at Augustin's never published a cookbook, Filippini of Delmonico's printed four recipes for frogs' legs in *The Table* (broiled, à la poulette, fried, and à l'espagnole); and Ranhofer printed seven recipes for frogs' legs in *The Epicurean* (à la d'Antin; à la Osborn; à la poulette with mushrooms; deviled; fried à la Orly; fried with cream sauce; and Royer).[1] Wister seems to have regarded Delmonico's as the epitome of polite civilization: in his short story "A Pilgrim on the Gila" (1895) he remarks: "What a country we live in, and what an age, that the same stars and stripes should simultaneously wave over [the Arizona desert] and our Delmonico's!"[2] At a dinner in Wister's honor at the Union League Club in New York the evening of January 14, 1896, a menu for which survives among his papers in the Library of Congress, he partook of such dishes as Consommé à la printanier, Boudins de chapon aux truffles, Filet de bass à l'Union League, Carré d'agneau du printemps, Sauce menthe, Térapène à la Maryland, Asperges en branches, Sauce hollandaise, and Salade de céleri aux pommes.[3] Unfortunately, the chef there never published a cookbook, so we cannot know the exact components in these recipes.

Lady Baltimore Cake

Owen Wister's second novel, set in Charleston, S.C., was titled *Lady Baltimore* (1906) after a type of cake baked at the Woman's Exchange in the city that the narrator often enjoys.

"I should like a slice, if you please, of Lady Baltimore," I said with extreme formality. I returned to the table and she brought me the cake, and I had my first felicitous meeting with Lady Baltimore. Oh, my goodness! Did you ever taste it? It's all soft, and it's in layers, and it has nuts—but I can't write any more about it; my mouth waters too much. Delighted surprise caused me once more to speak aloud, and with my mouth full, "But, dear me, this is delicious!"[4]

While the exact recipe for the cake baked at the Woman's Exchange in Charleston while Wister lived there cannot be established, he was later sent a recipe for Lady Baltimore that he approved. The recipe was later plagiarized in the *Boston Cooking School Magazine*.[5]

One cupful of butter, two cupfuls of sugar, three-and-a-half cupfuls of flour, one cupful of sweet milk, the whites of six eggs, two level teaspoonfuls of baking powder and one of rosewater.

Mix as you would white cake and bake in three layers.

Filling: Dissolve three cupfuls of granulated sugar in one of boiling water, cook until it threads, the pour it gradually over the whites of three eggs beaten to a standing froth, stirring constantly. Add to this icing one cupful of chopped raisins, one of nut meats (preferably pecans) and five figs, cut into very thin strips. Ice and emboss sides and top with the mixture.—*Anaconda Standard*, December 23, 1906, 4.

E. L. YOUMANS

E. L. Youmans (1821–1887) was the author of *Handbook of Household Science* (1864) and the founding editor of *Popular Science Monthly* in 1872.

Chetney of Chicken

Ingredients: One large or two small chickens, one-quart can of tomatoes, butter the size of a pigeon's egg, one tablespoonful of flour, one heaping teaspoonful of minced onion, one teaspoonful of minced pork, one small bottle of chetney (one gill).

Press the tomatoes through a sieve. Put the butter (one and a half ounces) into a stew pan, and when hot throw in the minced onions; cook them a few minutes, then add the flour, which cook thoroughly; now pour in the tomato pulp, seasoned with pepper, salt, and the minced pork, and stir it thoroughly with an egg whisk until quite smooth, and then mix well into it the chetney, and next the cooked chicken cut into pieces. The chicken may be *sautéd* (if young) in a little hot fat, or it may be roasted or boiled as for a fricassee. The chicken is neatly arranged on a hot platter, with the sauce poured over. Slices of beef (the fillet preferable) may be served in the same way with the chetney sauce.

This chetney is an Indian sauce, and can be procured at the first-class groceries.— Henderson, *Practical Cooking and Dinner Giving*, 177–78.

Curry of Chicken

Cut the chicken into pieces, leaving out the body bones; season them with pepper and salt; fry them in a *sauté* pan in butter; cut an onion into small slices, which fry in the butter until quite red; now add a teacupful of stock freed from fat, an even teaspoonful of sugar, and a tablespoonful of curry powder, mixed with a little flour; rub the curry powder and flour smooth with a little stock before adding it to the saucepan; put in the chicken pieces, and let them boil two or three minutes; add then the juice of half a lemon. Serve this in the center of a bed of boiled rice.

Veal, lamb, rabbits, or turkey may be cooked in the same way. The addition of half a cocoanut, grated, is an improvement.— Henderson, *Practical Cooking and Dinner Giving*, 178.

Notes

Preface

1. Hawthorne, *The Scarlet Letter* (1850; rpt. New York: Norton, 1988), 15–16.
2. Hall, *Their Ancient Glittering Eyes: Remembering Poets and More Poets* (Boston: Houghton Mifflin, 1992), 165.
3. Trollope, *Domestic Manners of the Americans* (1832; rpt. New York: Dodd, Mead, 1901), I, 68.
4. Cooper, *The American Democrat* (1838; rpt. Baltimore: Penguin, 1969), 213.
5. Waverley Root and Richard de Rochemont, *Eating in America: A History* (New York: Norton, 1995), 74.
6. Child, *The Frugal American Housewife* (Boston: Carter and Hendee, 1830), 3.
7. *Marion Harland's Autobiography* (New York and London: Harper and Bros., 1910), 169.

Bronson and Louisa May Alcott

1. Alcott, "Transcendental Wild Oats," *Independent*, December 18, 1873, 1569–71.
2. Alcott, *Little Men* (Boston: Roberts Bros., 1871), 217.
3. Root and de Rochemont, *Eating in America* 141.

Sherwood Anderson

1. Anderson, *Poor White* (New York: Huebsch, 1920), 294.

Anonymous

1. Thomas Jefferson was descended from the Randolphs of Virginia.

Susan B. Anthony

1. *Jennie June's American Cookery Book* (New York: American News, 1870), 330.

Catherine Beecher

1. Catharine Beecher and Harriet Beecher Stowe, *The American Woman's Home* (New York: J. B. Ford, 1869), 179.

2. Stowe, *Uncle Tom's Cabin* (Boston: Jewett, 1852), 304.
3. Beecher, *A Treatise on Domestic Economy* (New York: Harper and Bros., 1845), 109.
4. Beecher and Stowe, *The American Woman's Home* 184.
5. Hilaire Dubourcq, *Benjamin Franklin Book of Recipes* (Bath: Canopus, 2000), 181.

Henry Ward Beecher

1. Beecher, *Plain and Pleasant Talk about Fruits, Flowers, and Farming* (New York: Derby and Jackson, 1859), 181.

Elizabeth Bishop

1. Bishop, *One Art: Letters, Selected and Edited*, ed. Robert Giroux (New York: Farrar, Straus and Giroux, 1994), 348.

Edwin Booth — Breakfast at Delmonico's

1. "Honors to Edwin Booth," *New York Times*, June 16, 1880, 8.

Oliver Bell Bunce

1. Mrs. Oliver Bell Bunce, "Old Dominion Cakes," *Los Angeles Times*, April 13, 1893, 10.

Willa Cather

1. *Willa Cather in Person*, ed. L. Brent Bohlke (Lincoln: University of Nebraska Press, 1987), 83.
2. Rosowski, Foreword to *Cather's Kitchens* by Robert L. Welsch and Linda K. Welsch (Lincoln: University of Nebraska Press, 1987), x.
3. Robert L. Welsch and Linda K. Welsch, *Cather's Kitchens* (Lincoln: University of Nebraska Press, 1987), 152.

Lydia Maria Child

1. Elbert and Drews, Introduction to *Culinary Aesthetics and Practices in Nineteenth-Century Amer-*

ican Literature (New York: Palgrave Macmillan, 2009), 2.

2. Edwards, "Lydia Maria Childs' *The Frugal Housewife*," *New England Quarterly* 26 (June 1953), 243. See also Hildegard Hoeller, "A Quilt for Life: Lydia Maria Child's *The American Frugal Housewife*," *ATQ* 13 (June 1999), 89–104.

3. Child, *Hobomok* (Boston: Cummings and Hilliard, 1824), 121.

Irwin S. Cobb

1. Case, *Feeding the Lions: An Algonquin Cookbook* (New York: Greystone, 1942), 29–30.

2. Cobb, *Local Color* (New York: Doran, 1916), 49.

Rose Terry Cooke

1. Cooke, "Liab's First Christmas," in *The Sphinx's Children and Other People's* (Boston: Ticknor, 1886), 472.

Susan Coolidge

1. Mary Ronald, *The Century Cookbook* (New York: Century, 1895), 229.

Charles Dickens — Dinner at Delmonico's

1. Quoted in Root and de Rochemont, *Eating in America,* 322.

2. Harry Haff, *The Founders of American Cuisine* (Jefferson, N.C.: McFarland, 2011), 125.

3. "The Dickens Banquet," *New York Times,* April 19, 1868, 8.

4. Wilson, *The Twenties* (New York: Farrar, Straus and Giroux, 1975), 148.

5. *Alice B. Toklas Cook Book,* 60.

Emily Dickinson

1. Vivian R. Pollak, "Thirst and Starvation in Emily Dickinson's Poetry," *American Literature* 51 (March 1979), 33–49. See also Sandra M. Gilbert, "Dickinson in the Kitchen," *Emily Dickinson Journal* 15, ii (2006), 1–3.

2. A photograph of the original manuscript poem is available online at thehistorykitchen.com/2011/12/09/emily-dickinsons-coconut-cake.

Erna Fergusson

1. Fergusson, *Albuquerque* (Albuquerque: Armitage, 1947), 29.

2. Fergusson, *Mexican Cookbook* (Albuquerque: University of New Mexico Press, 1934), v.

3. *The Great American Writers' Cookbook,* ed. Dean Faulkner Wells (Oxford, Miss.: Yoknapatawpha, 1981), 46.

Benjamin Franklin

1. Franklin, *On the Art of Eating,* ed. Frank Chinard (Philadelphia: American Philosophical Society, 1958), 5, 25.

2. Evan Jones, *American Food: The Gastronomic Story* (New York: Dutton, 1975), 131.

3. Root and de Rochemont, *Eating in America,* 135.

4. *Alice B. Toklas Cook Book,* 5.

Allen Ginsberg

1. Ginsberg, *Howl and Other Poems* (San Francisco: City Lights, 1956), 23.

Sarah Josepha Hale

1. Susan Williams, *Food in the United States, 1820s-1890* (Westport, Conn.: Greenwood, 2006), 113–14.

2. Hale, *Northwood: A Tale of New England* (Boston: Bowles and Dearborn, 1827), 89.

Gail Hamilton

1. Hamilton, *Country Living and Country Thinking* (Boston: Ticknor and Fields, 1864), 147.

2. Hamilton, *Gala-Days* (Boston: Ticknor and Fields, 1863), 114.

Marion Harland

1. *Marion Harland's Autobiography* (New York: Harper and Bros., 1909), 337.

2. Jones, *American Food,* 141.

3. *Harland's Autobiography,* 344.

4. Harland, *The Carringtons of High Hill* (New York: Scribner's, 1919), 248.

5. *Harland's Autobiography,* 145.

6. Harland, *The Carringtons of High Hill,* 157.

7. Harland, *Jessamine* (New York: Carleton, 1876), 310.

8. Harland, *Judith* (New York: Fords, Howard and Hurlbert, 1883), 316–17.

9. Harland, *Judith,* 195.

10. *Harland's Autobiography,* 411.

11. *Harland's Autobiography,* 411.

12. *The Carringtons of High Hill,* 171.

13. *Harland's Autobiography,* 412.

14. *Harland's Autobiography,* 411–12.

15. *Harland's Autobiography,* 412.

16. Harland, *Judith,* 195.

Harvard Club of New York — Dinner at Delmonico's

1. Julian Hawthorne Collection, 87/23c scrapbook 1 (Bancroft Library, University of California, Berkeley).

2. "The Harvard Club," *New York Times*, February 23, 1871, 8.

Nathaniel Hawthorne

1. Hawthorne, *American Notebooks* (Columbus: Ohio State University Press, 1972), 16.

Lafcadio Hearn

1. Hearn, "The Last of the Voudoos," *Harper's Weekly*, November 7, 1885.
2. Quoted in Williams, *Food in the United States*, 125.
3. Haff, 78.
4. Root and de Rochemont, *Eating in America*, 381.
5. *The Food of a Younger Land* (New York: Riverhead, 2009), 109.

Ernest Hemingway

1. "Ernest Hemingway's Fillet of Lion," *Sports Illustrated*, December 26, 1955, 40–42.
2. Sterling North et al., *So Red the Nose, or Breath in the Afternoon* (New York: Farrar and Rinehart, 1935), n.p.
3. Tanner, "Hemingway's Trout Fishing in Paris: A Metaphor for the Uses of Writing," *Hemingway Review* 19 (Fall 1999), 86.

Thomas Jefferson

1. Root and de Rochemont, *Eating in America*, 65, 117.
2. Marie Kimball, *Thomas Jefferson's Cook Book* (1938; rpt. Charlottesville: University Press of Virginia, 1976), 10.
3. Jones, *American Food* 38; John Hailman, *Thomas Jefferson on Wine* (Jackson: University Press of Mississippi, 2006), 296.
4. Hailman, 13.
5. Hailman, 92.
6. Root and de Rochemont, *Eating in America*, 94.
7. Evan Jones, *American Food*, 40.

Jack Kerouac

1. *The Dharma Bums* (1958; rpt. New York: Penguin, 1976), 207.

Eliza Leslie

1. Leslie, *Althea Vernon, or The Embroidered Handkerchief to Which Is Added Henrietta Harrison, or The Blue Cotton Umbrella* (Philadelphia: Lea and Blanchard, 1838), 273.
2. Leslie, *Amelia* (Philadelphia: Carey and Hart, 1848), 33.

3. Leslie, *Althea Vernon to Which Is Added Henrietta Harrison*, 205.
4. Leslie, *Althea Vernon to Which Is Added Henrietta Harrison*, 310.

Meriwether Lewis and William Clark

1. Hallock, "Literary Recipes from the Lewis and Clark Journals: The Epic Design and Wilderness Tastes of Early National Nature Writing," *American Studies* 38 (Fall 1997), 48–49.

Jack London

1. London, *A Daughter of the Snows* (Philadelphia: Lippincott, 1902), 44.
2. London, *The Valley of the Moon* (New York: Macmillan, 1913), 351.
3. London, *John Barleycorn* (New York: Century, 1913), 341.

James Russell Lowell

1. http://www.tastearts.com/wp-content/uploads/2011/02/jamcs_russell_lowell.jpg

Charles Fletcher Lummis

1. *Landmarks Club Cookbook*, ed. Lummis (Los Angeles: Out West, 1903), iii–iv.

John D. MacDonald

1. MacDonald, *The Dreadful Lemon Sky* (1974; rpt. New York: Fawcett, 1996), 204.

Mary Peabody Mann

1. Julian Hawthorne, "Pies, Wisdom and Pandowdy," *Pasadena Star-News*, March 9, 1929, 5.
2. Mann, *Juanita* (Boston: D. Lothrop, 1887), 142.

H. L. Mencken

1. Cerwin, *Famous Recipes by Famous People*, 13.
2. *Baltimore Sun*, July 11, 1925; rpt. Positive Atheism, positiveatheism.org/hist/menck02.htm.

S. Weir Mitchell

1. Mitchell, *Fat and Blood* (Philadelphia: Lippincott, 1885), 97.

Vladimir Nabokov

1. Emerson, *The Conduct of Life* (Boston: Ticknor and Fields, 1860), 147.

Catherine Owen

1. See also Kim Cohen, "'True and Faithful in Everything': Recipes for Servant and Class Reform in Catherine Owen's Cookbook Novels," in *Culinary Aesthetics and Practices in Nineteenth-Century American Literature*, ed. Monika Elbert and Marie Drews (New York: Palgrave Macmillan; 2009), 107–22.

Katharine Anne Porter

1. Patricia Sharpe, "Saucy," *Texas Monthly* 25 (January 1997), 30.

Marjorie Kinnan Rawlings

1. "Marjorie Rawlings Hunts for Her Supper," *Saturday Evening Post*, January 30, 1943, 26.
2. Rawlings, *Cross Creek* (New York: Scribner's, 1942), 226.
3. Rawlings, *Cross Creek*, 232–33.
4. Rawlings, *Cross Creek*, 231.
5. Rawlings, *Cross Creek*, 215.
6. Rawlings, *Cross Creek*, 238.

Theodore Roosevelt

1. "What Roosevelt Told Jury," *New York Times*, May 28, 1913, 2.
2. "That One Country Club Julep," *St. Louis Post-Dispatch*, May 28, 1913, 12.

Saturday Club of Boston

1. E. W. Emerson, *The Early Years of the Saturday Club* (Boston and New York: Houghton Mifflin, 1898), 22–23.
2. Quoted in Root and de Rochemont, *Eating in America*, 346.

Upton Sinclair

1. Sinclair, "What Life Means to Me," *Cosmopolitan* 41 (October 1906), 594.

Gertrude Stein

1. *The Alice B. Toklas Cook Book,* 280, quoted in Sarah Garland, "'A Cook Book to Be Read. What About It?': Alice Toklas, Gertrude Stein and the Language of the Kitchen," *Comparative American Studies* 7 (March 2009), 34–56.
2. Malcolm, *Two Lives: Gertrude and Alice* (New Haven: Yale University Press, 2007), 4.
3. Simon, *The Biography of Alice B. Toklas* (Garden City, N.Y.: Doubleday, 1977), 219.
4. *Staying on Alone: Letters of Alice B. Toklas,* ed. Edward M. Burns (New York: Liveright, 1973), 222.
5. Toklas noted, "This leaf must come from

Apollo's Laurel (*Laurus Nobilis*), better known outside France as the bay."
6. *The Alice B. Toklas Cook Book,* 134.
7. Traci Marie Kelly, "Women's Culinary Autobiographies," in *Kitchen Culture in America: Popular Representations of Food, Gender, and Race*, ed. Sherrie A. Inness (Philadelphia: University of Pennsylvania Press, 2001), 263.

John Steinbeck

1. *The Great American Writer's Cookbook,* 102.

Bayard Taylor — Dinner at Delmonico's

1. "Bayard Taylor Honored," *New York Times*, April 5, 1878, 2.
2. *The Alice B. Toklas Cook Book,* 146.
3. Thomas Jefferson Murray, *A Book of Entrées* (New York: White, Stokes, and Allen, 1886), 12.

Mark Twain

1. Stoddard, "In Old Bohemia," *Pacific Monthly* 19 (March 1908), 262–63.
2. *Mark Twain's Letters,* ed. Michael B. Frank and Harriet Elinor Smith (Berkeley: University of California Press, 2002), VI 3.
3. Jones, *American Food*, 115.
4. Andrew Beahrs, *Twain's Feast* (New York: Penguin, 2010), 24.
5. Julian Hawthorne Papers, 87/23c scrapbook 1 (Bancroft Library, Berkeley).
6. "Celebrate Mark Twain's Seventieth Birthday," *New York Times*, December 6, 1905, 1.
7. Howells, *Selected Letters, 1902–1911*, ed. David Nordloh et al. (Boston: Twayne, 1983), 138, 140.
8. Matthew Rodriguez, "Mark Twain's 70th birthday dinner menu," sundancechannel.com/sunfiltered/2010/12/mark-twains-70th-birthday-dinner-menu.

Carl Van Vechten

1. Van Vechten, *The Merry-Go-Round* (New York: Knopf, 1918), 156–57.

Sam Ward

1. Kathryn Allamong Jacob, *King of the Lobby: The Life and Times of Sam Ward, Man-About-Washington in the Gilded Age* (Baltimore: Johns Hopkins University Press, 2010), 78.
2. Haff, 130.

Robert Penn Warren

1. *The Great American Writers' Cookbook,* 186.

Booker T. Washington

1. *New York Times*, October 27, 1901, 1.

George Washington

1. Haff, 19. See also *Dining with the Washingtons: Historic Recipes, Entertaining, and Hospitality from Mount Vernon*, ed. Stephen McLeod (Mt. Vernon: Mt. Vernon Ladies Association, 2011).

2. Root and de Rochemont, *Eating in America*, 94.

3. Case, *Do Not Disturb* (New York: Stokes, 1940), 216.

4. "Wets Have Gala Day in Capitol's Shadow," *New York Times*, February 23, 1926, 16; "Representative Hill Reads Beer Recipe," *Atlanta Constitution*, February 23, 1926, 2.

5. "Washington's Recipe for Making Beer," *Washington Post*, March 2, 1926, 1, originally published in "Washington's Note Book: Selections from a Newly Discovered Manuscript," ed. Victor Hugo Paltsits, *Bulletin of the New York Public Library* 24 (August 1920), 435.

6. "Beer Recipe Causes Blanton to Demand Action by Coolidge," *Washington Post*, March 3, 1926, 1, 8; "Congressional Wets Denounced by Upshaw," *Washington Post*, March 5, 1926, 4.

7. "Washington's Beer Recipe Now in Congressional Record," *Atlanta Constitution*, March 12, 1926, 2.

Eudora Welty

1. These files, dated 1939–1941, are stored in boxes A829–A833 of the Federal Writers' Project: Special Studies and Project, 1691–1942. See also *The Food of a Younger Land*, ed. Mark Kurlansky (New York: Riverhead, 2009), 102.

2. *The Food of Younger Land*, 108.

3. *Southern Sideboards* (Jackson, Miss.: Junior League of Jackson, 1978), 272.

4. *Jackson Cookbook* (Jackson, Miss.: Symphony League of Jackson, 1971), n.p.

5. *What There Is to Say We Have Said: The Correspondence of Eudora Welty and William Maxwell*, ed. Suzanne Marrs (Boston: Houghton Mifflin, 2011), 72.

6. *What There Is to Say We Have Said*, 452n1.

Walt Whitman

1. *Cincinnati Gazette*, February 21, 1882, 10. See also Louis Szathmary, "The Culinary Walt Whitman," *Walt Whitman Quarterly Review* 3 (Fall 1985), 28–33.

A. D. T. Whitney

1. *The Living of Charlotte Perkins Gilman* (New York: D. Appleton-Century, 1935), 64.

2. Whitney, *The Other Girls* (Boston: Osgood, 1873), 5–6.

Owen Wister

1. Alessandro Filippini, *The Table* (New York: Charles Webster, 1889), 211; Charles Ranhofer, *The Epicurean* (New York: Ranhofer, 1894), II, 407.

2. Wister, *Red Men and White* (New York: Harper and Bros., 1895), 229.

3. Menu in Owen Wister Collection, box 43 (Library of Congress).

4. Wister, *Lady Baltimore* (New York: Macmillan, 1906), 17.

5. "Some Good Recipes," *Christian Science Monitor*, August 27, 1909, 6.

Further Reading

Agrell, Isabel Lewis. *Sinclair Lewis Remembered.* Crosslake, Minn.: privately printed, 1996.

Alcott, Abigail May. *Receipts and Simple Remedies,* ed. Nancy Kohl. Concord, Mass.: Louisa May Alcott Memorial Association, 1980.

Angelou, Maya. *Great Food, All Day Long.* New York: Random House, 2010.

_____. *Hallelujah! The Welcome Table.* New York: Random House, 2004.

Archer, Mary. *Belgian Relief Cook Book.* Reading, Pa.: Reading Eagle, 1915.

Barr, Beryl, and Barbara Turner Sachs. *Artists' and Writers' Cookbook.* Sausalito, Cal.: Contact Editions, 1961.

Barthelme, Donald. *The Teachings of Don B.,* ed. Kim Herzinger. New York: Turtle Bay, 1992.

Beahrs, Andrew. *Twain's Feast.* New York: Penguin, 2010.

Beecher, Catharine. *Miss Beecher's Domestic Receipt Book.* New York: Harper and Bros., 1850.

_____, and Harriet Beecher Stowe. *The American Woman's Home.* New York: J. B. Ford, 1869.

Bégué de Packman, Ana. *Early California Hospitality.* Fresno, Cal.: Academic Library Guild, 1952.

Beilenson, Evelyn L. *Early American Cooking: Recipes from America's Historic Sites.* White Plains, N.Y.: Peter Pauper, 1985.

Bellow, Saul. "Saul Bellow's Meat Sauce." *Esquire* 140 (October 2003), 68.

Berry, Ryan. *Famous Vegetarians and Their Favorite Recipes.* New York: Pythagorean, 1993.

Boreth, Craig. *The Hemingway Cookbook.* Chicago: Chicago Review Press, 1998.

Bosse, Sara, and Onoto Watanna. *Chinese-Japanese Cook Book.* Chicago and New York: Rand McNally, 1914.

Bower, Anne L., ed. *Recipes for Reading: Community Cook Books, Stories, Histories.* Amherst: University of Massachusetts Press, 1997.

Bradford, Ned, and Pamela Bradford. *Boston's Locke-Ober Café: An Illustrated Social History with Miscellaneous Recipes.* New York: Athenaeum, 1978.

Brose, Nancy Harris. *Emily Dickinson: Profile of the Poet as Cook.* Amherst: privately printed, 1976.

Buck, Pearl S. *Oriental Cookbook.* New York: Simon and Schuster, 1972.

Burr, Hattie. *The Woman Suffrage Cook Book.* Boston: Burr, 1890.

Campbell, Helen. *The Easiest Way in Housekeeping and Cooking.* Boston: Roberts Bros., 1893.

Case, Frank. *Feeding the Lions: An Algonquin Cookbook.* New York: Greystone, 1942.

Cerwin, Herbert. *Famous Recipes by Famous People.* San Francisco: Lane, 1940.

Chávez, Denise. *A Taco Testimony: Meditations on Family, Food and Culture.* Tucson, Az.: Rio Nuevo, 2006.

Child, Lydia Maria. *The Frugal Housewife.* Boston: Carter and Hendee, 1830.

Coe, Sophie D. *The Kirmess Cookbook.* Boston: Women's Educational and Industrial Union, 1887.

Croly, Jane C. *Jennie June's American Cookery Book.* New York: American News, 1870.

DeWitt, Dave. *The Founding Foodies: How Washington, Jefferson, and Franklin Revolutionized American Cuisine.* Naperville, Ill.: Sourcebooks, 2010.

Dubourcq, Hilaire. *Benjamin Franklin Book of Recipes.* Bath: Canopus, 2000.

Eichner, Bill. *The New Family Cookbook.* White River Junction, Vt.: Chelsea Green, 2000.

Elbert, Monika, and Marie Drews, ed., *Culinary Aesthetics and Practices in Nineteenth-Century American Literature.* New York: Palgrave Macmillan, 2009.

Ellet, Elizabeth Fries. *The Practical Housekeeper.* New York: Stringer and Townsend, 1857.

Ephron, Nora. *Heartburn.* New York: Knopf, 1983.

Erdrich, Louise. *Blue Jay's Dance.* New York: HarperPerennial, 1996.

Fergusson, Erna. *Mexican Cookbook.* Albuquerque: University of New Mexico Press, 1945.

Filippini, Alessandro. *The Table.* New York: Charles L. Webster, 1889.

Fitchett, Laura S. *Beverages and Sauces of Colonial Virginia.* New York and Washington: Neale, 1906.

Fitzgerald, F. Scott. "Turkey Remains and How to Inter Them with Numerous Scarce Recipes," in

The Crack-Up, ed. Edmund Wilson (1936; rpt. New York: New Directions, 1956), 193–95.

Flagg, Fannie. *Original Whistle Stop Cafe Cookbook*. New York: Fawcett Columbine, 1993.

Fowler, Damon Lee. *Dining at Monticello: In Good Taste and Abundance*. Charlottesville: Thomas Jefferson Foundation, 2005.

Franklin, Benjamin. *On the Art of Eating*, ed. Frank Chinard. Philadelphia: American Philosophical Society, 1958.

Gillette, F. L. *The White House Cookbook*. Chicago: Peale, 1887.

Gopnik, Adam. "Cooked Books: Real Food from Fictional Recipes," *New Yorker*, April 9, 2007, 80–85.

Hailman, John. *Thomas Jefferson on Wine*. Jackson: University Press of Mississippi, 2006.

Hale, Sarah Josepha. *The Good Housekeeper*. Boston: Weeks, Jordan, 1839.

Hamilton, Gail. *Country Living and Country Thinking*. Boston: Ticknor and Fields, 1862.

Harland, Marion. *Common Sense in the Household*. New York: Scribner's, 1884.

_____. *The Distractions of Martha*. New York: Scribner's, 1906.

_____. *Jessamine*. New York: Carleton, 1873.

_____. *Judith*. Philadelphia: Our Continent, 1883.

Hearn, Lafadio. *La Cuisine Creole*. New Orleans: Hansell, 1885.

Hellman, Lillian, and Peter Feibleman. *Eating Together: Recipes and Recollections*. Boston: Little, Brown, 1984.

Hemingway, Ernest. "Fillet of Lion," *Sports Illustrated*, December 26, 1955, 40–42.

Hemingway, Mary. "Life with Papa," *Flair* 1 (January 1951), 29, 116–17.

Henderson, Mary F. *Practical Cooking and Dinner Giving*. New York: Harper and Bros., 1877.

Hill, Janet McKenzie. *Dainty Desserts for Dainty People*. Johnstown, N.Y.: Knox, 1909.

Hillyard, Kay. *The Steinbeck House Cookbook*. Salinas, Cal.: Valley Guild, 1964.

Hirtzler, Victor. *The Hotel St. Francis Cook Book*. Chicago: Hotel Monthly, 1919.

Hogan, Louise E. *Children's Diet in Home and School*. New York: Doubleday, Page, 1910.

Inness, Sherrie A. *Dinner Roles: American Woman and Culinary Culture*. Iowa City: University of Iowa Press, 2001.

_____, ed. *Kitchen Culture in America: Popular Representations of Food, Gender, and Race*. Philadelphia: University of Pennsylvania Press, 2001.

Johnson, Ronald. *The Aficionado's Southwestern Cooking*. Albuquerque: University of New Mexico, 1968.

_____. *The American Table: More than 400 Recipes that Make Accessible for the First Time the Full Richness of American Regional Cooking*. New York: Morrow, 1984.

_____. *Company Fare*. New York: Simon and Schuster, 1991.

_____. *Simple Fare: Rediscovering the Pleasures of Real Food*. New York: Simon and Schuster, 1989.

Jones, Evan. *American Food: The Gastronomic Story*. New York: Dutton, 1975.

Kimball, Marie. *Thomas Jefferson's Cook Book*. Charlottesville: University Press of Virginia, 1976.

Kleber, L. O. *Suffrage Cook Book*. Pittsburgh: Equal Franchise Federation of Western Pennsylvania, 1915.

Kurlansky, Mark, ed. *The Food of a Younger Land*. New York: Riverhead, 2009.

Leonardi, Susan J. "Recipes for Reading: Summer Pasta, Lobster à la Riseholme, and Key Lime Pie," *PMLA* 104 (May 1989), 340–47.

Leslie, Eliza. *Directions for Cookery*. Philadelphia: Carey and Hart, 1840.

Lincoln, Mrs. D. A. *Mrs. D. A. Lincoln's Boston Cookbook*. Boston: Roberts Bros., 1883.

Longone, Jan. "The Mince Pie That Launched the Declaration of Independence and Other Recipes in Rhyme." *Gastronomica* 2 (Fall 2002), 86–89.

Lummis, Charles F. *Landmarks Club Cookbook: A California Collection of the Choicest Recipes*. Los Angeles: Out West, 1903.

MacCaffrey, Anne, ed. *Cooking Out of This World*. New York: Ballantine, 1973.

Magid, Annette, ed. *You Are What You Eat: Literary Probes into the Palate*. Newcastle: Cambridge Scholars, 2008.

Mann, Mary Peabody. *Christianity in the Kitchen*. Boston: Ticknor and Fields, 1858.

Matthews, Brander. "Recipes in Rhyme." *Harper's Bazar* [sic] 38 (February 1904), 188–92.

McCabe, Victoria. *John Keats's Porridge: Favorite Recipes of American Poets*. Iowa City: University of Iowa Press, 1975.

McLeod, Stephen, ed. *Dining with the Washingtons: Historic Recipes, Entertaining, and Hospitality from Mount Vernon*. Mt. Vernon: Mt. Vernon Ladies Association, 2011.

Moses, Kate. *Cakewalk: A Memoir*. New York: Dial, 2012.

Moss, Maria. *A Poetical Cookbook*. Philadelphia: Caxton, 1864.

Mosser, Marjorie. *Good Maine Food: Ancient and Modern New England Food and Drink*. Intro. Kenneth Roberts. New York: Doubleday, Doran, 1939.

North, Sterling, et al., *So Red the Nose, or Breath in the Afternoon*. New York: Farrar and Rinehart, 1935.

Oates, Joyce Carol. "Celebrating the Boys with a Birthday Dinner." *Gourmet* 59 (January 1999), 28–29.

Owen, Catherine. *Choice Cookery*. New York: Harper and Bros., 1889.

_____. *Ten Dollars Enough*. New York: Houghton Mifflin, 1886.

Parloa, Maria. *The Appledore Cook Book*. Boston: A. Γ. Graves, 1880

_____, et al. *Universal Common Sense Cookery Book*. Boston: Brown, 1892.

Piatti-Farnell, Lorna. *Food and Culture in Contemporary American Fiction*. Hoboken: Taylor and Francis, 2011.

Proulx, Annie, and Lew Nichols. *Cider: Making, Using and Enjoying Sweet and Hard Cider*. Pownal, Vt.: Storey, 1997.

Ranhofer, Charles. *The Epicurean*. New York: Ranhofer, 1894.

Rawlings, Marjorie Kennan. *Cross Creek Cookery*. New York: Scribner's, 1942.

Reardon, Joan, ed. *As Always, Julia: The Letters of Julia Child and Avis DeVoto*. Boston: Houghton Mifflin, 2010.

Reiger, Barbara, and George Reiger. *Zane Grey Cookbook*. Englewood Cliffs, N.J.: Prentice-Hall, 1976.

Roberts, Kenneth. *Trending into Maine*. Boston: Little, Brown, 1938.

Romines, Ann, ed. *At Willa Cather's Tables*. Red Cloud, Neb.: Cather Foundation, 2010.

Ronald, Mary. *The Century Cook Book*. New York: Century, 1895.

Sanders, Dori. *Dori Sanders' Country Cooking: Recipes and Stories from the Family Farm Stand*. Chapel Hill, N.C.: Algonquin, 1995.

Schofer, Yvonne, ed. *A Literary Feast: Recipes and Writings by American Women Authors from History*. Madison, Wisc.: Jones, 2003.

Shillaber, Lydia. *Mrs. Shillaber's Cookbook: A Practical Guide for Housekeepers*. New York: Crowell, 1887.

Shurman, Carrie V. *Favorite Dishes*. Chicago: Donnelley, 1893.

Sigourney, Lydia. *Lucy Howard's Journal*. New York: Harper and Bros., 1858.

Smith, Elaine. "Of Coconut Cake and Consommé: Willa Cather's School of Cookery." *Willa Cather Newsletter and Review* 54 (Fall 2010), 77–80.

Smith, Jacqueline Harrison, ed. *Famous Old Receipts*. Philadelphia: Winston, 1908.

Stout, Rex. *Nero Wolfe Cookbook*. New York: Viking, 1973.

Stratton, Florence. *Favorite Recipes of Famous Women*. New York and London: Harper and Bros., 1925.

Styron, William. "Clam Chowder." *Esquire* 102 (November 1984), C16.

Toklas, Alice B. *The Alice B. Toklas Cook Book*. New York: Harper and Bros., 1954.

Tschirky, Oscar. *The Cook Book by "Oscar" of the Waldorf*. Chicago and New York: Werner, 1896.

Victor, Metta. *Beadle's Dime Novel Cook Book*. New York: Beadle and Adams, 1868.

Webb, Nancy, and Jean Francis Webb. *Plots and Pans: Recipes and Antidotes from the Mystery Writers of America*. New York: Wynword, 1989.

Wells, Dean Faulkner, ed. *The Great American Writers' Cookbook*. Oxford, Miss.: Yoknapatawpha, 1981.

_____. *The New Great American Writers' Cookbook*. Jackson: University Press of Mississippi, 2003.

Welsch, Robert L., and Linda K. Welsch. *Cather's Kitchens*. Lincoln: University of Nebraska Press, 1987.

Wiggin, Kate Douglas. "Three Literary Recipes." *Harper's Bazar* [sic] 46 (September 1912), 435.

_____, ed. *A Book of Dorcas Dishes*. Cambridge: privately printed, 1911.

Wilcox, Estelle Woods. *Buckeye Cookery*. Minneapolis: Buckeye, 1877.

Williams, Susan. *Food in the United States, 1820s–1890*. Westport, Conn.: Greenwood, 2006.

_____. *Savory Suppers and Fashionable Feasts*. New York: Pantheon, 1985.

Wolfe, Linda. *The Literary Gourmet*. New York: Random House, 1962.

Young, Kevin, ed. *The Hungry Ear: Poems of Food and Drink*. New York: Bloomsbury, 2012.

Index of Recipes